Christ Church
T012642

D1610199

THE POEMS OF ROBERT SIDNEY

Although Robert Sidney's poems probably circulated during the 1590s among the same circle of 'private friends' as were also reading Shakespeare's sonnets, his poetry remained concealed from the world at large until our own time. In avoiding public recognition as a poet, Robert was perhaps influenced by a wish to avoid invidious comparisons with his dead brother Philip. The modest notebook, unsigned though entirely in his own handwriting, in which his poetry has survived, was acquired in the middle of the nineteenth century for the library at Warwick Castle, where it remained—disguised under a false attribution—for over a hundred years. The dispersal of the library during the 1960s brought the notebook to the attention of its present editor, who identified the hand and thus restored Robert Sidney to his place among the Elizabethan poets.

The notebook contains the largest body of original verse to have survived in the handwriting of any English poet of the period, and affords a unique insight into the construction of an Elizabethan love sequence. This edition contains the first complete and authoritative publication of Robert's notebook: an exact transcript, recording all deletions and revisions, is printed in parallel with a modernized text.

Concerning the private lives of most Elizabethan poets we know almost nothing, but for Robert a wealth of original material survives among the family papers in the possession of Viscount De L'Isle. The Introduction and Commentary to this edition use this intimate insight into Robert's life to illuminate his poetry.

Peter Croft is Librarian of King's College, Cambridge, and a Fellow of the college.

THE POEMS OF ROBERT SIDNEY

Edited from the Poet's
Autograph Notebook
with Introduction
and Commentary
by

P. J. CROFT

CLARENDON PRESS · OXFORD

1984

Oxford University Press, Walton Street, Oxford OX2 6DP
London Glasgow New York Toronto
Delhi Bombay Calcutta Madras Karachi
Kuala Lumpur Singapore Hong Kong Tokyo
Nairobi Dar es Salaam Cape Town
Melbourne Auckland
and associated companies in
Beirut Berlin Ibadan Mexico City Nicosia

Oxford is a trade mark of Oxford University Press

Published in the United States
by Oxford University Press, New York

British Library Cataloguing in Publication Data
Sidney, Robert
The poems of Robert Sidney.
I. Title II. Croft, P.J.
821'.3 PR2339.S/
ISBN 0-19-812726-X

Library of Congress Cataloging in Publication Data
Sidney, Robert.
The poems of Robert Sidney.
Includes bibliographical references and index.
I. Croft, P. J. (Peter John) II. Title.
PR2344.S35A114 1984 821'.3 83-21971
ISBN 0-19-812726-X

Typeset by Joshua Associates, Oxford
Printed in Great Britain
at The Alden Press, Oxford

In Memoriam

J. D. C.

Cor ad cor loquitur

CONTENTS

ILLUSTRATIONS

CHRONOLOGICAL TABLE

NB (1) The system of changing the year-number on 1 January is consistently followed. (2) Robert Sidney himself is referred to as RS, his first wife is referred to simply as Barbara.

1554 (30 Nov.) Birth of Philip Sidney (brother).
1561 (27 Oct.) Birth of Mary Sidney (sister).
1563 (19 Nov.) Birth of RS.
1569 (25 Mar.) Birth of Thomas Sidney (brother).
1575 RS matriculates at Christ Church, Oxford.
1577 (21 Apr.) Mary Sidney marries Henry Herbert, Earl of Pembroke.
1579 (Feb.)–1582 (Mar.) RS travelling on the Continent (returning briefly to England in the summer of 1581).
1581 (1 Nov.) Penelope Devereux (Philip Sidney's Stella) marries Lord Rich.
1583 (21 Sept.) Philip Sidney marries Frances, daughter and heiress of Sir Francis Walsingham.
1584 (23 Sept.) RS marries Barbara, daughter and heiress of John Gamage of Coity, Glamorgan.
1585 (Nov.–Dec.) RS accompanies his brother Philip to Flushing (Nov.) or possibly follows him there in the train of his uncle the Earl of Leicester (Dec.).
1586 (5 May) Death of Sir Henry Sidney (father).
(9 Aug.) Death of Lady Sidney (mother).
(22 Sept.) Battle of Zutphen.
(7 Oct.) RS knighted at the Camp near Zutphen for his valiant conduct in the battle.
(17 Oct.) Death of Philip Sidney at Arnheim from wound received at battle of Zutphen.
1587 (18 Oct.) Birth of Mary Sidney (eldest daughter).
*c.*1588–1602 Birth of ten more children to RS and Barbara, namely three sons (William, Henry, Robert) and seven daughters (Katherine, Elizabeth, Philip, Bridget, Alice, Barbara, Vere).
1588 (Aug.–Sept.) RS in Scotland on a diplomatic mission to James VI, Barbara remaining in England.
(4 Sept.) Death of Robert Dudley, Earl of Leicester (uncle).
1589 (July) RS appointed Governor of Flushing.
1590 (21 Feb.) Death of Ambrose Dudley, Earl of Warwick (uncle).
First publication of Philip Sidney's *Arcadia*.
Philip Sidney's widow marries Robert Devereux, Earl of Essex.
1590 (May)–1592 (Dec.) RS and Barbara in Flushing.
10 Nov. 1590 Birth at Flushing of William Sidney (eldest son).
May–July 1592 Siege and eventually successful assault on the

Spanish-held town of Steenwyck, in the course of which RS is slightly wounded.

1594 (Jan.–Apr.) RS in France on a diplomatic mission to Henry IV, Barbara remaining in England.

1595 (26 July) Death of Thomas Sidney (brother).

1595 (Aug.)–1596 (Jan.) RS in Flushing, Barbara remaining in England.
(1 Dec.) Birth at Baynard's Castle in London of Robert Sidney (youngest son and eventual heir: the only son to survive his parents).
(10 Dec.) RS writes from Flushing to Burghley explaining that he cannot honourably satisfy the Queen's wishes concerning the suspected spy Patrick Segrave.

1596 (Aug.)–1598 (Mar.) RS in Flushing, Barbara remaining in England until June 1597.
early May 1597 Roels, pensionary of Middelburgh and RS's best friend among the Dutch, dies from the plague.
June 1597 Barbara sails from England and joins RS in Flushing.
24 Jan. 1598 RS plays a distinguished part in the routing of the Spanish army at Turnhout.

1599 (Aug.)–1600 (Oct.) RS in Flushing, Barbara remaining in England.
28 Nov. 1599 Birth at Baynard's Castle in London of Barbara Sidney (daughter).

1600 Publication of Robert Jones's *First Book of Songs and Ayres* with dedication to RS.

1601 (19 Jan.) Death of Earl of Pembroke (brother-in-law).
(7 Feb.) Rebellion in London led by Earl of Essex: RS chosen to parley with the rebels and procure their surrender at the end of the day.
(25 Feb.) Earl of Essex beheaded.

1603 (24 Mar.) Death of Queen Elizabeth.
(13 May) RS created Baron Sidney of Penshurst.
RS appointed Chamberlain to the Queen Consort, Anne of Denmark.

1604 (9 Feb.) Death of the dowager Countess of Warwick (uncle's widow).
(27 Sept.) Mary Sidney (daughter) marries Sir Robert Wroth.

1605 (6 Jan.) Mary Wroth dances at the Whitehall Banqueting House in Ben Jonson's *Masque of Blackness*, the Queen's Twelfth Night entertainment.
(4 May) RS created Viscount L'Isle.

1610 Publication of Robert Dowland's *Musicall Banquet* with dedication to RS.

1612 (3 Dec.) Death of Sir William Sidney (eldest son).
Publication of Ben Jonson's *The Alchemist* with dedication to Mary Wroth.

1614 (14 Mar.) Death of Sir Robert Wroth (son-in-law).

1616 (May–June) Cautionary towns of Flushing and the Brill restored to the Dutch: termination of RS's appointment as Governor of Flushing.

(7 July) RS installed Knight of the Garter.
Publication (in *The Workes*) of Ben Jonson's poem 'To Penshurst' praising the lord and lady of the house (i.e. RS and Barbara).
1618 (2 Aug.) RS created Earl of Leicester.
1619 (2 Mar.) Death of Queen Anne of Denmark.
1621 (May) Death of Barbara.
(25 Sept.) Death of the dowager Countess of Pembroke (sister).
Publication of Mary Wroth's romance *The Countesse of Mountgomeries Urania.*
1625 (27 Mar.) Death of James I.
(25 Apr.) RS marries Sarah, widow of Sir Thomas Smyth of Bidborough, Kent.
1626 (13 July) Death of RS.

PREFACE

Seldom can we know a man who lived four hundred years ago in the way that we can know Robert Sidney: it would be difficult to name another Elizabethan who has both left us a similarly coherent body of verse and whose everyday life comes through to us from the surviving documents in such intimate detail. No full account of Robert's life has yet seen the light of print, but—even had I felt equal to the task—the inclusion of a full-scale biography would have overbalanced this edition, whose essential aim is to define the nature of Robert's achievement as a poet: in discussing his life I have concentrated, therefore, on those aspects which seem most relevant to an understanding of the impulses which lie behind the poetry.

The Elizabethans had a strong sense that human life is acted against an eternal background, and those who spent their lives in the service of a Queen who was regarded as semi-divine may illustrate with particular vividness the universal truth that the man of creative imagination leads 'a life of Allegory' on which his works are the commentary.[1] The lives of Philip Sidney and Walter Ralegh can both be seen as examples in their different ways, and Robert's outwardly less glamorous career can also be seen in the same light.

I have not attempted to pass judgement either on Robert's life or on his poetry—his achievement must in the end be assessed by each reader for himself—but I hope that this edition will persuade the reader that Robert's sequence is a more sophisticated work of art than would be apparent were it seen only as a collection of individual poems and its underlying design were thus overlooked. A single arrangement of all the poems is not established by the only text we possess, but the element of ambiguity in the notebook's testimony can be seen as the poet's own way of intimating that we may be misguided when we seek one 'perfect' order in a sequence designed to portray the shifting moods of love (cf. p. 112).

[1] Cf. John Keats's journal letter to George and Georgiana Keats, written 14 Feb.–3 May 1819: the relevant passage occurs in the entry for 18 Feb.

The letters by Robert which contain the closest parallels with his poetry were mostly written in the period 1595–8, and the parallels cluster particularly around the first half of 1597. This may indicate the period when many of the poems were being composed, but does not necessarily tell us when Robert began (firstly) to collect them in the surviving notebook, and (secondly) to revise them and to expand the sequence—though the evidence of the different inks in the notebook suggests that this whole process may itself have spread over a considerable time.[2] In this connection it should be observed:

(1) that the closest parallels with the letters all occur within the sequence as originally conceived, i.e. occur in poems before Sonnet 35;

(2) that two stages of expansion can be discerned, each stage immediately preceded by a few poems unconnected with the sequence;

(3) that the last change which is clearly a revision—as distinct from changes which could be mere corrections of transcriptional errors—occurs at Sonnet 32: 10;

(4) that the unrevised versions of two lines can be recognized behind the echoes of them by others (Sonnet 25: 4 and Song 10: 3, echoed respectively by Shakespeare and by Mary Wroth—see Appendix B and Appendix C). This suggests that the poems circulated in their unrevised forms among Robert's 'private friends', and consequently that some time may have elapsed before he began to revise them.

The letters from Robert to his wife Barbara and the letters to him from various correspondents which are quoted in this edition have all remained among the family papers. These are currently on deposit in the Kent Archives Office at Maidstone: they remain the property of Viscount De L'Isle, VC, KG, whose permission should be obtained by those wishing to consult them.

Robert's letters to the Earl of Essex, and some of his letters to Burghley and to Robert Cecil, are among the Cecil Papers at Hatfield House.

[2] The notebook consists of paper with an armorial watermark of the same type as Briquet 2291 and Heawood 481: watermarks of this general type were widespread in the period and have been found e.g. in six letters from Robert to Barbara dated October–December 1596. The watermark evidence is consistent with a date of paper manufacture some time during the 1590s, but one cannot claim more than that.

The sources for other letters quoted in the Introduction are given where the quotations occur.

Letters are quoted from the originals—i.e. from the actual documents sent. (In the few cases where the only known authority is an early transcript, this is stated.) While the spelling has been preserved, abbreviations have been silently expanded (in a manner consistent with the writer's practice elsewhere) since it would be futile to try to reproduce in print the graphic idiosyncrasies of different correspondents, usually writing in haste, always absorbed in the business of the moment and with no thought that their words would one day be printed.

Poetry presents a quite different case, and we are usually dependent for our best texts of Elizabethan poetry on early printed editions whose 'accidentals' reflect the habits of different compositors and printing houses: therefore, where verse is cited in the Introduction, Commentary, and Appendices, spelling and punctuation have been modernized where appropriate.

Quotations from Marsilio Ficino's Commentary on Plato's *Symposium* are from the original Latin text, first published in 1484. Ficino's own Italian translation—produced in the hope of bringing his work within reach of a wider public—remained unpublished until 1544 and never really superseded the original Latin. The Latin text was frequently reprinted and widely disseminated during the sixteenth century, and is the text represented among the books purchased with Robert's own donation to the Bodleian in 1600 (see p. 60).

See also the general head-note to the Commentary.

A substantial selection from the Sidney papers was published in 1746 by Arthur Collins in the two folio volumes which he entitled *Letters and Memorials of State*. Comparison of Collins's text with the originals reveals his skill in accurately deciphering a whole range of sometimes difficult hands—but it also reveals that he silently omitted many passages from the letters which he printed and even (on rare occasions) cobbled together passages from different letters. In these respects he was, of course, merely conforming to the usual eighteenth-century practice in such matters. Collins performed his editing on the originals themselves—crossing through passages to be omitted, indicating how the gaps thus created were to be closed, inserting between the lines his own readings of particularly difficult words—all evidently done for the guidance of an amanuensis engaged to transcribe the material for the printer. These eighteenth-century tamperings, however, have complicated for today's student the task of deciphering the originals.

The next large-scale publication of the Sidney papers was undertaken by the Historical Manuscripts Commission in the six volumes of the *Report on the Manuscripts of Lord De L'Isle & Dudley* issued at intervals between 1925 and 1966. A basic problem which faced the Commission was the fact that it was going over ground which had already been covered, though inadequately, by Arthur Collins. The second of the HMC volumes, which comes down to December 1602 and thus covers the period of Robert's life with which the Introduction to the present edition is mainly concerned, appeared in 1934 and its text had been prepared by C. L. Kingsford. Kingsford died before he was able to complete his task, and the Introduction which was supplied for the published volume by W. A. Shaw examines some of the shortcomings to Kingsford's editorial method. Those who compare the extracts from Robert's correspondence quoted from the original manuscripts in the following Introduction with the corresponding passages as they appear in HMC will be able to test for themselves how far the full flavour of the originals is sometimes lost in Kingsford's versions. (Those interested in trying this exercise might begin with the section of the Introduction called 'Robert and Other Women'.)

The use made of the Sidney papers in the Introduction will reveal to the reader how deeply we are indebted to Rowland Whyte for our intimate knowledge of Robert's life during the years 1595–1600 when he was so often in Flushing. During these prolonged absences Whyte acted as Robert's agent and at crucial periods wrote to him several times a week—often in the midst or at the end of a hard day at court—reporting the latest news from England. His letters were preserved by Robert and they survive today as a vivid witness both to the daily life of the Elizabethan court and to the domestic life of the Sidney family at Penshurst and in London.

Rowland Whyte was the son of Griffith Whyte and the grandson of John Whyte (alias Wynne) who had served the

Earl of Pembroke. It was probably through this connection that Rowland's uncle Harry Whyte had entered the service of Sir Henry Sidney. We may gather that Harry Whyte's nephew and Robert Sidney grew up together, since letters written in October 1575 to Philip Sidney by Robert Dorsett, canon of Christ Church, indicate that Rowland had accompanied the young Robert to Oxford.[3] Five years later, on 18 October 1580, Philip wrote from London to his younger brother, then travelling on the Continent, a long and tender letter (see 'Philip and Robert') which contains a passage showing that Rowland was accompanying Robert at the time:

> I cannot write now to H. White, doe yow excuse me. For his Nephew they are but passions in my father, which wee must beare with Reverence, but I am sory he should returne till he had the fruite of his travell, for yow shall never have such a servant as he would prove, use your owne discretion therin.

It is good to know that Philip Sidney's confidence in the young Rowland Whyte was to prove so amply justified.

In the brief Preface to her *Period Piece: a Cambridge childhood* (1952) Gwen Raverat tells us that it does not matter in which order her chapters are read since 'it is all going on at the same time, sticking out like the spokes of a wheel from the hub, which is me'. The overlapping which the reader will discover between the various sections of the following Introduction may serve as a reminder that the different aspects of Robert's life were likewise 'all going on at the same time'.

June 1983 P. J. CROFT

Postscript. While this edition was in the press, I learned that a biography of Robert Sidney by Millicent V. Hay is to be published in the United States under the imprint of the Folger Shakespeare Library in the course of 1984.

[3] Dorsett wrote in Latin: the original letters are now at Christ Church, and English versions of them are printed in James M. Osborn, *Young Philip Sidney* (1972).

ACKNOWLEDGEMENTS

First among those debts which can be listed, though they cannot be adequately described, I am happy to name the encouragement of Viscount De L'Isle, VC, KG, the present head of the Sidney family, a man who cares for his heritage and in whom the time-honoured tradition of Penshurst's hospitality still lives. I am indebted to Dr Nicholas Pickwoad, bookbinder and conservator, for his expert physical examination of Robert Sidney's notebook, the results of which are embodied in Appendix D. I owe much to Peter Davidson and to my daughter Caroline for their generously shared musical knowledge and for bringing to life with their 'good voices' Robert's Song 6 and Song 12 as they may well have been heard in the family circle at Penshurst. The first stanza of Song 6 set to the tune of 'Walsingham', and the first stanza of Song 12 set to the tune of 'Où êtes vous allées', are reproduced in the Commentary below (pp. 313 and 322–3): the former was written out for this edition by Peter Davidson, the latter by my daughter Caroline. My grateful thanks to Dilly Bradford for being so much more than just an efficient typist: for the editor of Robert Sidney's poems she realized Dr Johnson's idea of the reader 'uncorrupted by literary prejudices' with whom the critic finally rejoices to concur. To others I am indebted for discussions, not indeed concerned with Robert Sidney nor strictly tied to any theme at all, but engendering insights which illuminate precisely because they are not trying specifically to 'explain'. Although their very nature requires that such debts remain nameless, they are by no means unremembered.

INTRODUCTION

PROVENANCE

It is possible that a few at least of Robert's poems had been handed about among his literary friends before he collected them in the surviving notebook, but if so the manuscripts concerned have disappeared as completely as have the manuscripts of Shakespeare's 'sugred Sonets' which we know were circulating during the 1590s, probably in the same private circle (see Appendix B). Of the few published contemporary allusions to Robert's interest in poetry, the earliest seems to be that contained in Thomas Moffett's *The Silkewormes and their Flies* (1599):

> *Sydneian Muse*: if so thou yet remain,
> In brother's bowels, or in daughter's breast,
> Or art bequeath'd the *Lady of the plain*. . . .

(Moffett was a member of the Countess of Pembroke's household at Wilton and habitually referred to her as *the Lady of the plain.*) One of the many dedicatory sonnets appended by George Chapman to his *Iliads* (1609) is addressed to Robert, then Viscount Lisle, and hails him in its heading as 'the most Learned and Noble Concluder of the *Warres* Arte and the *Muses*', while in a poem included in *The Scourge of Folly* (1611) John Davies of Hereford addresses Robert thus:

> Learning and arms, together with the Muse
> (Which trinity of powers Art's heaven set forth)
> Thy brother did into thy breast infuse
> As to the heir of all his matchlesse worth:
>   Then sith Sir Philip still in thee abides
>   There's more in thee than all the world besides.

Each of these references is in itself slightly veiled: those who knew Robert to be a poet would see in each a compliment to his own verse, but the uninitiated need perceive no more than a compliment to his discernment in the art of poetry. That this ambiguity reflects Robert's own wish not to be publicly identified as a poet is suggested by two other contemporary allusions. Robert's eldest son died unmarried in December 1612 at the age of twenty-two, and in the following year the poet Joshua Sylvester added to a new edition of his *Lachrymae Lachrymarum* mourning Henry, Prince of Wales, 'An Elegie-&-Epistle Consolatorie, against immoderate sorrow for th'immature Decease of Sr William Sidney Knight, Sonne and Heire apparant to The Right Honorable, ROBERT, LORD SIDNEY, L. Vi-Count Lisle' (etc.). There is a joint dedication to the bereaved parents and their surviving offspring and the prefatory sonnet opens with a reference to their eldest daughter:

> Although I know None, but a Sidney's Muse,
> Worthy to sing a Sidney's Worthyness: Anagram
> None but Your Owne *AL-WORTH, Sidnëides, *LA:WROTH
> In whom, Her Vncle's noble Veine renewes.

This shows that Mary Wroth was known as a poet some eight years before the publication of her work in 1621: more interesting, however, is the evidence implicit in the overt allusion to the daughter's Muse that the bereaved father himself was not publicly known to be a poet, for had he been so it is inconceivable that his own poetry should be completely ignored on such an occasion. While Joshua Sylvester, however, dutifully evokes the illustrious example of Mary Wroth's uncle Philip and seems entirely unaware that her father was also acquainted with the Muse, that Mary Wroth herself was familiar with her father's poetry is revealed by the unmistakable echoes thereof in her own verse (see Appendix C). In the year after the publication of Mary Wroth's work Henry Peacham referred to her in his *Compleat Gentleman* (1622, pp. 161–2) in terms which are closely comparable to those which had been used by Joshua Sylvester in 1613. Peacham chose for one of his armorial illustrations the Sidney arrowhead contained in a lozenge and he explains:

> This forme of bearing, is tearmed a Lozenge, and is proper to women never marryed, or to such in courtesie as are borne Ladies; who though they be married to Knights, yet they are commonly stiled and called after the Sirname of their fathers, if he be an Earle; for the greater Honour must ever extinguish the lesse: for example, the bearer hereof is the Lady *Mary Sidney*, the late wife of Sir *Robert Wroth* Knight, and daughter of the right Honourable, *Robert* Lord *Sidney* of *Penshurst*, Viscount *Lisle*, Earle of *Leicester*, and companion of the most noble Order of the Garter, who

seemeth by her late published *Vrania* inheritrix of the Diuine wit of her Immortall Vncle.

Robert's own verse often evokes his elder brother's in the way he consciously diverges from it, and it may be that the first such conscious divergence is to be recognized in the brief inscription *For the Countess of Pembroke* which Robert wrote on the first page of the notebook. The impersonality of this is underlined when we recall the terms of Philip's dedication of his *Arcadia* to the same lady in an epistle headed *To my Dear Lady and Sister the Countess of Pembroke* and beginning 'Here now have you (most dear, and most worthy to be most dear, lady) this idle work of mine'. Robert by contrast merely uses the standard form employed when superscribing the outside of a letter or packet for delivery by hand, and the absence here of any hint of brotherly intimacy seems to imply that Robert wanted his sister to read his poems as she had Philip's, but to do so free from any embarrassing suggestion that the younger brother was trying to rival the elder.

The many blots, smudges, and deletions which Robert made in the course of first transcribing and later revising the text indicate that the surviving notebook can hardly itself have been designed for presentation. A presentation manuscript at this period would be copied out fair—a task usually assigned to an amanuensis—and the decorum appropriate to the occasion would have discouraged the author from then marring the fair appearance by subjecting the text to revision. The essentially private nature of Robert's notebook is further suggested by the fact that it is unsigned and by its total lack of calligraphic pretension: it is written throughout in the vigorous and highly individual Italic which Robert had developed by his mid-twenties and which remained essentially unchanged thereafter for the rest of his life. The earliest complaint we have about Robert's handwriting occurs in Philip's letter to him of 18 October 1580 (cf. 'Philip and Robert') where among a wealth of good advice the elder brother does not forget to admonish him affectionately on this subject—'I would by the way your worship would learne a better hand, yow write worse than I, and I write evell enough'. Robert never reformed, however, and complaints about his adult handwriting recur throughout his correspondence. His faithful agent warned him how the ageing Burghley—

whose own handwriting is hardly a model of clarity—grumbled at his letters:

> My Lord Treasurer saies that you have no reason to put hym to such paines as you doe to reade your ciphres, he knowes you can wryte a better hand, and desires you to use yt unto hym or to let some other wryte them for you. Mr. Hix tells me that he was angry because he cold not reade yt, and cast yt ofte from hym; your lordship may doe very well to have a care to please hym yf you meane to have your letters reade. (Rowland Whyte to Robert, 4 March 1596/7.)

We are indebted to Rowland Whyte for other glimpses of Robert's correspondents reacting to the challenge of his handwriting. Roger Manners went to the window and from one corner to the other for more light and at last called Whyte over and said 'he wold not take 100 li. to read this letter. I was faine to read yt for hym' (29 November 1595), though on another occasion Queen Elizabeth actually managed to read the whole of a letter from Robert to Lady Warwick, stumbling only at three words which Lady Warwick 'was faine to help her in' (13 September 1599). When entering his poems into the surviving notebook Robert made no attempt to subdue the spontaneous characteristics of a hand which caused his contemporaries such evident difficulty.

It is conceivable that a presentation manuscript for the Countess of Pembroke was actually prepared by an amanuensis, and the fact that Robert has ticked the upper margin of every page throughout his own notebook may mean that he was checking it against the scribe's work (though an alternative possibility is that he was simply checking it against his own drafts before destroying them).

If a formal manuscript were presented, it seems that the Countess followed Robert's wishes in keeping it closely to herself. In any case, no such manuscript is now known and if it ever existed we may suppose either that it was included in the auction of books and pictures arranged by the creditors of Philip, fifth Earl of Pembroke (see John Aubrey, *The Natural History of Wiltshire*, ed. John Britton, 1847, pp. 85–6) or else that it perished in one of the fires to which Wilton has fallen victim over the years.

Some sidelight on the indications that Robert's own notebook remained at Penshurst may be gained if we consider another volume of similar format but miscellaneous content and written in a variety of late sixteenth- and early seventeenth-century hands. The core of this volume (now British Library, Add. MS 15232) comprises twenty-four sonnets and two songs from *Astrophil and Stella* in a text slightly superior even to that published with the co-operation of the Countess of Pembroke in 1598 (see p. 19). The volume also contains anonymous poems, two of which echo poems by Philip (*Astrophil and Stella* viii and *Certain Sonnets* 27) while another contains one line (see fo. 18^{v})

But nowe I finde to trewe

which seems directly to echo Robert's Song 11: 75

and now I finde to true.

Inserted in the volume is an autograph letter from Mary, Countess of Pembroke, dated from Wilton, 9 September 1590, addressed to Robert's wife Barbara who was then at Flushing with her husband expecting the child which was to prove their first-born son William (the letter concerns the nurse whom the Countess was sending over to attend her sister-in-law, and concludes 'with my blessing to my pretey Daughter'—i.e. the writer's god-daughter Mary, Robert and Barbara's eldest child). In the early nineteenth century the volume was acquired by the collector B. H. Bright who recorded on a flyleaf his own guess as to its provenance: *I suspect that this MS volume belonged to Wilton & that I have in it the writing of Sir P.S. and his sister.* Bright does not mention the autograph letter, a critical examination of which readily exposes the falsity of his hopeful suspicion since the Countess's handwriting no more resembles any of the hands in the volume than does her brother Philip's. Bright's silence on the matter suggests that he was not personally responsible for inserting the letter in the volume but that he found it there and then jumped to the conclusion that the volume itself must have come from Wilton. Had Bright reflected, he might have realized that the letter's presence actually points to Penshurst rather than Wilton as the source of the volume. The apparent immaturity of several of the hands involved—including that which transcribed the *Astrophil and Stella* poems in a careful Italic—may indicate that members of Robert's growing family took part in the compilation. The volume is no longer attached to the early eighteenth-century calf binding, stamped with the arms of Charles Montagu, first Baron Halifax, whose covers are still preserved. Robert's second daughter Katherine (died 8 May 1616) became the first wife of Sir Lewis Mansell, baronet, who married as his third wife Lady Elizabeth Montagu, aunt of the first Baron Halifax: this could explain how the volume left Penshurst and eventually passed into the Montagu family. No unquestionable examples of Katherine Sidney's handwriting have been traced, but she may herself be the author of some poems which an immature-looking hand has drafted in the volume.

There is good reason to believe that Robert's own notebook remained at Penshurst until the late eighteenth or the early nineteenth century, by which time the estates (which had passed from the direct male line on the death of the improvident seventh Earl in 1743) were falling into decay. Exact details remain unknown concerning the discreet dispersal of selected items from the Sidney papers which must have occurred during this period (the selection was mainly confined to literary manuscripts and to letters of the kind which contemporary taste termed 'choice Autographs', while the bulk of the family correspondence was fortunately left intact). The collectors who benefited most directly from the Penshurst dispersal were James Bindley and Thomas Lloyd, if we may judge from the subsequent sale catalogues of their own collections (see *British Library Journal*, i, 1975, pp. 108-9: for Thomas Lloyd see also A. N. L. Munby, *Phillipps Studies: 3*, 1954, p. 152). Between 1819 and 1843 Thomas Lloyd figures both as a buyer and a seller at London auctions. The sale at Sotheby's on 10 May 1828 of material from Lloyd's collections included letters which had been at Penshurst when they were published by Arthur Collins in his *Letters and Memorials of State* (2 vols., 1746). Robert's notebook made what seems to have been its first public appearance as lot 603 in a later—this time anonymous—sale of Lloyd's material (Sotheby's, 22 February 1833) which included various manuscripts, for example Thomas Nevitt's memorial of his services to Robert Sidney (lot 651), which must have come from Penshurst.

In this sale the notebook was catalogued as 'Sonnets by Robert, first Earl of Leycester (brother to Sir Philip Sidney) in his own handwriting, addressed to his Sister Mary "For the Countess of Pembroke"' and was purchased by the dealer Thomas Thorpe who included it as item 944 in a catalogue he issued later in 1833. Thorpe there described the volume as 'Sonnets, Songs, Elegies and Pastorals, in the Autograph of Robert Sidney, First Earl of Leicester, 4to. *vellum*' and he added the comment:

> Some of the lines have interlineary corrections, but it would appear that these beautiful verses, for such many of them are, were not the original compositions of Sir Robert Sidney, but transcripts from the loose papers of Sir Philip Sidney. Some of the shorter poems are exquisite gems. At p. 29, commences a song, The Lady and Pilgrim, [the first eight lines are quoted] many stanzas in length, which the writer does not remember to have seen printed.

By the following year, when the poems appeared as item 601 in Thorpe's *Catalogue of an extraordinary assemblage of genealogical and heraldic manuscripts*, the cataloguer had decided that 'the circumstance of these alterations being in his autograph, places the first Earl of Leicester within the pale of poets of the sixteenth century, a distinction to which it has not hitherto been supposed he was entitled'.

Each catalogue up to this point correctly identifies the handwriting. Various manuscripts of this period still among the Sidney papers contain identifications added by later members of the family or by Arthur Collins, and some such identification was probably written on the vellum binding which then covered Robert's notebook, since no trade cataloguer of the early nineteenth century was seriously expected to 'research' a manuscript. In the same Sotheby sale of 22 February 1833 which contained Robert's notebook as lot 603, lot 616 is catalogued simply as 'Ancient Manuscript, ON VELLUM, *in the original binding*' and the comparison nicely illustrates how the level of description in auction catalogues of this period directly reflects the extent to which a manuscript readily identified itself to the cataloguer.

From Thorpe's 1834 catalogue Robert's notebook was acquired by Viscount Kingsborough (1795–1837), better known as a collector of Mexican antiquities though he also owned a number of English literary manuscripts. While in Kingsborough's possession the volume was stripped of its vellum binding (which may well have been the original wrapper) and reclothed in its present binding of tooled green morocco: in its re-bound state the author is identified only on the spine, which is lettered simply 'Sonnets by the Earl of Leicester. MS.' The obscuring of Robert Sidney's authorship had thus begun, and on the volume's next public appearance, as lot 606 of the Kingsborough sale in Dublin on 1 November 1842, the cataloguer dutifully followed the spine title and identified the author simply as the Earl of Leicester. The notebook was purchased at the Dublin sale by the bookseller Thomas Rodd and he, as we learn from Frederic Madden's note in the British Museum copy of the sale catalogue, transferred it to Thomas Thorpe who thus reacquired it after a lapse of some eight years. The catalogues issued by Thorpe between 1843 and 1848 reveal that he had forgotten his firm's previous description of the volume, for it now reappears firmly attributed to Robert Dudley, Earl of Leicester. The confusion is easily understandable, not only because Robert Dudley is so much better known than Robert Sidney in the annals of English history, but because Robert Dudley was in fact the only Earl of Leicester during Elizabeth's reign (the title was not revived in Robert Sidney's favour until 1618). The attribution to Dudley received apparently authoritative confirmation in 1848 from the Post Office official William Blott when he wrote to H. J. Cooke, agent for the next purchaser Lord Brooke, later fourth Earl of Warwick. Blott's letter is now inserted in the volume and reads:

General Post Office
Jan[y] 24 1848

My Dear Sir,

You have my full permission to assure Lord Brooke that I am persuaded in my own mind that the Volume of Manuscript Poems you exhibited to me some days since was written by Robert Dudley, Earl of Leicester.

At the same time it is right that I should mention that I have no grounds for arriving at this conclusion other than the great resemblance the writing bears to the facsimile of the Earl of Leicester's writing, published in John Gough Nicholl's 'Autographs of Royal Noble and Learned Personages'

I am
my D[r] Sir
yours most Sincerely
W. Blott

H. J. Cooke, Esq[r.]

Nichols's *Autographs of royal, noble, learned and remarkable personages conspicuous in English history* had been published in 1829 and reproduces parts of over six hundred letters, including examples of both Robert Dudley and Robert Sidney: any reader who has tried to use this handsome folio, however, will know the difficulty of referring from the Index to the plates and will understand how a hurried consultation might lead to confusion. Of Nichols's two examples of Robert Sidney's hand, one consists of the end of a letter signed *Leycester* and Blott must have come across this and jumped to the wrong conclusion—though had he noticed the date included in the facsimile (*At penshurst the 16 of Jan: 1623*) he might have realized his error in time and have made instead a correct identification.

The volume was acquired for Lord Brooke in 1848 and placed in the Local Library of Warwick Castle, two of whose book-plates it still bears. The volume presumably gained its place in the self-styled Local Library (one of three distinct libraries at Warwick Castle) by virtue of its supposed authorship—an association which would have seemed enhanced by the inscription to Robert Dudley's niece, the Countess of Pembroke, on the first page.

The attribution to Robert Dudley, which a critical comparison with any of that nobleman's surviving autographs would have exposed as false, seems nevertheless to have discouraged further investigation into the true authorship for the next century and more. The volume remained at Warwick Castle until the late 1960s, when a discreet dispersal of books and manuscripts preceded the public sale of the celebrated Fulke Greville MSS (Christie's, 19 June 1968, lot 136) and the eventual sale of the Castle itself to Madame Tussauds Ltd. As a result of the preliminary dispersal, Robert's notebook was entrusted for examination to the present writer who eventually succeeded in identifying the hand, or rather—had I but known this at the time—in re-identifying it. The notebook was described and illustrated in my *Autograph Poetry in the English Language* (1973, no. 22) and subsequently appeared as lot 390 in Sotheby's sale catalogue of 19 November (Robert Sidney's birthday) 1974: in January 1975 it was acquired by the British Library, where it is now Additional MS 58435. We may believe that Robert Sidney has at last been permanently restored—as Sotheby's and Thorpe's catalogues had briefly restored him in 1833-4—to his rightful place 'within the pale of poets of the sixteenth century'.

THE REVISIONS

Robert did not use the notebook for original composition. The state of the text shows that a version of every poem already existed before he began to enter it in the notebook, but the process of transcription—from drafts now lost—inaugurated a new stage in the evolution of the text. The physical condition of the manuscript—the use of various inks and the frequent blots offset from facing pages—constitutes a body of evidence indicating that throughout the period Robert was using the notebook he often closed and often resumed it.

In the first place, Robert was prone to errors of transcription, frequently the result of anticipating some similar word in the poem he was copying. This tendency to scribal error explains the occasional presence (Pastoral 2: 42 and 52, Sonnet 26: 10, Song 11: 32, Sonnet 30: 9, Pastoral 14 heading, Song 18: 21–2) of false starts immediately smudged out, while the ink was still wet, and the correct version written directly on top of the smudge before proceeding. In other cases, scribal errors were deleted with a stroke of the pen and the correction written above, also during the course of the original transcription. In the second place, as he worked through his drafts Robert sometimes decided to revise a word or phrase which he had just transcribed. In the third place, Robert often returned to revise at subsequent sessions many of the poems he had previously entered.

The above account will explain why it may occasionally be impossible to decide whether a particular alteration corrects a slip of the pen or represents a deliberate revision. The final word of Elegy 16: 9 was originally *run* in the notebook but here the rhyme shows that *run* is a scribal aberration and that *flow* must already have stood in the draft. It is equally clear from the sense that the first *pains* at Song 5: 16 is a slip and that *wrongs* must always have been intended. On the other hand, in the last line of Song 20 where the poet is addressing his own senses, Robert began to write *yowr* but broke off before he had completed the third letter and substituted *her*. In this case it is possible that *yowr* (Robert's habitual spelling of *your*) stood in the draft, for in most *presence/absence* references the poet is thinking of his own variable position in relation to the place where the beloved (by implication) permanently abides: in Song 20, however, *your presence* could suggest that the poet's senses had procured their own blessing and the substitution of *her*, which makes unambiguously clear that it is the beloved's presence which bestows the blessing, may be a deliberate revision.

The reader must assess for himself the likely status of some alterations, but it is manifest that the majority represent deliberate revisions of the text which had been achieved in the lost drafts. One or more of several motives can usually be discerned in each revision: a wish (1) to clarify and/or strengthen the meaning, (2) to refine harmony of expression by removing minor infelicities or incongruities, (3) to introduce verbal plays or sharpen existing ones, (4) to improve the rhythm, and (5) to improve euphony.

A few examples will serve to illustrate what has just been said.

Song 1 introduces the theme of absence into the sequence and employs the metaphor which receives its most extended treatment in Song 6—that of absence as a kind of death (Song 1: 19 *to all delights quite dead*, 21 *to living burial led*, 31–2 *when that gone I am / To mine unjust decay*). This underlying metaphor probably explains why the expression in line 30 *doth think his life his hell* came to be considered incongruous: in revising the line Robert both removed the incongruity and replaced a merely subjective verb with an active image: *doth bear with him his hell.*

At Sonnet 6: 4 the change from *conquer* to *comfort* introduces a gentler image and one more in keeping with the subjective view of night which this sonnet presents.

The revision of Sonnet 14: 10 from

> Destiny's foresight, love's strength, my will's end,

to read

> Destiny's foresight, Love's justice, Will's end

brings in the concept of *justice* which is more in keeping with the poem as a whole (cf. the reference to *your judgement* in line 3) and eliminates the possessive pronoun which belittles the essentially supra-personal concepts being enumerated. The revision also slows the movement of the line and creates a rhythm whose bold irregularity stands out in its context and focuses attention on the meaning.

Song 6: 59 as originally written represents death as *tearing* the lady's joys from her, an image whose violence clashes with the lady's welcoming of death in neighbouring lines (54 *Death now fair name doth prove*, 61 *Faithless life, true death*, 64 *Death me to him shall give*). The violent action of *from me doth tear* is accordingly softened in the revision to *will not forbear.*

Differences of ink show that the twentieth quatrain of Song 6 (77–80) was revised on two distinct occasions, and that *miss* was replaced by *err* at the end of the quatrain's second line in the course of the original transcription. The original reading *miss* might be a scribal aberration but alternatively could mean that the quatrain stood in the draft Robert was transcribing—

> To find her be not afraid
> See, and thou canst not miss,
> What worth of all else is said
> All is said true of this

—though while still copying the quatrain Robert decided to substitute *err* for *miss* at the end of the second line and so before reaching the end of the fourth line had already avoided the rather clumsy use of *this* to signify the beloved.

The second stage of revision produced a final version:

> To find her will be small pain
> See, and thou canst not err:
> What worth of all else men feign
> Is all proved true in her

which sharpens the expression by introducing the *feign/true* antithesis: the worth which men pretend to find elsewhere is truly found only in the beloved. The new version strengthens the connection between Song 6 and Song 1 (see below, p. 80) and incidentally helps us to perceive how Robert's thought here is essentially the same as that which informs Shakespeare's lament for the departure from this world of perfect love:

> Truth may seem, but cannot be,
> Beauty brag, but 'tis not she,
> Truth and Beauty buried be.
> (*The Phoenix and Turtle*: 62–4.)

The unfortunate suggestion that the lady might frighten the pilgrim was removed by Robert in revising the first line of the quatrain quoted above, and the same notion is softened in the revision of *beware* to *mark well* at Song 6: 87. Such revisions—like those at Pastoral 7: 23 and Sonnet 28: 5—show Robert toning down elements in his work of the kind which Keats, using the colloquial language of his day in reference to his own poetry, was to label 'smokeable'.[1] Robert shared Keats's

[1] Keats to Richard Woodhouse, 21 Sept. 1819 (with reference to *Isabella*).

wish 'to use more finesse with the Public'—although Robert's envisaged audience must have been a more select group than Keats's 'Public'.

The reference to *rich Ton's sandy bed* in the original version of Song 6: 74 can be recognized as a 'literary' allusion to the river which flows through Tonbridge: the name however is purely fanciful, the etymology of *Tonbridge* not being really analogous to that of, for instance, *Edenbridge* and *Cambridge*. The use of the river's real name in place of the fanciful allusion is more in keeping with the popular ballad style which Song 6 evokes, and adds solidity to this unique intimation of an actual lady's real identity. The 'honest' naming of the Medway enhances at a touch an effect which is without parallel in the sequence, just as the wholly mutual love which Song 6 portrays is itself unique therein. It seems worth describing therefore the physical evidence which tells us that this particular revision was made during the course of the original transcription rather than during one of the subsequent sessions when revisions were introduced.

The blots offset from facing pages show that throughout the whole period of transcription and revision Robert's notebook was often closed before the ink was dry on the last page to be reached or amended. Differences of pen and ink show that there was a break in the transcription of Song 6 after line 104 (the sixth line on fo. 18^{r}), and the fact that the revision *Medwayes* in line 74 is—unlike the revisions in lines 77, 79–80, and 87 on the same page (fo. 17^{v})—in the same pen and ink as that used for transcribing the poem down to line 104, combined with the fact that the tail of the *y* in *Medwayes* has blotted on fo. 18^{r}, proves that this revision represents the last writing of this particular session: it must have been made just before Robert closed the book while the ink of *Medwayes* was still wet and Song 6 not yet transcribed beyond line 104.

The revisions at Sonnet 20: 7–8 include the replacement of *darkness* with *mourning* which more accurately realizes the image implicit in *widow sky*, while the replacement of *Sun's departure* by *husband-Sun's loss* represents an attempt both to clarify the meaning and to mitigate the clumsiness inherent in the *sun/son* homophone by exploiting the unavoidable pun for calculated effect rather than allowing the passage to appear insensitive to the pun's latent presence.

The revision of Pastoral 9: 35 introduces the *his own/unknown* verbal play and removes the clumsiness of *others* concerning which it remains unclear whether a genitive singular or a plural was intended. The revision in Song 10: 3 introduces the *know/no* verbal play and the revision of Sonnet 30: 12, which mainly serves to strengthen the rhythm, also sharpens the chiasmal play *care to see/see my cares* (see p. 41).

At Pastoral 8: 46 *floods* was replaced by *streams* because the former word primarily connotes a high tide, a sense directly at odds with that intended. In view of the rather obvious incongruity of *floods* here, we may suspect that Robert nevertheless chose that word in the first instance because he wanted to avoid excessive use of 'hissing' *s*, a sound to which other revisions suggest that he became particularly sensitive. The revision in this line suggests that Robert was alive to the sound of his verse but where he perceived a clash between the claims of sound and sense he tended finally to prefer the latter.

The revision of Song 4: 18 softens the jarring assonance of *is his bliss*, and there are revisions which seem mainly or wholly prompted by the wish to prune occurrences of hissing *s* at Pastoral 8: 13, Sonnet 20: 9, Pastoral 9: 28, 30, and 38; Sonnet 32: 10.

Sonnet 28 was subjected to the most extensive detailed revision of any poem in the notebook and the revisions here, while they serve various specific purposes, all combine to enhance the sonnet's artistic harmony. The rhythm of lines 3-6 was improved, an improvement assisted by the creation of pleasing alliterations —in lines 3-4 centring round the chiasmal *st m : m st* sequence in *storms and mists*, in lines 5-6 lightly carried on the thrice-repeated hard *g*. The idea of the *foul* strikes a discord in this Maytime poem which aims at perfect harmony, and in the revision of line 3 the word itself was purged from the poem. (Sonnet 28's value as refreshing relief, and specifically the value of this particular purging, are jointly reinforced by the betrayal sonnets placed on either side of it in the sequence, both of which consciously evoke a foul atmosphere.) The more specific *rosy* was substituted in line 4 for the generalized *flowery* which merely echoes *flower* in line 2. The first-person pronoun in line 5 was removed and any infelicitous suggestion thereby avoided that the air proceeds from the poet himself rather than from the fragrant place of leaves and flowers where he is. The removal of *rose(s)* and *violet(s)* (lines 6 and 11), together with the introduction of *myrrh* and *amber* (line 11), refines the poem's appeal to the lower triad of senses (see 'Robert's Use of the Sequence as a Form') and gets rid at the same time of an unfortunate disyllabic pronunciation—of *violet(s)*—in which some will hear the 'Cockney whine' and which in a formal metre[2] always tends to grate on the sensitive ear. The replacement of *Lysa* with *Charys* (line 8) may have been partly prompted by a sense that the threefold alliteration on *l* in this line was too heavy, and partly by a sense that the name *Lysa*—which evokes the *fleur de lys*, the type of pure whiteness—does not altogether harmonize with *ruby lips*. (See ' "Lysa" and "Charys" ' for another possible motive in this revision.)

The most important single aspect of Robert's revisions in Sonnet 28, however, consists in the pruning of three occurrences of *sweetness* (in lines 2, 10, and 13, replaced with *comfort, fairness*, and *richesse* respectively) and one of *sweet* (line 12, replaced with *dear*). The sense of sweetness which permeates the poem is paradoxically enhanced by the pruning of the word itself, which in the final version survives only in the close-set reiteration of its key syllable at the heart of the sonnet. The use of *sweet* in the sixth and eighth positions (the third and fourth stresses) of line 7

That in their bosoms sweet, they sweeten thee

exemplifies the favourite Sidneian device of repetition with variation, and represents a more restrained use of the figure employed in lines 1-2 of *Astrophil and Stella* 79.

Pastoral 9 is a unique case of a poem which was significantly expanded (in two stages) after its original version had been entered in the notebook. Robert's habit of making a terminal flourish below each completed poem shows that Pastoral 9 was originally complete in four stanzas and that stanza 5 and stanza 6 are successive afterthoughts, stanza 5 being written across the terminal flourish originally made below stanza 4 and stanza 6 being written across that made below stanza 5. The original four-stanza version, which consists entirely of the Shepherd's monologue, leaves him at the end embittered at the beloved's treachery but still in bondage to her. At the start of stanza 5 the

[2] The distinction can be observed in Shakespeare, the looser rhythms of whose dramatic verse can accommodate the disyllabic pronunciation (the most famous example being Perdita's 'violets dim') while the word always receives its full trisyllabic extension when it occurs in the formal metre of the Sonnets and *Venus and Adonis*.

Shepherd has finished speaking and looks up to notice his faithful flock: this stanza introduces into the sequence an entirely new theme, that of the lover's rejection of his bondage. The introduction of this theme underlines the significance of the revision in stanza 5's opening line to make it more rhythmically expressive by heightening the emphasis on its two key words *now* and *new* (see 'The Metrical Aspect', p. 40). The decision to expand the poem further by adding stanza 6 was probably prompted in part by a sense that stanza 5 had not by itself brought the new theme to a strong enough climax, and in part by a wish to make Pastoral 9 exactly equal in length (480 syllables) to Pastoral 8, whose all-patient Shepherd is balanced by the embittered Shepherd of Pastoral 9, the two poems standing on either side of the longest uninterrupted run of sonnets in the sequence (see p. 109).

The theme of escaping from love's bondage reappears in the sequence in Song 10 and in Song 12, and further evidence of deliberate design can be detected in the way both these latter poems treat the same theme as the expanded Pastoral 9 but in a contrasted tone—a tone of buoyant disengagement (see p. 109). The inauguration of the notebook probably marks the inauguration of a plan to collect the poems into a sequence, though there are various indications that Robert's design was not fully formed at the outset but is gradually taking shape as he compiles the notebook. This is indicated not only by the way Pastoral 9 has been expanded, but also by the evidence that first Sonnet 35 and later Elegy 16 formed the conclusion of the sequence at successive stages in the course of its development (see pp. 25 and 104). These indications of an evolving design are further borne out by the evidence of the various inks, which shows that the poems through Sonnet 18 were not given numbers at the time they were entered in the notebook but had their numbers added by Robert later, whereas beginning with Sonnet 19 most poems were numbered as they were entered. Occasional exceptions include Elegy 16 and Song 17 where in each case the whole heading is in a different ink from the text, and Song 23 where again the number alone is in a different ink.

THE FORMAL ASPECTS OF THE POETRY

The system employed for numbering the poems in the main sequence is based on the distinction between sonnets and poems in diversified forms. Each of the twenty-four 'diversified' poems in the sequence is classified in its heading as either *Song* (seventeen poems), *Pastoral* (five poems), or *Elegy* (one poem)—except the last poem in the notebook which has no heading but clearly belongs to the sequence and should have been headed *Song 24*. Although thus variously headed, these 'diversified' poems form collectively a single series running—like the Songs in *Astrophil and Stella*—parallel to the series of sonnets with which the 'diversified' series is intermixed to compose the sequence as a whole. That they were conceived in this way is shown not only by the fact that they are numbered through consecutively (*Song 1, Pastoral 2, Song 3*, etc.) but also by the fact that within this series Robert never repeats the same stanzaic pattern, so that these twenty-four poems represent twenty-four different verse forms.

Sonnets

Although by the mid-1590s sonnets divided into three quatrains and a couplet had become the most popular variety in England, all of Robert's sonnets—like the majority of Philip's—conform to the Italian variety consisting of an octave and a sestet. The dominant English variety—that favoured by Daniel, Drayton, Shakespeare, etc.—has an inherent tendency to set off and emphasize the final couplet. The Sidneian sonnet is more flexible: of the four rhyme-schemes used in Robert's sestets the two most frequently employed both conclude with a rhymed couplet, yet the design of these sestets is less stereotyped than can be gathered from their rhyme-schemes alone, since varying degrees of emphasis are given to the final couplets depending in each case on whether—and how strongly—the sense pattern accords with, or is counterpointed against, the rhyme pattern.

The combination of rhyme schemes used by Robert in his sonnets more frequently than any other—his invariable abbaabba octave followed by a cdcdee sestet—is also the combination most favoured by Philip: it occurs in sixteen of Robert's thirty-five sonnets and in sixty of the 108 sonnets in *Astrophil and Stella*. Of the three other sestet rhyme-schemes used by Robert two also occur in *Astrophil and Stella*, and although the third (cdcede) does not occur anywhere among the wide variety of sonnet forms used by Philip it does appear in several of the sestets in Henry Constable's *Diana* (1592) where it is possible that

Robert found it: in this connection it may be significant that eight sonnets by Philip himself first reached print (anonymously) in the second edition of Constable's collection (*c.*1594). At all events, this is the most 'interwoven' scheme used in any of Robert's sestets, which probably explains why he chose it for all four sonnets in his (unfinished) Crown. Similarly interwoven schemes are used in several of Philip's sestets, the most closely comparable being the cddece scheme in *Astrophil and Stella* 29.

Robert's sestets, however, are formally differentiated not only by their rhyme-schemes but also by the different ways they are spaced on the page, and in each case the spacing is related to the sense pattern. The eleven sonnets employing the cdcd ee rhyme-and-spacing scheme (see Table of Verse Forms) conclude with a strongly set-off final couplet, but in most cases Robert counterpoints the sense pattern against the rhyme by introducing a sense break at the end of the sestet's third line, a pattern often found in conjunction with a running over of the sense from the sestet's fourth line into the fifth (i.e. into the first line of the final couplet). This pattern can be clearly seen in, for example, Sonnets 9, 15, 21, and 27, and the tendency in all such cases is to bind the final couplet more closely into the sestet as a whole.

In two cases, and in two cases only, Robert's layout leaves the sestet undivided, namely in Sonnets 6 and 7 which occupy facing pages in his notebook. Both these sonnets use the cdcdee scheme for the sestet and in both the sense pattern corresponds with that just described—a break after the sestet's third line and an enjambment from its fourth line into the penultimate line. These sestets should probably be spaced on the page as are those of Sonnets 15, 21, and 33, and it may be that when Robert transcribed Sonnets 6 and 7 into his notebook he had not yet decided to subdivide sestets using this particular combination of sense and rhyme patterns.

In breaking the sense after the third line of the sestet Robert was following Philip's usual practice in *Astrophil and Stella.* Comparison suggests that both brothers shared the same feeling about the 'strong' final couplet—namely, that while it could be occasionally effective it should not be used too often, and that the degree and kind of emphasis given to the final couplet should be varied in order both to avoid monotony and to preserve the unity of the sestet. The most authoritative complete text we possess of Philip's sequence is that appended to the edition of the *Arcadia* published with the help of his sister in 1598, and in that text the sestets are regularly divided by a space after the third line: the same arrangement is found in a notebook (British Library, Add. MS 15232) containing twenty-four of the *Astrophil and Stella* sonnets in a text which Ringler recognized as superior even to the edition of 1598. (Reasons for supposing that this notebook may have originated in Penshurst are given above, pp. 5–6.) Modern editions ignore the formal spacing within these sonnets, and indeed it is possible that the 1598 printer's invariable spacing of the *Astrophil and Stella* sestets into equal halves is too mechanically regular and that some sestets (e.g. those of 54, 66, and 68) should be divided into four and two as eleven of Robert's are. Comparison with the best surviving texts of *Astrophil and Stella* suggests, at all events, that Robert was following the example he found in Philip's (now lost) authorial manuscripts when he decided to space his own sonnets on the page so as to reflect the carefully designed sense patterns which they embody.

The importance of structure in Robert's poetry reinforces the significance of those enjambments which with unusual boldness cross the formal divisions within the sonnets concerned. In Sonnet 17 the sailing metaphor introduced in line 7 is continued from octave into sestet: here the movement of the verse helps to realize the sensation of pressing forward against resistance which is being described. In Sonnet 35 the enjambment of the sestet's quatrain into the final couplet creates a strong caesura in the penultimate line which heightens the rhetorical effect of the triumphant conclusion.

The device known in English since the nineteenth century as enjambment was vividly described by Samuel Daniel at the start of the seventeenth century from the viewpoint of a practising poet. In his *Defence of Rhyme* (1603) Daniel gives it as his opinion that 'sometimes to beguile the ear with a running out, and passing over the rhyme, as no bound to stay us in the line where the violence of the matter will break through, is rather graceful than otherwise'. Daniel imbibed the cultural atmosphere of the Sidney circle when serving in the household at Wilton during the 1590s, and his description aptly suggests the spirit in which Robert Sidney uses enjambment to increase the variety and expressiveness of his verse.

Rhyme

Although Robert eschews feminine rhyme in his sonnets, he uses it in seven out of his eighteen 'Songs' (not counting the one such rhyme occurring in the unique prosody of Song 6). Both in avoiding feminine rhyme in his sonnets, and in using it in his Songs only as a regular structural element of the stanzaic pattern, Robert was conforming with Philip's mature practice as exemplified in *Astrophil and Stella*. One may guess from Daniel's *Defence of Rhyme* that Philip's practice came to represent within the Sidney circle the orthodox standard in such matters. Daniel records how Hugh Sanford (tutor and secretary at Wilton) had warned him of the 'deformity' of mixing 'uncertainly' feminine rhymes with masculine, and explains how he has himself come to believe that feminine rhymes are 'fittest for ditties, and either to be set for certain, or else by themselves', i.e. fittest for songs and to be used either (1) alternating with masculine rhyme in a set pattern, or (2) in stanzas employing feminine rhyme only. The development of Daniel's views on this matter is reflected in the textual history of his sonnet sequence *To Delia*, the original (1592) version of which abounds in feminine rhyme but was subjected in later editions to successive revisions largely in order to rid the sonnets of such rhymes.

Robert's rhyming practice requires some mention here of lines 5-6 of the seventh stanza of Pastoral 2

Lips of cherries
Hands of lilies

which has somewhat the effect of feminine rhyme though in fact the rhyme is on the final syllables only of these particular short lines which a metrical inversion has turned into trochaics, whereas the corresponding lines in every other stanza are (like the whole poem) iambic. In this type of verse 'where the structure forces us to appreciate each syllable'[3] such minor freaks in a metrical design may produce effects which in a less disciplined prosody would be blurred or lost.

Pronunciation

Robert's use of rhyme calls for special consideration of those words which possess in actual pronunciations a variable syllabic

[3] *The Journals and Papers of Gerard Manley Hopkins* (1959), p. 85.

value. During the sixteenth century the termination *-ion* was in the process of losing its full disyllabic value. The formal or old-fashioned pronunciation is illustrated in Philip's *Defence of Poetry* where he cites *motion* : *potion* as the English example of putting the rhyme in the antepenultimate syllable 'which the Italian term *sdrucciola*'. For Philip, then, the *-ion* termination —at least in the rhyming position—retains its full disyllabic extension, so that words ending thus, having their main stress on the antepenultimate syllable, can be used for trisyllabic rhymes. Philip himself used trisyllabic rhyme only in the *terza rima* of four *Old Arcadia* poems (cf. Ringler, p. 572) and in each case includes rhymes ending in *-ion*. In regular iambic verse, however, a stress on the antepenultimate entails at least a secondary (metrical) stress on the final syllable, and words ending in *-ion* may thus be used for masculine rhyme. The strict syllabic structure of Robert's verse reliably distinguishes between formal and informal pronunciations of the same word and tells us that the formal pronunciation of words ending in *-ion* occurs in only one situation, namely where such words are used *as the rhyme words in sonnets*. In that situation the formal pronunciation is always used, although otherwise it does not occur in Robert's verse. Thus we find in Sonnet 3 (lines 10, 12) *devótións* : *perféctións* and in Sonnet 22 (lines 9, 12) *condítión* : *stáy puts ón*, where in each case the rhyme is masculine, i.e. on the last syllable only. In the octave of Sonnet 25, however, are three trisyllabic rhymes, *inféctións* : *perféctións* : *afféctións* (lines 2, 6, 7) though the other rhyme word of the set *afflíctións* (line 3) carries the rhyme on its last syllable only and so may be thought of as preserving the 'decorum' of the Sidneian sonnet, which strictly admits only masculine rhyme. The trisyllabic rhymes in the octave of Sonnet 25—the only occurrence of such rhymes in Robert's verse—were probably a calculated licence to bring out the octave's abnormally 'smart' and ironic tone: it is important to notice, however, that these audacious rhymes never infringe the sonnet's decasyllabic structure.

In all other contexts words in *-ion* exhibit the more familiar pronunciation wherein the ending has lost its full value and counts merely as a monosyllable in the metrical scheme. Thus we find

If those devotions now no more (Song 5: 1)

From whose least motion thousand graces flow (Sonnet 10:12)

The brave directions of your lips divine (Sonnet 15: 11)

Alas my love from no infections free (Sonnet 26: 7)

And joyful hither your oblations move (Sonnet 32: 7)

And of afflictions no end see (Song 18: 20).

In this condition such words are available to the Songs for feminine rhyme, and they are so used in the third stanza of Song 20.

The word types represented by (1) *heaven*, (2) *power*, and (3) *prayer* already possessed in the sixteenth century the variable phonetic values which they still retain, allowing them to be freely used in verse as either monosyllables or disyllables. In practice, such words always count as monosyllables in Robert's verse—except that each of the three representative words just cited occurs once, and once only in each case, as a disyllable. The normal monosyllabic value of these words is illustrated in, for example,

Beauties born of the heavens, my soul's delight
(Sonnet 3: 1)

You heaven's equal, who alone (Song 22: 10)

And no power left, that comfort may the night
(Sonnet 6: 4)

You that have power to kill, have will to save
(Sonnet 15: 1)

Only of vows and prayers done sacrifice
(Sonnet 16: 4)

Hither your rites by day, your prayers at night
(Sonnet 32: 14).

The unique occurrences of each as a disyllable are as follows:

For well you know you shine for heaven's grace
(Sonnet 1: 11)

All power is under heavier power set
(*Translated out of Seneca*: 6)

Straight my proud will did unto prayers turn
(Sonnet 9: 9).

In *Translated out of Seneca*: 6 the first *power* is metrically a monosyllable and the second a disyllable: this line may be compared with Shakespeare's Sonnet 124: 4

> Weeds among weeds, or flowers with flowers gathered

where the metrical scheme similarly determines that the first *flowers* counts as one syllable and the second as two. Robert's Sonnet 1 itself contains an example of *heaven* as a monosyllable (line 8) and two occurrences of *heavenly* (lines 2, 13) with the corresponding disyllabic pronunciation (i.e. counting *heaven* as the first syllable). Sonnet 1 may be compared with Sonnet lxxii of Spenser's *Amoretti* which contains two occurrences of *heaven* (both monosyllabic) and two of the possessive *heaven's* (both disyllabic). All such examples lend substance to the notion that Elizabethan poets sometimes brought together two pronunciations of the same word for deliberate effect (cf. *Shakespeare's Sonnets*, ed. Stephen Booth (1977), pp. 288–9): for the device to work properly, both variants must have actually existed at the time in natural pronunciations.

The word *even* occurs only as an adverb in Robert's verse and is always a monosyllable. The ease with which unstressed *e* is elided between consonants in Robert's verse agrees with normal Elizabethan pronunciations, as we may learn from Gabriel Harvey's letter to Spenser on 'our English reformed versifying' (cf. p. 42) wherein he complains of the 'absurdities' of 'yl-favoured *Orthographye*' which distorts natural pronunciations. 'Have we not', he asks indignantly, '*Mooneth*, for *Moonthe*: *sithence*, for *since*: *whilest*, for *whilste*: *phantasie*, for *phansie*: *euen*, for *evn*: *Diuel*, for *Divl* . . . and a thousand of the same stampe.'

The word *flattering* has two distinct values in Robert's verse: in the refrain of Song 12 it has its full extension

> Ah whither will you lead me flattering delight

but elsewhere it is a disyllable—

> And leave fond flatt'ring toys (Song 6: 38)
>
> Feels not more sure the scourge of flatt'ring skill
> (Sonnet 17: 5)
>
> As a flatt'ring winter's day (Pastoral 14: 32).

We may compare the treatment of *flattery* in Shakespeare's Sonnet 114, where the word has its full form in line 2

> Drink up the monarch's plague, this flattery

and in line 9 its elided form

> O 'tis the first, 'tis flatt'ry in my seeing.

Formal Variety

Robert inherited his concern for formal variety from Philip. *Astrophil and Stella* with its eleven diversified songs provides the most obvious comparison with Robert's own sequence, but the most extensive example of Philip's technical virtuosity is provided by his metrical versions of Psalms 1–43: in devising a different verse form for each psalm, Philip in his turn was emulating the example set by his immediate model the Marot-Beza French Psalter of 1562, and the same principle was continued by his sister the Countess of Pembroke when completing the metrical Psalter which her elder brother had begun.

None of the eleven verse forms represented in the eleven *Astrophil and Stella* songs was repeated by Robert in his own sequence —and indeed of Robert's twenty-six non-sonnet forms (two of them found only in poems outside the numbered sequence) only six occur anywhere in Philip's considerable output. Five of these six forms, as reference to the Table of Verse Forms will show, are composed of regular iambics: the one exception is Song 4, to be discussed below (pp. 32–4). Both the complex stanza of Song 4 and the heroic couplets of Elegy 16 are technical experiments of considerable interest, for comparison in each case with the relevant poem by Philip suggests that in his own poem Robert was consciously aiming at a different effect from that obtained by his brother within the same outward form.

Philip's only poem in continuous heroic couplets (OA 27) is a stylized dialogue wherein the lines alternate regularly between the two speakers, each line is a sense unit, and the second line of each couplet responds to the first. The heroic couplets of Elegy 16 are in strong contrast, for Robert deliberately counterpoints the sense pattern against the rhyme pattern. The design of Elegy 16 can be analysed thus:

lines 1–6: *exordium*, divided into two parts, the first part concerning the beloved, the second part (beginning with the seventh syllable of line 3) concerning the speaker but returning to the beloved in line 6.

lines 7–18: *central section*, a succession of four three-line sense units, each of the first three revolving round a particular feature in the beloved (at one pole) and the speaker (at the opposite pole): 7–9 *your eyes . . . mine* [*eyes*]; 10–12 *your heart . . . my heart*; 13–15 *your face . . . my face*. The fourth sense unit, 16–18, climactically celebrates the beloved as the unchanging embodiment of all that is fair.

lines 19–22: *peroration*, echoing the *exordium*, lines 19–20 recalling lines 1–2, lines 21–2 recalling line 4 and line 6 respectively.

The counterpointing of sense pattern against rhyme pattern in the central section may be expressed: aab; bcc; dde; eff. These 3-line sense units linked by rhyme are reminiscent of *terza rima*, which was a favourite form with Philip but does not occur in Robert's known work.

Patterns

The circular movement of Elegy 16 reinforces the evidence from its position in the notebook that, at one stage in the evolution of Robert's design, the Elegy was intended to be the final poem in the numbered sequence (cf. p. 104). The circular Song i of *Astrophil and Stella* ('Only in you my song begins and endeth') indicates that a celebratory poem of this kind is most appropriate either to begin or to end a love sequence. It may be because the Song series in *Astrophil and Stella* begins in this way that Robert for his part chose at one stage to end his sequence with a 'circular' poem in celebration of his beloved (before, that is, he decided to add the block of eight Songs which conclude the notebook as we now have it). Another (no doubt deliberate) difference is that while the last quatrain of Astrophil's Song i is identical with the opening quatrain, Robert's Elegy—apart from the repetition of line 2 as line 20—echoes, rather than literally repeats, its opening in its conclusion.

The circle, the figure which 'knows no end', symbolizes both *eternity* and the *crown* which adorns not only those who intrinsically exist to be celebrated (a deity, the beloved) but also those who have brought their earthly trials to a triumphant conclusion ('Finis *coronat* opus'). These significances are present in the first stanza of Song 10, behind which can also be discerned the hymn quoted by Marsilio Ficino in his Commentary on the *Symposium* (II. ii), 'Amor circulus est bonus a bono in bonum perpetuo revolutus'. Yet the circle which symbolizes eternal bliss can also symbolize eternal despair, and it is this baleful significance which informs Sonnet 17, the only poem in the sequence apart from Elegy 16 whose conclusion verbally echoes its opening. Sonnet 17 opens with 'The endless alchemist'—an arresting use of the adjective which probably contains a reminiscence of Philip's phrase 'endlessly despairing' (*Astrophil and Stella* 97) and which in context refers to the alchemist's endless pursuit of an endlessly receding mirage. Sonnet 17's opening *endless* is echoed in its last line about the hapless poet-lover who finds

> Nor end with joys, nor end from cares in love

and the sonnet's circular movement thus represents the antithesis of the eternal circle evoked in Song 10's opening stanza where the happy lovers 'know no end of joy' and wear 'a crown of pleasure'.

Robert did not complete the Crown of sonnets which he began in praise of his beloved: signs of strain might be detected towards the end of the fragment we have, and on the surface it appears that the creative impulse flagged and expired prematurely. But if so, Robert had the option of simply discarding his failure: instead, he chose to transcribe it into his notebook and to number it as part of both the main and the alternative sequences. He even chose to retain the opening quatrain of the Crown's abandoned fifth sonnet, thus gratuitously (it would seem) emphasizing the abortive nature of the undertaking. The probable explanation is that Robert saw the unfinished Crown as symbolizing the condition of the hapless lover, who fails not only to win for himself 'the crown of true desire' (Song 18) but fails also to carry out his beloved's command as described in the Crown's opening sonnet—though in attempting to do so he at least proves his 'obedience' as well as his 'folly'. Robert's inclusion of a self-confessed failure in his sequence may also represent another calculated divergence from Philip whose own Crown (OA 72) is, of course, completed. Robert's note at the end of his broken Crown—*The rest of the 13 sonnets doth want*—

raises the question why 13? Philip's Crown is in ten ten-line stanzas (plus four-line envoy) and on this analogy—the number of units corresponding to the number of lines per unit—Robert's Crown should consist of fourteen sonnets, as indeed his daughter's completed Crown actually does.[4] All the evidence indicates that Robert was alluding to the unluckiness of thirteen in popular belief, and that the same allusion lies behind the 'conceit' of constructing out of poems which he selected from the main sequence an alternative sequence consisting of thirteen items in all wherein the ill-fated Crown is itself positioned as the centrepiece (see p. 112). The wording of Robert's terminal note to the Crown certainly shows that he had abandoned any idea of completing it—but also raises for us the question whether he ever really intended to do so.

The most pervasive figure in Robert's poetry is the chiasmus, i.e. the pattern formed when a series of elements is first stated and then repeated back in reverse order, as in a mirror image (the rhyme-scheme abbaabba used in the octaves of all Robert's sonnets exemplifies this pattern). In the first two quatrains of Song 21 the sense pattern is carefully matched to the chiasmal rhyme-scheme. The outer lines of Song 21's first quatrain refer to the morning, the outer lines of the second quatrain refer to the moon, while the inner lines of both these quatrains concern the beloved, here presented as the source of all beauty in the created universe so that the cosmic images (the morning, the moon) which represent the beauty of the outer world are compared to her rather than she to them. The same matching of sense pattern to rhyme-scheme occurs again in the final quatrain of Song 21 where *eyes* and their corresponding verb *see* span the outer lines while *heart* and its corresponding verb *love* are contained in the inner lines.

The chiasmal figure is to be recognized in much of the poetry's verbal detail. Thus in the paradox expressed

> I present, absent am; unseen in sight (Sonnet 30: 4)

unseen corresponds with (and glosses) *absent* while *in sight* has the same relationship to *present*, and in

> Of wretched monsters I most monstrous wretch
> (Sonnet 19: 3)

[4] Lady Mary Wroth, 'Pamphilia to Amphilanthus', pp. 36–41 (see head-note to Appendix C).

the chiasmal verbal pattern is ingeniously combined with an adjective-noun/noun-adjective interchange. In the conclusion of Song 22

> Beauty and love, which only true
> Wretch are in me, and in blest you

the centrally placed *true* governs both pairs of matched elements (*Beauty* = *blest you* : *love* = *wretch me*) while by separating the pairs into their constituent elements and arranging these chiasmally the beloved is made both to begin and to end this climactic couplet.

Such poetry may manipulate syntax so as to allow the creation of aesthetically pleasing and expressive patterns not possible within the constructions and word order of ordinary prose. The commonest kind of manipulation involves simple transposition, as in the last line of Sonnet 23

> As present pain than absent joy is worse

which could easily be rearranged

> As present pain is worse than absent joy

though the final emphasis thus placed on *joy* would be out of harmony with the emotional tone of the whole poem. Similarly, the lines

> As only that he liveth
> His sense of pain doth show (Song 13: 12–13)

involve only a simple transposition from the normal prose order 'As only his sense of pain doth show that he liveth', which however would leave a lingering emphasis on the idea of *living* whereas it is the sense of living *pain* which the poetry stresses. One more example

> That of sense not led astray
> Only she should be desirèd (Song 20: 41–2)

will suffice to illustrate how transposition may help to ensure that the concluding emphasis—whether of stanza or whole poem—falls where emotionally it belongs.

Some degree of syntactical flexibility is intrinsic to the language of poetry itself: although such devices as transposition can become mechanical, in both Philip's and Robert's verse they are generally used to enhance the expressive value of a highly disciplined poetic language. To describe this feature in purely negative terms as 'a tendency to tortured syntax' which 'slows the reader down' (*British Library Journal*, i, 1975, p. 116) is equivalent to seeing in the stylized steps of a ballet dancer nothing more than a series of stilted movements.

The concern with pattern, with formal design, is fundamental to Robert's poetry. The elaborate correlative structure of Pastoral 9 can hardly escape notice: some other controlling structures, however, are less immediately apparent, and it may be worth pointing out some further examples of a feature which the Elizabethan reader was conditioned to recognize more readily than might today's reader.

Pastoral 2 is a dialogue poem which revolves entirely round the theme announced in its opening—the Nymph's attempt to make the Shepherd define how much he loves her. Having in the first line of stanza 2 rejected mere words as a proof of love, the Nymph proceeds to name a series of four things which the Shepherd is challenged to prefer to herself. These four things are arranged in ascending order and a stanza is devoted to each—*thy good flock* (stanza 2), *thine eyes* (stanza 3), *thy life* (stanza 4), *thyself* (stanza 5). Having rejected all these in turn as unworthy of comparison with his love, the Shepherd declares in stanza 6 that his love for the Nymph can be compared only to herself—

> Like thyself, like nothing else, is
> My love to thee.

In the final stanza (stanza 7), the Shepherd, at the Nymph's request, defines the meaning of this climactic statement.

The key word of Song 6 is *joys* and the Song's theme is the total reciprocity of the love it celebrates—the Lady's love for the Knight exactly equals the Knight's love for the Lady. On learning of the Knight's death the Lady declares (lines 57–60 = stanza 15)

> Of my life the limits were
> The joys his love did lend,
> Which since death will not forbear
> Desire of life doth end

which is matched by the Knight's declaration (lines 97–100 = stanza 25)

Buried deep in joyless grave
This carcass is of mine,
For the world is a dark cave
Where her lights do not shine

and both declarations are fully answered, once the Knight has been buried in the Lady's breast, in the conclusion (lines 133–6 = stanza 34)

The most loving, most beloved,
To death by absence pressed,
By no time to be removed
At full joys here doth rest.

The balanced intervals which separate these counterbalancing stanzas—nine stanzas intervening between the first and second and eight between the second and third—reinforce the underlying design of the poem.

In stanzas 1 and 2 of Pastoral 8 the Nymph ironically reproaches the Shepherd with having been led astray by other women since their last meeting: in the following stanzas her rejections of him become more and more decisive, the mounting progression being emphasized by the verbal links between them —*believed/belief* (stanzas 3–4), *scorn/scorn* (stanzas 4–5), *scorn, hate/scorn, hate* (stanzas 5–6), *go away/then I will go* (stanzas 7–8).

In addition to the patterns *within* individual poems are the latent patterns which may be discovered in the relationships *between* individual poems: these are discussed below in the section 'Robert's Use of the Sequence as a Form'.

The Metrical Aspect

It may prove helpful at this point to recall an inherent characteristic of iambic metres in English, namely that 'reversal of the first foot and of some middle foot after a strong pause is a thing so natural that our poets have generally done it, from Chaucer down, without remark' and that this habit hardly produces a formal change of rhythm 'but rather is that irregularity which all natural growth and motion shews' (Gerard Manley Hopkins, *Author's Preface* to MS B of his poems). Since reversal of the first foot is so normal, whereas the second foot (as Hopkins also remarked) is sensitive and cannot easily be disturbed, the alternate-stress metres may most readily be distinguished according to whether the regular stress falls on the third syllable (trochaic metre) or on the fourth (iambic metre).

The essential distinction between trochaic and iambic verse consists in the striking difference of effect between falling and rising rhythms: it is this difference which is ignored when trochaic lines are explained, as in theory they might be, as iambics lacking the initial syllable (the point is well made by Robert Bridges, *Milton's Prosody*, revised final edition, Oxford (1921), p. 54). That Robert Sidney distinguished between the two metres is clear from the way he developed the device of employing both trochaic and iambic lines in the same poem, always as a regularly recurring element of the stanzaic pattern. Philip had used the same device, though there is a major difference of emphasis between the two brothers in this respect: of Philip's fifteen trochaic poems only four include iambic lines, while iambic lines are included in all but one of Robert's seven trochaic poems.

In Song 10's six-line stanza every line is catalectic (i.e. contains an odd number of syllables) so that the regular alternation between trochaic and iambic lines produces a corresponding alternation between masculine rhyme (trochaic lines) and feminine rhyme (iambic lines):

> Yóu who fávour dó enjóy
> And spénd and kéep love's tréasure,
> Yóu who knów no énd of jóy
> Nor límits fínd nor méasure,
> Yóu whose cáres triúmphing ón annóy
> Give yóu a crówn of pléasure.

In each six-line stanza of Song 22 lines 5–6 are iambic while lines 1–4 are in a well-known metre which had already enjoyed a long and distinguished history in Latin verse—a trochaic tetrameter wherein every other line is catalectic so that eight-syllable lines with feminine endings alternate with seven-syllable lines with masculine endings.[5] In Latin verse each eight-syllable/

[5] This 'trochaic tetrameter catalectic' is the metre of the first two stanzas of the Ode which concludes Samuel Daniel's sequence *To Delia* (1592). Philip Sidney was probably the first poet consciously to use the metre in English: it appears in lines 1–4 of the eight-line stanza employed for his version of Psalm 42, as well as in *Astrophil and Stella* ii, in lines 1–2 of each quatrain, lines 3–4 of which repeat the pattern in reverse order ($a_8b_7b_7a_8$).

seven-syllable pair was usually written as one long line with caesura after the eighth syllable—a method sometimes adopted for this metre in English verse (e.g. Tennyson's *Locksley Hall*). A variant of this metre appears in the refrain to Song 3 (a refrain whose trochaic beat is determined by its second line)

> Lóve not whó have nót loved
> Ánd who dó love, lóve no móre.

Both the switch from the iambics employed within the stanzas, and the fact that this refrain represents the only unrhymed verse anywhere in Robert's poetry, combine to draw attention to the metre here. Song 3's refrain is an inverted verbal echo of the refrain of the *Pervigilium Veneris*

> Crás amét qui núnquam amávit
> quíque amávit crás amét

and Robert's refrain echoes not just the words but also the 'trochaic catalectic' metre of that famous late-Classical poem.[6] The imitation extends to the way Song 3's refrain is used, like the refrain of the *Pervigilium Veneris*, to begin the poem as well as to conclude each stanza.

Robert's sophisticated handling of standard metres provides the necessary background against which to assess the exceptional case of Song 4, within whose six-line stanzas there is continual fluctuation (fluctuation not governed by any set pattern) between disyllabic and trisyllabic feet. The disyllabic feet are essentially iambs (occasionally subject to 'natural' reversal in the first foot) and the trisyllabic feet, while mainly anapaests, are sometimes modified into feet more naturally scanned as amphimacers and at least once into a foot more naturally scanned as a dactyl. Thus we get lines composed of such combinations as

[6] The Latin refrain is here printed in two lines to facilitate comparison with Song 3's refrain. The *Pervigilium Veneris* was not rediscovered until the sixteenth century and was first printed as a four-page pamphlet in 1577. The first generally accessible text was published at Antwerp in 1580 in Justus Lipsius, *Electorum Liber I*, pp. 35–46. The printings which followed from 1587 to 1592 are mostly included in one-volume collected editions of Catullus, Tibullus, and Propertius, and append to the *Pervigilium Veneris* the note 'quod quidam Catullo tribuunt'.

Béautў's sphére,|thróne ŏf lóve [amphimacer + amphimacer]
Héart ănd eýes|Ĭ dŏ túrn [amphimacer + anapaest]
Phóenĭxlĭke|jóy ănd búrn [dactyl + amphimacer].

The mixed metre is established in the first stanza, where lines 1–2 and 4–5 are iambics (with reversed initial foot in line 5) while the only natural scansion of line 3 is anapaestic, which metre also provides the best scansion of line 3's structural counterpart, line 6:

My sóul in púrest fíre
Doth nót aspíre
To rewárd of my páin
True pléasure ís in lóve
Ónly to lóve
And not séek to obtáin.

In this first stanza variations in the scansion are matched to the rhyme-scheme, iambic lines rhyming with iambic and anapaestic with anapaestic, but these two stress-patterns are variously modified and variously combined in succeeding stanzas.

Two features of Song 4 are notable: (1) the rhythms suggested by the sense must help to determine how any given line is to be read, though variant scansions of some lines still remain possible; (2) these shifting rhythms are held within a fixed pattern of syllables and rhyme.

The only poem by Philip to employ a similarly mixed metre (including iambs and anapaests) is *Certain Sonnets* 24. Philip's poem, however, is written to a named tune, 'The smokes of Melancholy', and although in the absence of that tune the metrical scheme cannot be established with certainty (cf. Ringler, p. 431) it presumably contains a more regular stress pattern than Song 4. That Robert, nevertheless, had his elder brother's mixed-metre poem in mind is indicated by another kind of reminiscence, the verbal echo of the conclusion of Philip's poem in Song 4's conclusion.

There is one other poem by Philip besides *Certain Sonnets* 24 which Robert must have had specifically in mind when composing Song 4. As reference to the Table of Verse Forms will show, Song 4 is the only place where Robert uses a complex stanza form which had also been used by Philip, and we may detect here the same concern with metrical experiment on Robert's part as comparison between the heroic couplets of the two brothers has already suggested. Philip's version of Psalm 33 is composed in regular iambics and moves stiffly within the strait-jacket of its intricate stanza: it can hardly be a coincidence that Robert adopted the same rare stanza for his mixed-metre poem, and we may deduce that he did so in a deliberate attempt to achieve a more flexible rhythm than his brother had achieved within the same outward pattern of syllables and rhyme.

Where notation is supplied to the lines quoted in this Introduction it is intended as no more than an outline guide to the reading of the verse, with a particular view to suggesting how far variations of rhythm may be accommodated within the formal metrical structures which enclose each poem. There is no attempt—even supposing a notation adequate for the purpose could exist—to distinguish varying degrees of stress, or those shades of expression which will always differentiate one reading from another. Any reading may be valid which responds to the sense of the words and the emotion behind them, and no two readings can (or should) be identical in all respects.

From the metrical point of view Song 4 can be seen as the 'literary' counterpart of Song 6, a homespun ballad whose apparent *naïveté* is in reality the product of conscious art. Like all Robert's poems, Song 6 has a fixed outward structure, in this case consisting of quatrains whose pattern is $a_7b_6a_7b_6$. This, the longest of Robert's poems, was designed to have a special value within the sequence, and one aspect of that value consists in the poem's special relationship to the rhythms of ordinary speech. The 'ground rhythm' is given in lines 5–6

Áged fáther só to thée
Thy trávail wórk thy rést

where, in conventional prosodic terms, the first line is 'trochaic tetrameter catalectic' and the second 'iambic trimeter'. While this alternating pattern is never absent for long, the rhythms of natural speech are continually playing across it in such a way as to forbid the imposition of a formal scansion on the poem as a whole. The speech rhythms are allowed free play, yet for its total effect Song 6 depends on the fact that its flexible rhythms are contained within a set pattern of syllables and rhyme. The opening lines

> Yónder cómes a sád pílgrim
> From the Eást he retúrns

establish at the outset that this poem is not going to fit into any regular stress-pattern—and incidentally illustrate how the prosody here allows the rhyme to be carried on an unstressed syllable, as it is again in

> Mány óne see wé lády (line 9)

and

> Súch a óne I sáw lády (line 21).

Song 6 when heard as speech depends for its proper effect on preserving the natural speech accent of the words, and to prevent any uncertainty in this case the natural pronunciations of *pilgrim* and *lady* are clearly demonstrated elsewhere within the poem:

> Pilgrim he is well to know (line 13)
>
> Lady know truth, truth to be (line 37)
>
> Pilgrim said he to me (line 70)
>
> Tell the lady that doth rest (line 73).

Another symptom of Song 6's special prosody is the fact that it is able to include a feminine rhyme (*pleasure* : *treasure*, lines 50, 52) without infringing the strict syllabic structure of the verse.

The coming together of stressed monosyllables creates expressive rhythms natural to English speech but excluded by the standard metres of English verse when these are strictly observed. Such rhythms occur freely in Song 6, intermixed with the ground rhythm of alternating stress.

Song 6 is effective and moving when heard as speech, but there is an alternative and equally moving way of hearing it. The form of the dialogue between lady and pilgrim, the shape of the stanzas, and the verbal echoes all combine to show that Robert's poem was inspired by the popular 'Walsingham' ballad whose original words are lost though fragments of them can be recognized in the first three of those 'snatches of old tunes' chanted by

Ophelia in her madness (*Hamlet*, IV. v). The popular ballad also inspired the well-known version attributed to Sir Walter Ralegh, though the Ralegh version betrays itself as in part a 'literary' sophistication. The shifting metre of that version involves the singer in some rather awkward manipulations when all its eleven stanzas are sung to the same tune: the first two stanzas seem to be closely modelled on the lost original, but with the third stanza the metre begins to shift and—most significantly—a man recounting his experience of woman's falsehood appears in place of the faithful loving lady who can be recognized as the central figure of the popular ballad behind the snatches thereof sung by Ophelia. That Song 6 is independent of the sophisticated Ralegh version and draws its inspiration directly from the popular ballad is suggested by the fact that Robert's poem likewise has for its central figure a faithful lady enquiring for news of her absent lover. A notable feature of Song 6 is its reiterated use of the term 'lady', a word not found at all in the male-centred Ralegh version (nor, significantly, anywhere in Robert's own poetry outside Song 6). Comparison of Ophelia's

> He is dead and gone, lady,
> He is dead and gone
> (*Hamlet*, IV. v)

with Robert's

> Such a one I saw lady,
> I once saw such a one,
> But him no more see shall I,
> He is now dead and gone
> (Song 6: 21–4)

suggests that the language and rhythms of Robert's poem are closely akin to the popular ballad which Ophelia recalls. Although the words of that ballad are mostly lost, the tune to which it was sung has enjoyed a better fate. The tune of 'Walsingham', indeed, was widely known in late Elizabethan England if we may judge by the surviving settings for lute and for various keyboard instruments.[7] Robert must have had the tune in his head when composing Song 6 for his words can be sung to it, and the

[7] William Byrd's setting is preserved in Cambridge, Fitzwilliam Museum, Virginal MS. The setting by Francis Cutting reached print in William Barley's *A new book of tablature* (1596).

haunting ballad air repeated throughout the poem's thirty-four stanzas imparts a compelling sadness to the alternating speeches of Lady and Pilgrim. Peter Davidson, to whose generously imparted musical knowledge I am much indebted, acutely comments that the rising musical phrase in the first half of the tune's last line continually emphasizes important monosyllables in the most expressive manner. (See Commentary for the 'Walsingham' tune fitted to Robert's words.) When Song 6 is actually sung in dialogue the alternation of female voice and male voice poignantly brings out the poem's most distinctive feature—the fact that the woman, so far from being the scornful nymph or unattainable goddess she is throughout most of the sequence, is as deeply involved in this poem as her male lover.

Philip Sidney's confession (see 'Robert and Music') of how he was moved at hearing 'the old song of Percy and Douglas' should bring home to us how Elizabethans could enjoy hearing a lengthy narrative sung to a repeated ballad tune, though modern ears might find that experience unduly monotonous. We do not know what version of *Chevy Chase* was heard by Philip but it probably exceeded in length the thirty-four quatrains of Song 6 which can be comfortably sung through in about ten minutes. The way Robert has laid out Song 6 in the notebook, with alternate lines indented but no regular spaces between the quatrains, reflects the way a popular ballad would be sung—straight through, without strong pauses between its stanzas. Robert must have expected his readers to recognize the native 'Walsingham' tune as implicit in the phrasing of his own poem, and in omitting explicit reference to that tune he was leaving readers the option of hearing Song 6 either as speech or as song.

The case is different with Song 12, the only poem in the notebook which explicitly announces itself as written to a named tune. The actual tune which Robert had in mind is discussed in the section 'Robert and Music', but it may be observed here that the popular tune in this case is of French origin, and that the unusual metrical form of Song 12 was evidently devised to fit its foreign tune. Song 6 is effective whether spoken, or sung to its native tune; Song 12 needs to be sung to achieve its proper effect. Those poems in Robert's sequence which are classified in their headings as 'Songs' do in fact evoke the singing voice. Seven of the eleven Songs in *Astrophil and Stella* exist in late sixteenth- or early seventeenth-century musical settings, but these settings all date from after Philip's death and witness, not to any specific tune which Philip himself may have had in mind (so far as we can tell), but rather to the inherently singable quality of the verse. I am not aware of positive evidence that any of Robert's poems, except Song 6 and Song 12, were specially composed to particular tunes: it is probably true in the case of Robert's 'Songs', as of those in Philip's sequence, that while the verse runs easily into song it does not usually depend on particular tunes for its proper effect.

The realization that Robert's poetry admits expressive variations of rhythm needs to be balanced against a realization that he shared with his contemporaries a more formal conception of metre than is commonly held today. The effect of this in practice is twofold, (1) the regular metre will sometimes be found to reinforce the sense in ways which the modern reader might miss, and (2) the special effects produced by departures from that metre may also prove to be unexpectedly meaningful.

A few examples may help to illustrate what has just been said, though the reader will understand that the metrical effect of isolated lines can no more be fully appreciated than can their sense until the lines are restored to their contexts. It will be as well to remember also that any detailed examination of a poet's prosody runs the risk of seeming to suggest that the poet himself was more fully aware of all its details than in reality he is likely to have been. While there can be no doubt that Robert was a highly conscious craftsman, *exactly* how far he analysed his metrical effects remains an open question: instinct must be trusted for some things, and a poet instinctively knows that to analyse too curiously is to risk falling into the ditch like the centipede when asked to explain how he managed his feet.

In the line

Thése are but wórds, I múst prove thée (Pastoral 2: 11)

the metrical stress on both *words* and *thee* is required to bring out an important antithesis, and in

Which láte prayed fór the lánd, now ón it díes (Sonnet 23: 4)

the metrical stress on the two prepositions similarly underlines a significant antithesis. In the opening line of Sonnet 24

Canst thóu turn fróm the háven óf thy rést

the metrical stress again falls on a significant preposition—the image is essentially about turning *away from* rest towards danger. The metrical stress on *thou*, both here and in line 3

> Canst thóu forsáke the míne whose gólden stóre

should also be respected since it underlines the comparison on which the octave turns between the addressee and the speaker, the subjects respectively of the first and second quatrains.

A line which can best be read as containing both Hopkins's 'natural' reversals is

> Yóu for yoursélf, mýself for yóu I lóve (Sonnet 3: 14)

where reversal of the first foot is unquestionable and reversal after the 'strong pause' of the caesura is suggested by the play on *yourself/myself*. George Puttenham's quaint explanation of his own verbal plays *Prove/reprove* : *excuse/accuse* can be adapted to fit Robert's less naïve example—'by reason one of them [the two words involved] doth as it were nicke another, and have a certaine extraordinary sence with all, it behoveth to remove the sharpe accent [in *myself*] from whence it is most naturall, to place it where the nicke may be more expressly discovered' (cf. *The Arte of English Poesie* (1589), p. 111). The reversal also heightens the next regular stress by placing *two* weak syllables before it. The key word *you* occurs in both the first and the eighth positions in the line and the (heightened) stress on the eighth position balances the naturally strong stress on the first position. The stress pattern of the whole phrase underlines the chiasmal pattern formed by the words themselves. It is instructive to compare Robert's line with the metrically simple line which probably suggested it

> I loved my self, because my self loved you.[8]

The repeated stress on the repeated *you* in the line quoted from Sonnet 3 may be compared with

> Neárer to mé than whát with mé was bórn
> (Sonnet 26: 10)

[8] *The Phoenix Nest* (1593), p. 72, where the whole poem appears (anonymously). The line in question—like Robert's, the final line of its poem—had been quoted in 1589 by George Puttenham (p. 168), who described it as coming from 'a most excellent dittie written by Sir *Walter Raleigh*'.

where the most expressive reading involves retaining the metrical stress on *me* in both places: when both these stresses are observed they become the two dominant stresses in the line, symmetrically balanced on either side of the central (and solely metrical) stress on *what*.

The accenting of *myself* in the line quoted from Sonnet 3 may be contrasted with

> Show mé untó mysélf in a trúe líght (Sonnet 6: 8).

Here the verbal play suggests retaining the metrical stress both on *me* and on *myself*—where of course the metre coincides with the natural stressing of the word. The most striking feature of the line, however, is the irregularity of its second half, occasioned by the fact that its 'fourth foot' (*in a*) refuses even the beat supplied by the metre so that in any natural reading a strong 'accentual spondee' will conclude the line. In a formal English metre such a foot constitutes a bold irregularity—in this case matching the bold paradox that only in darkness is the speaker revealed to himself in a true light.

An interesting comparison is afforded by a line which Robert revised precisely in order to enhance its metrical effect. As it originally stood in the notebook the first line of stanza 5 of Pastoral 9 read

> Thís sáid, the shépherd ás with nów new éyes

where, after the opening spondee *This said* (an absolute construction), the line invites a regular scansion wherein *new* carries no stress and the rhythmic pattern suggests taking *now new* as a compound epithet (*now-new*). Robert later revised the line to read

> Thís sáid, the shépherd as nów with néw éyes

which separates *now* from *new* and achieves a strong stress on each of these (in the context) keywords—the stress on *now* heightened by its irregularity and the fact that it follows two weak syllables (which in theory constitute the third foot), the stress on *new* heightened by the boldness of the accentual spondee which—balancing the opening spondee—now concludes the line (cf. 'The Revisions').

Another line which Robert revised to make it more rhythmically expressive is worth considering. The notebook reveals that line 12 of Sonnet 30 originally stood

> Ábsent I wánt what Í care móst to sée

which Robert later revised to read

> Ábsent I wánt áll what I cáre to sée.

The change strengthens the meaning and at the same time enlivens the rhythm by (1) strengthening the caesura, (2) reversing the foot immediately following the caesura and supplying the dominant stress (*all*) which the line previously lacked, and (3) replacing the rather awkward metrical stress on the second *I* with a firm stress on *care*. The stress on *care* combines with the removal of *most* to sharpen the chiasmal word-play with *see my cares* in the next line.

The foregoing examples suggest that Robert was less interested in smoothness for its own sake than in the creation of expressive rhythms, and this is borne out by two irregular lines whose special metrical 'difficulty' must be designed to focus attention on their meaning:

> Which áre what Í ám, and Í what théy áre (Sonnet 4: 4)
>
> Déstiny's fóresight, Lóve's jústice, Wíll's énd
> (Sonnet 14: 10).

Both of these are central lines in statements of the Platonic 'truth' or essence of the poet's love (for the revision which finally produced the latter, see 'The Revisions').

Not all Robert's metrical effects will be equally to everyone's taste, and it would be unreasonable to suggest that he never perpetrates irregularities which fail to justify themselves by their expressiveness. Since no two readers, however, will 'hear' a poem in exactly the same way, these matters must finally be judged by each reader for himself.

Robert inherited Philip's concern with technical innovation, but he was not content merely to extend metrical variety within the categories represented in his elder brother's work. In Song 4 and in Song 6 Robert created poems whose stress patterns are more freely varied than any to be found in Philip's verse—yet these two poems remain disciplined works of art, their variations held within set patterns of syllables and rhyme.

Robert's poetry calls for a reading which acknowledges its formal aspect without suppressing the rhythms of natural speech. Any reading which does not recognize *both* claims will inevitably be the poorer: the challenge is to find an appropriate balance between them. Gabriel Harvey's letter to Edmund Spenser on 'our English reformed Versifying' transcends his habitual pedantry and deserves to be better remembered:

we are not to goe a Tittle farther, either for the *Prosody*, or the *Orthography*, (and therefore your Imaginarie *Diastole* nothing worthe) then we are licenced and authorized by the ordinarie vse, and custome, and proprietie, and Idiome, and, as it were, Maiestie of our speach: which I accounte the only infallible and soueraigne Rule of all Rules.[9]

Harvey is here thinking primarily of those experiments with quantitative metres which were fashionable in some circles during the 1570s and early 1580s though they ultimately proved abortive: his strong words, however, can still bring home to us that native Elizabethan prosody, for all its concern with pattern and technique, may be more flexible, more accommodating to the tones and rhythms of ordinary speech, than an exclusively formal view of it would allow.

PHILIP AND ROBERT

. . . But what do I blunder at thyes thyngys, follo the dyrectyon of your most lovyng brother, who in lovyng you, is comparable with me, or excedyth me. Imitate hys vertues, exercyses, Studyes, & accyons; he ys a rare ornament of thys age, the very formular, that all well dysposed young Gentlymen of ouer Court, do form allsoe thear maners & lyfe by. In troth I speake yt wythout flatery of hym, or of my self, he hathe the most rare vertues that ever I found in any man. . . . Ons agayn I say Imytate hym.

Thus his father[10] advising the young Robert to become like his brother, and as we read the paternal exhortations we begin to realize how it must sometimes have felt to be the younger brother

[9] *Three proper, and wittie, familiar Letters* (1580). The recently discovered author-corrected copy now on deposit in Cambridge University Library (Peterborough G. 3. 6) shows that the passage should read as above, though in all editions *Tittle* is misprinted *little*.

[10] The letter survives among the Sidney papers only in an eighteenth-century transcript apparently made for Arthur Collins, who printed it in his *Letters and Memorials of State* (1746), I. 246–7. Collins's text agrees with the transcript in dating the letter 25 March 1578, though some passages point to a date not earlier than 1580–1.

of Philip Sidney in an age when fathers did not hesitate to administer stiff doses of good advice or to hold up shining examples for emulation.

Robert's birthday fell on 19 November and he was almost exactly nine years younger than the brother (born on 30 November) who from adolescence had been 'the observed of all observers'. The two surviving letters from Philip himself to Robert bear witness, both in their content and in the physical form in which we possess them, to the contemporary taste for the didactic, since both are long letters of advice to Robert while travelling on the Continent and both survive only in early transcripts. What is evidently the earlier of the two letters is undated and survives in numerous transcripts: the other is dated 18 October 1580 (see 'Robert and Music'), contains passages which are more personal, and survives only in an early seventeenth-century transcript among the Sidney papers. Both letters glow with Philip's love of learning, but in the second letter affection and the play of humour suffuse—though in no way do they blunt—the elder brother's eagerness to instruct.

The father's anxiety about Robert's expenditure while abroad strikes a familiar note:

> I fynd by Harry Whyte, that all your money is gon, whych wyth sum wunder displeaseth me; and if you cannot frame your Charges, according to that proportyon I have appoynted you, I must & wyll send for you home. I have sent order to Mr. Languet for one hundryth poundys for you, whych is Twenty pound more than I promysed you; and thys I looke & order, that it shall sarve you tyll the last of March 1580. Assure your self I wyll not Inlarg one grote, therfore looke well to your Charges.

Thus wrote Sir Henry in the letter already quoted, and the tender way in which Philip refers to the same notoriously delicate subject reveals—all the more strongly by contrast with the heavy paternal admonishments—the bond of affection between the two boys. 'My deere Brother', begins Philip's second letter to Robert, 'for the mony yow haue receaued, assure your selfe (for it is true) there is nothing I spend so pleaseth me as that which is for yow.' Philip returns to the subject later in this letter and one sentence—'The odd 30^{li} shall come with the hundred or els my father and I will iarle'—shows that the elder brother, now nearly twenty-six years of age, was prepared to stand up to his father on Robert's behalf if he judged it appropriate.

Robert was present at Arnheim throughout the three and a half weeks that Philip lay there after receiving at Zutphen on 22 September 1586 what eventually proved his death wound. The event which left Robert the head of his family shortly before his twenty-third birthday must have been his most intimate experience of tragedy. Elizabethan decorum, which discouraged open expressions of private grief, helps to explain the sparseness of Robert's own direct references to Philip. Writing to Robert Cecil on 12 January 1600/1 from Wilton, where he was attending his brother-in-law the Earl of Pembroke who was to die just one week later, Robert confessed that he was about to lose the man 'to whome of all men (my father and mine elder brother eccepted) I have bin most bownd vnto'. Robert's surviving letters do not enlarge on the debt to Philip which he here parenthetically acknowledges, nor is any elucidation thereof immediately vouchsafed by Robert's own poetry. On closer examination, however, Robert's sequence not only discloses many echoes of Philip's verse but further discloses metres and forms inherited from Philip being handled so as (1) to create consciously differentiated prosodic effects, and (2) to portray a different view of love.

Song 17, the shortest poem in the sequence, is an example of what Puttenham[11] called 'a full Allegorie' or 'long and perpetuall Metaphore':

> The sun is set, and maskèd night
> Veils heaven's fair eyes:
> Ah what trust is there to a light
> That so swift flies.
>
> A new world doth his flames enjoy,
> New hearts rejoice:
> In other eyes is now his joy,
> In other choice.

If this lyric existed in isolation—if it were not set in the sequence—the reader might well see it as Robert's lament for his brother The favourite image for the female beloved in Neoplatonic poetry, however, is the inherently masculine image of the sun and that dominant image is continually used throughout Robert's sequence in a way which illustrates the characteristically Neo-

[11] *The Arte of English Poesie* (1589), p. 156. Sonnets 20 and 31 of Robert's sequence are other examples of 'full Allegorie'.

platonic indifference to the anomaly involved. Compare, for example, Robert's Pastoral 8: 21–4, or Sonnet 4 of Henry Constable's *Diana* (1592) which describes the poet's beloved as she sleeps and concludes

> I feel my sun's heat, though his light I miss.

When Song 17 is set in context it is seen as the poet's lament for his beloved's absence. Philip's *literary* presence can be recognized in the background, however, for Robert's lyric starts as a variation on a theme supplied by lines 3–4 of the opening quatrain of *Astrophil and Stella* 91:

> Stella, while now by honour's cruel might
> I am from you, light of my life, misled,
> And that fair you my sun, thus overspread
> With absence' veil, I live in sorrow's night.

In considering the macabre images which Robert's poetry contains, the modern reader needs to bear in mind that disease and death were familiar realities to the Elizabethan and that Robert in particular was closely surrounded by them in Flushing, that plague-spot where he spent so much of his time during the 1590s. Robert's younger brother Thomas died in July 1595 at the early age of twenty-six, and his best friend among the Dutch died of the plague at Middleburg in May 1597 (see 'Ideal Beauty'). These losses were fresh in Robert's experience during the years 1595–7 which other evidence suggests as the period when the poems were mainly being composed (see in particular 'The Betrayal Theme'). While the macabre images may ultimately reflect the physical reality of Philip's last illness some ten years before, we should expect Robert's memory of that event to have blended with other griefs by the time he began composing his poetry.

According to Greville's account, Philip assured the doctors when they began to dress his wound 'that while his strength was yet entire, his body free from feaver, and his mind able to endure, they might freely use their art, cut, and search to the bottome'.[12] Yet the doctors failed to amputate Philip's injured leg when gangrene set in and amputation might have given him

[12] Fulke Greville, *The Life of the Renowned Sir Philip Sidney* (1652), p. 146.

his only chance of life. Robert seems to be recalling this in the opening of Sonnet 26:

> 'Ah dearest limbs, my life's best joy and stay,
> How must I thus let you be cut from me,
> And losing you, myself unusefull see,
> And keeping you, cast life and all away'
>
> Full of dead gangrenes doth the sickman say
> Whose death of part, health of the rest must be.

While the physical reality of Philip's last illness seems to lie behind these lines, we should equally recognize the probable contribution made by Philip's pastoral romance, where it is said of the constant man 'for the saving of all his body he will not spare the cutting off a limb'. These words of Pyrocles in Book IV of the *Arcadia* (Robertson, p. 296) may have seemed to Robert in retrospect ironically to anticipate the reality of Philip's own death. The real and the imagined in such a case become inextricable. At all events, Robert has assimilated the image of the man infected with gangrene to the purposes of his own poetry, for in Sonnet 26 that image becomes a symbol of the poet's hopeless love.

Greville's wish to edify is manifest throughout his *Life* of Philip and inevitably influenced his description of the deathbed, where Robert's human weakness is used as a foil to the fortitude in the face of death shown by Philip himself:

> The last scene of this Tragedy was the parting between the two brothers: the weaker shewing infinite strength in suppressing sorrow, and the stronger infinite weakness in expressing of it. So far did invaluable worthinesse, in the dying brother enforce the living to descend beneath his owne worth, and by abundance of childish tears, bewaile the publique, in his particular loss.[13]

While recognizing that conscious design has shaped this description we can still acknowledge the essential truth it contains and recognize therein the reason why Robert failed to produce his own elegy on Philip: he was himself too close to the painful reality to be able to turn the experience into art.

The contemporary elegists distance Philip's death under various pastoral disguises, but all make some allusion to his valour or his martial prowess and thereby acknowledge that he died

[13] Fulke Greville, op. cit., p. 159.

a hero's death. Spenser's *Astrophel*, which was not published until 1595, presents Philip as an Adonis figure who while hunting *salvage beasts* was pierced in the thigh by a boar's *fell tooth* —a transparent allegory of Philip's actual death, from a bullet wound received in the thigh while fighting his country's enemies.

Philip's nineteen-year-old wife, who had joined him at Flushing in June, nursed him through his final days: the Earl of Leicester wrote after Philip's death to her father Sir Francis Walsingham to say that she 'is here with me at Vtrickt, till she may recouer some strength, for she is wonderfully ouerthrowen thorow hir longe care since the beginning of her husbandes hurt' (Leicester to Walsingham, 25 October 1586).[14] The presence of Philip's wife at his bedside during his last days is poetically represented in Spenser's pastoral elegy where the shepherds carry the wounded Astrophel to his *lovèd lass* who stays with him lamenting until he departs this life. As it develops, Spenser's elegy merges the image of the woman whom Philip had celebrated in his poetry with that of the girl whom he had married in 1583 when she was still only in her sixteenth year: Spenser's merging of the two loves of Philip's life is symbolized in the fact that the elegy which says of Stella

> Her he did love, her he alone did honour,
> His thoughts, his rimes, his songs were all upon her

is dedicated *To the most beautiful and vertuous Ladie, the Countesse of Essex*, who (as the initiated would realize) was actually Philip's widow, by now remarried.

It should be clear that—despite previous suggestions to the contrary—the Knight in Robert's Song 6 who dies solely of grief for his absent love cannot represent Philip. There are clues in the text of Song 6 which taken together covertly point to the Flanders coast as the place where the Knight pines to death—but the text also contains clear indications that this is a metaphorical death. The way the Knight speaks of himself as already dead and buried in the *dark cave* which the world itself has become in the absence of his beloved should tell the reader that the *living burial* towards which the parting lover goes in Song 1 has in Song 6 actually taken place (cf. 'Robert and Barbara').

[14] *Correspondence of Robert Dudley, Earl of Leycester*, ed. John Bruce, Camden Society xxvii (1844), pp. 445–7.

Song 6 is founded on a metaphor to which Philip's own poetry had given memorable expression, and in a single line of Philip's

Absence is death, or worse, to them that love

can be recognized the seed from which Robert's longest poem was to grow. This seminal line marks in fact the culminating point of one of Philip's most elaborately structured poems, which is echoed several times in Robert's sequence (Ringler, *Other Poems*, 5). Another of Philip's poems (*Certain Sonnets* 20) is founded on the metaphor of departure from the beloved as a death.

Viewed from another angle, Song 6 evokes Song viii of *Astrophil and Stella*: both are the longest poems of their respective sequences, and in both the woman reveals that she is as much in love as the man and thus adds a dimension to a male-centred genre. The comparison thus implicitly invited, however, brings out important differences between the situations portrayed in the two poems (cf. p. 62).

Discernible just below the surface of Robert's sequence are the frustrations which he experienced in his private life and in his public career during the 1590s. Although some images probably reflect Robert's memory of the tragedy which took place at Arnheim in October 1586, it is not ultimately the dying Philip but Philip the living poet whom Robert's sequence recalls—and recalls most tellingly in the way the elder brother's work is evoked to help define a different view of love. In avoiding public recognition as a poet, Robert was probably influenced by a wish to avoid invidious comparisons with his brother. In choosing nevertheless to be both a poet himself, and something more in that capacity than a mere imitator of Philip, Robert in his own way continues Philip's aim to extend the range and variety of English verse.

ROBERT AND MUSIC

The letter which his elder brother wrote to him from London on 18 October 1580 (cf. Preface and 'Philip and Robert') contains the most personal of the few references we possess to Robert's skill in music. The letter was written a month before Robert's seventeenth birthday and while he was still on the Continent, where he had already been travelling for the better part of two years. After a wealth of serious advice Philip proceeds to lighten the tone and *inter alia* urges 'Now sweete Brother take a delight to keep and increase your Musick, you will not beleive what a want I finde of it in my Melancholie times.' Although familiar to students of Philip, the sentence has been imperfectly understood. It has been seen as evidence that the writer himself lacked the skill to perform on a musical instrument (James M. Osborn, *Young Philip Sidney* (1972), p. 81) though it is improbable that Philip really lacked such a standard accomplishment of the Renaissance courtier. An alternative suggestion had previously been made that Philip was referring to music in general and 'could very well mean no more than that he enjoyed the solace of music when he was feeling sad, whether played by himself or another' (John Buxton, *Sir Philip Sidney and the English Renaissance* (1954), p. 113). There is no obvious reason, however, why Philip—though deprived for the time of Robert's music—should be missing music in general at the period when he wrote the letter.

The various poems he wrote to named tunes demonstrate Philip's interest in musical technique, and near the end of the long letter of advice[15] which he wrote to Edward Denny on Whit Sunday 1580 Philip requests 'that you remember with your good voyce, to singe my songes for they will one well become an other'. Since Philip wished his friend Ned Denny to sing his songs, it is natural to suppose that he would likewise have wished his own beloved and musical younger brother to do so. The request to Denny suggests that we should take literally the references in *Astrophil and Stella* to Stella (Penelope Rich) delighting Philip with her singing—and specifically with her singing of his own songs (see sonnets 57 and 59, also Song iii). Most readers of *A Defence of Poetry* remember Philip's confession of his own 'barbarousness' at being moved more than with a trumpet when he heard 'the old song of Percy and Douglas' (i.e. the *Ballad of Chevy Chase*) sung by a blind fiddler. In fact, we have Philip's own ample testimony, in both prose and verse, that he enjoyed listening to music, and that to him music primarily meant singing.

The whole of Philip's letter to Robert of 18 October 1580 is

[15] Printed by James M. Osborn, *Young Philip Sidney* (1972), pp. 537-40. The letter survives only in a transcript, now in the Bodleian, made *c.*1600 by John Mansell, subsequently President of Queens' College, Cambridge.

eloquent of the elder brother's tender concern for the younger's education and welfare. Only when it is seen in context, and only when we remember how long Robert had already been abroad and recall how Philip was moved by the sound of singing, does that letter's reference to 'your music' become fully intelligible. Philip wants Robert to return home improved in all accomplishments, and as a special inducement for him to improve his music Philip confesses how much he himself is missing, during Robert's prolonged absence from the family circle, the pleasure of hearing him play and sing. Once the full meaning of the passage is grasped, its intimacy may surprise us: it opens a small window into the household where Robert grew up to become a poet.

The more intimate aspects of Elizabethan life can usually be recaptured only by means of such incidental glimpses, and through piecing together scattered fragments of information. The Sidney family papers include a series of accounts for payments made on behalf of Robert when he was a boy and these record that in April 1576 Richard Lant was paid 6*s.* 8*d.* 'for his paines taken in teaching him to singe'. Robert was twelve and a half years old at this time and was already up at Christ Church, Oxford, where he seems to have entered into residence as early as June 1575. Richard Lant[16] was then master of the choristers at Christ Church and the fact that the Sidney family paid him to give Robert singing lessons suggests that they recognized the boy's musical talent and wanted him to bear his part at social and family gatherings when music was being performed.

Among the various volumes dedicated to Robert in later life are two music books, Robert Jones's *First Book of Songs and Ayres* (1600) and the anthology *A Musicall Banquet* (1610) compiled by John Dowland's son Robert. That both these dedications eulogize Robert's patronage of the arts is no more than predictable, but the latter dedication actually vouchsafes a tantalizing nugget of real information, for Robert Dowland therein reminds the dedicatee (and thus reveals to his readers) that it was with 'your Lordship undertaking for mee' that 'I was

[16] Richard Lant was one of at least four members of the Lant family to join the Christ Church choir during the third quarter of the sixteenth century (see Joseph Foster, *Alumni Oxonienses*). They may have been related to Thomas Lant (*c.* 1556–1600: see *DNB*) who began his career as servant to Philip Sidney and who made the famous drawing of Philip's funeral procession in 1587 which was engraved and published in 1588.

made a member of the Church of Christ, and withall received from you my names'. Nothing is known of Robert Sidney's acquaintance with John Dowland beyond the one fact that Robert—who like Dowland was born in 1563—agreed to become godfather to the composer's son (born *c.*1590). *A Musicall Banquet* begins with a piece by John Dowland which is listed in the Table of Contents as 'Syr Robert Sidney his Galliard' while the heading of the page containing the piece itself refers to him by his more recent titles: 'The Right Honourable the Lord Viscount *Lisle*, Lord Chamberlaine to the Queenes most excellent Maiestie, his Galliard'. The piece is an impressive set of divisions on a tune which is closely related to the tenor part of the immensely popular chanson 'Susanne un jour', and the connection is confirmed by the version in Cambridge University Library, MS Dd. 2. 11, which is actually entitled 'Susanna Galliard' (cf. Diana Poulton, *John Dowland* (1972), pp. 149–50).

It may throw light on Robert's association with the galliard to recall how his eldest daughter performed before the ageing Queen during the Christmas festivities of 1602. On 28 December of that year his faithful agent Rowland Whyte reported to Robert that 'Mistress Mary on St. Stevens day in the after noone dawnced before the Queen two galliards with one Mr. Palmer, the admirablest dawncer of his tyme; both were much comended by her Maiestie: then she dawnced with him a corante.' Robert's eldest daughter, who married Sir Robert Wroth in 1604 and in 1605 appeared at court in Ben Jonson's *Masque of Blackness*, was also to follow in her father's footsteps as a poet and was evidently the leading dancer and musician of her generation in the Sidney family. Her musical skill is commemorated in the portrait, painted in the early seventeenth century and still at Penshurst, where she is depicted full length holding a fine theorbo: when she was still a child Rowland Whyte reported from Penshurst to her father 'God bless her, she is very forward in her learning, writing and other exercises she is put to, as dawncing and the virginalls' (23 October 1595). The same theme reappears in a letter over four years later in the great series from Rowland Whyte; writing from Baynard's Castle in London, and having retailed the latest political news, Whyte concludes by reassuring Robert that his wife and family 'are well, and pray for you. They are kept at ther bookes, they dance, they sing, they play on the lute, and are carefully kept vnto yt' (9 February 1599/1600). The picture evoked is of a household where both Philip's and Robert's songs might readily find performers.

In choosing as their dedication piece to Robert a galliard based on a popular chanson the two Dowlands may have been alluding to a special interest on Robert's part in French music. There are other indications of such an interest, which may have begun during Robert's embassy to France early in 1594 when he gained for himself the personal affection of Henri IV and his beloved mistress Gabrielle d'Estrées ('Madame'). The letter (*Paris*, 15 July 1598) wherein the English diplomat Thomas Edmondes assures Robert of Madame's continued affection for him (see 'Robert and Other Women') concludes with a postscript which illustrates the familiar friendship between Robert and the Earl of Southampton and discloses that the twenty-five-year-old nobleman—who was in Paris at the time as a member of Cecil's embassy—had agreed to act as an intermediary between Robert and the Parisian music-seller Léon Cavellat.[17] Edmondes's postscript mentions certain enclosures which unfortunately are no longer present: '. . . I send your Lordship a letter & certeine songes which were delyvered me by my lord of Southampton to convey to your Lordship from Cavelas. His Lordship comendeth himself most kindlie to you and would have written to you if it had not ben for a litle sloathfullnes.'

These Parisian connections may explain why Song 12 of Robert's sequence, the only one of his poems which he explicitly tells us is written to a tune, is in fact *To a french Tune/Ou estes vous allez mes belles amourettes*. No early version of a tune so called has yet been traced, but there is good reason to suppose that the tune none the less survives in a collection of popular songs entitled *Chansonnier, ou Recueil de Chansons Anecdotes* which was being compiled in France around the year 1700 (British Library, MS Egerton 815). On fo. 350 of that volume is a tune called 'Où êtes vous allées mes belles Amours', fitted to satirical verses dated 1705, beginning 'Gens de Cour qui ne Scavez pas / Ce qui se passe à la Ville'. There is nothing unusual about a popular tune persisting for a century or more, and *The Beggar's Opera* provides a famous English example,

[17] Léon Cavellat carried on his trade in Paris from 1577 until his death in 1610. He acquired the stock of Nicholas du Chemin on the latter's death in 1577.

dating from about a generation after MS Egerton 815, of a whole treasury of traditional melodies surviving into the eighteenth century and then being set to topical verses. Although in the space of a century a tune might undergo some modifications, it looks very much as if the chanson in MS Egerton 815 is to the same tune—at least in essentials—as that to which Robert fitted his verses. The unusual metrical shape of Song 12 chimes with the surviving version of the tune: the musical phrases correspond with the verse lines, and among those features of the melody which accord well with Robert's words is the fact that the peak of the musical phrase, in the first and in the second line of each stanza, coincides with the eighth syllable (see Commentary for the air from MS Egerton 815 fitted to Robert's words).

In composing Song 12 to the tune of *Ou estes vous allez* Robert can scarcely have been unmindful that of the eight poems by his brother to named tunes—all eight included in the collection published as *Certain Sonnets*—not one is to a French tune.[18] A more revealing difference from Philip is represented by Robert's Song 6, which in its form and in its phrasing evokes the native ballad tune of 'Walsingham' (see 'Formal Aspects': 'The Metrical Aspect'). Although Philip himself never wrote a ballad, his passing reference to 'the old song of Percy and Douglas' in *A Defence of Poetry* remains one of the most vivid tributes we possess to the vitality of the popular oral tradition in Elizabethan England. The disparaging element in Philip's tribute need not be glossed over: the ballad which moves his heart more than with a trumpet is yet sung 'but by some blind crowder, with no rougher voice than rude style; which being so evil apparelled in the dust and cobwebs of that uncivil age, what would it work trimmed in the gorgeous eloquence of Pindar?' All the same, it is that blind crowder with his rough voice who lingers in the imagination.[19] Philip's candour lets through the truth of his feelings and allows us to perceive that he was more

[18] The eight tunes used by Philip are respectively Dutch (one), English (one), Italian (five), and Spanish (one). Cf. Ringler, p. xliii.

[19] Philip's description of this incident has the ring of genuine autobiography and may indeed preserve a boyhood memory. The accounts of his servant Thomas Marshall record that on 8 September 1566, some three months before his twelfth birthday, at Chipping Norton on the return journey from Oxford to Shrewsbury, twelve pence was given 'by Mr. Philip's commandment to a blind harper who is Sir William Holles man in Nottinghamshire'. It is difficult not to believe that this 'blind harper' and the 'blind crowder' of *A Defence of Poetry* are one and the same.

deeply moved by that old song than the Renaissance courtier in him could readily explain. In seeking to reform and revitalize English poetry Philip looked to continental and classical models and turned his back on the native tradition (cf. Ringler, p. lii). Robert's poetry likewise looks to classical and continental models, but in his case there is one important exception: in Song 6, the longest and most deeply felt of his poems, Robert echoes a ballad tradition whose roots go back into pre-Reformation and pre-Renaissance England.

NEOPLATONIC LOVE

Not only is the overall design of Robert's sequence modelled on that of *Astrophil and Stella*, but Robert's familiarity with his elder brother's work is reflected in the many detailed verbal echoes of it in his own verse. Robert's intimate knowledge of Philip's poetry may sometimes be most tellingly revealed, however, precisely where he diverges from it. One aspect of the paradox is illustrated in the way Robert handles certain verse forms with the aim—or so comparison suggests—of creating effects consciously differentiated from those obtained by Philip within the same forms (see 'Formal Aspects': 'Formal Variety' and 'The Metrical Aspect').

The most fundamental difference between the two sequences, however, resides not in their outward forms but in their divergent attitudes towards the Neoplatonic philosophy of love to which both allude. Both brothers acknowledge love's heavenly origin, are aware that the lover is granted a glimpse of the eternal Beauty. Philip, however, refuses to submit patiently to the Neoplatonic doctrine's strict insistence that love must transcend the body. The conflict which dominates *Astrophil and Stella* is the conflict between idealized love and sexual desire, and the cynicism which is one of the strands running through Philip's sequence is the cynicism of a sensual young man who knows the impossibility of carrying out in practice the uncompromising precepts of Neoplatonic love. By contrast, sexual desire is scarcely avowed as an active element in Robert's sequence, which owes all its variety to the changing moods experienced by a lover who is at heart always an idealist. The cynicism which appears in Robert's sequence is inspired by the beloved's betrayal of her lover: it is the cynicism of the disillusioned idealist.

That Robert portrays this reverse side of idealism with conscious art as an integral aspect of his sequence can be seen from Song 10, the most buoyant and worldly of the cynical poems. It opens with an ideal vision of the lovers who have attained a paradise of endless joy, but this vision is merely used within the poem to underline the complete reversal which begins with the second stanza where the same lovers are told to make the most of their joy since it cannot last.

The way the difference between the brothers' sequences is brought out by the fact that they share the same Neoplatonic frame of reference can be illustrated from *Astrophil and Stella* 46—a sonnet wherein Philip is transparently pleading his own cause under the guise of taking the 'scholar' Cupid's part against his severe 'schoolmistress' Stella:

> I cursed thee oft, I pity now thy case,
> Blind-hitting boy, since she that thee and me
> Rules with a beck, so tyranniseth thee
> That thou must want or food, or dwelling place.
>
> For she protests to banish thee her face
> (Her face?—O Love, a rogue thou then must be)
> If Love learn not alone to love and see,
> Without desire to feed of further grace.
>
> Alas poor wag, that now a scholar art
> To such a schoolmistress whose lessons new
> Thou needs must miss, and so thou needs must smart.
>
> Yet dear, let me his pardon get of you
> So long (though he from book miche to desire)
> Till without fuel you can make hot fire.

The harsh command of schoolmistress Stella is echoed by the Shepherd in Robert's Pastoral 8 when he assures the scornful Nymph

> My soul to love and look, naught else affects
> (Pastoral 8: 36)

—but while Robert's Shepherd voluntarily accepts the condition, Philip's sonnet is a protest against the perversity of a command which if obeyed would merely get the pupil lover into fresh trouble, since if Cupid confined himself to seeing 'Without desire to feed of further grace' he would miss the next stage of his education. Philip therefore entreats that even if Cupid runs away to desire he should be granted an indefinite pardon, that is, a pardon until Stella herself can perform the inherently impossible task which she enjoins on her pupil, namely to kindle fire without proper fuel.[20]

The idea that the lover should find sufficient reward in the mere sight of his beloved can be traced back to the medieval tradition of courtly love, as Chaucer's *Knight's Tale* may remind us where Arcite laments the fate which has liberated him from the prison whence he could behold Emily:

> Oonly the sighte of hire whom that I serve,
> Though that I nevere hir grace may deserve
> Wolde han suffised right ynough for me.

Renaissance Europe was still steeped in the observances of courtly love, though the ancient traditions needed the rejuvenation which they received from their fusion with the fashionable Neoplatonism of Marsilio Ficino whose Commentary on the *Symposium*, written in Latin *c.*1468–9, was first printed in the translation of Plato's *Dialogues* published at Florence in 1484, and became the most influential textbook of the new philosophy. In his Commentary Ficino decisively asserts that the perception of physical beauty involves sight alone and that the lover of such beauty can require no other gratification:

> Lucem illam corporis, non aures, non olfactus, non gustus, non tactus, sed oculus percipit. Si oculus solus agnoscit, solus fruitur. Solus igitur oculus corporis pulchritudine fruitur. Cum vero amor nihil aliud sit nisi fruendae pulchritudinis desiderium, haec autem solis oculis comprehendatur, solo aspectu amator corporis est contentus (II. ix).

This passage was probably Philip's immediate source for Stella's harsh command that love must learn 'alone to love and see' and the 'book' mentioned in the penultimate line of *Astrophil and Stella* 46 may properly be thought of as an edition of Plato's *Symposium* containing Ficino's Commentary. One way of expressing the difference between the brothers' sequences would be to say that while poet-lover Philip continually deserts Ficino's

[20] Philip's poem has been imperfectly understood by recent editors, who have unnecessarily emended *his pardon* in line 12 (the reading of the authoritative 1598 edition) to *this pardon* although the whole sonnet shows that it is precisely a pardon for *Cupid* which Philip entreats.

teaching and gives way to sexual desire—continually plays truant from the Neoplatonic textbook—poet-lover Robert attends closely to it.

Another passage of Ficino's Commentary extends the statement quoted above by explaining that beauty is threefold—of the *soul*, of the *body*, and of the *voice*—and that these three aspects are perceived respectively by the *mind*, by the *sight*, and by the *hearing*. The lover of beauty will therefore find total gratification in these three alone:

Cum ergo mens, visus, auditus sint, quibus solis frui pulchritudine possumus, amor vero sit fruendae pulchritudinis desiderium, amor semper mente, oculis, auribus est contentus. Quid olfactu? Quid gustu vel tactu opus est? (I. iv).

The mind cannot be counted as a sense and the poets usually held therefore that the beauty of the soul was expressed in the voice and perceived by the hearing. Shakespeare's Venus is thus being perfectly orthodox when she tells Adonis

> Had I no eyes but ears, my ears would love
> That inward beauty and invisible.
> (*Venus and Adonis*: 433–4.)

Sight and hearing, the two senses which operate at a distance from their objects, were considered as belonging to a higher category than the other three (smell, taste, touch) which all depend on physical contact and were not allowed any role in the perception and enjoyment of beauty.

Ficino's theory of love is the key to Robert's sequence, and the gist of Ficino's theory is its insistence that love is nothing but the desire to enjoy beauty and that only the higher senses are involved therein. The purity of Ficino's scheme is qualified in Robert's sequence only by Sonnet 28 with its deftly calculated appeal to the lower triad of senses (see 'Robert's Use of the Sequence as a Form'). Sonnet 28 was skilfully designed to be the exception which confirms the rule that beauty is revealed only to sight and hearing. How deeply this rule is implicit in the sequence as a whole may be illustrated from Song 20 which addresses the poet's senses and is in practice concerned only with eyes and ears. Sonnet 28 employs the device of the air mediating between the poet and his beloved to avoid any suggestion of direct physical contact, and *kisses* are mentioned within the numbered sequence itself only in reference to the metaphorical kisses of the air (Song 3: 43–5 and Sonnet 28: 9) and of the brooks on the meadows (Sonnet 31: 9). Except in Sonnet 28, where they are the source of fragrance, lips are primarily regarded as the source of speech (thus at Song 12: 5 'from those sweetest lips flow words of nectar right'). The unnumbered poem 'Once to my lips', which describes an actual kiss, would have broken the decorum of the sequence had it been incorporated therein. The embrace in Pastoral 7—and the mere mention of folding 'with glad arms her body dear' may come in this context almost as a physical shock—is scarcely realized as a physical experience in the verse, which stresses how the shepherd lad uses his proximity to gratify his sense of sight:

And with broad eyes he thousand beauties drank.

The reader versed in Ficino's philosophy would realize that when in Sonnet 22 the poet, expecting his beloved's arrival, says that hitherto he has been

Blest in your sight, and but in sight yet blest,

he is now hoping that his hearing will also be blest, and when he continues

I wait to'adore, in rays as sweet as bright,
The sun lodged in your eyes, heavens in your breast

the first of the two balanced phrases in the latter line refers to her outward beauty (perceived by the sight) and the second to her inward beauty (revealed in her voice and perceived by the hearing).

Sonnet 25 is a witty exercise modelled on the Neoplatonism expounded by Ficino, and cannot be properly understood unless its intellectual background is recognized. The idea of the beloved as a type or reflection of the deity, implicit in the second quatrain's stressing of her *perfections* and her *sovereignty*, is more esoterically developed in the sestet, which alludes to Ficino's teaching that it was the divine power's wish to propagate its own perfection—a kind of love for itself—which created the universe. ('Cupiditas perfectionis propriae propagandae amor quidam est.' III. ii.) The entreaty to the beloved in the sestet's first line

O love yourself: be you yourself your care

directly echoes Spenser's line, itself echoing Ficino, describing how the 'high eternal power' begot the universe:

It loved itself, because itself was fair.[21]

The term *acts* in line 10 of Robert's sonnet is adopted straight from Ficino, where *actus* is the term used for the divine power as manifested in creation:

> Eodem modo primus ille actus omnium, qui deus dicitur, spetiem actumque rebus singulis producendo largitus est. . . . Ut est actus omnium roboratque, bonum dicitur. Ut vivificat, lenit, mulcet et excitat, pulchrum. . . . Denique ut bonum, procreat, regit et complet. Ut pulchrum, illuminat gratiamque infundit. (II. ii.)

Lines 10–11 of Sonnet 25 are modelled closely on this, Robert's *good* corresponding to Ficino's *bonum* while *fair* and *lovely* correspond to Ficino's *pulchrum*.

The sonnet's final couplet involves the familiar comparison of the beloved to the sun and thus gives a fresh turn to the continued idea of her as a reflection of the divine creator, and the same paragraph of Ficino's Commentary must have prompted Robert here too:

> sed divini solis perpetua et invisibilis lux una semper omnibus adstat, fovet, vivificat, excitat, complet et roborat. (II. ii.)

(The way Renaissance poetry constantly uses the inherently masculine image of the sun as a symbol for the beloved recalls the asexuality of orthodox Neoplatonism.) The astronomical image in this final couplet emphasizes once more the vast distance between beloved and lover, for the lover calls himself a *point* (Latin *punctum*) in just the same sense as Milton's Adam calls the earth 'this punctual spot' when he views it in relation to the whole universe (*Paradise Lost*, VIII. 23). We may incidentally note how Sonnet 25 illustrates, as do Sir John Davies's *Orchestra* and Milton's *Paradise Lost*, the continued hold of the

[21] 'An Hymne of Heavenly Love', line 29: first published in 1596 in the volume *Fowre Hymnes*. The volume is prefaced with a joint dedication to the Countess of Cumberland and the Countess of Warwick wherein Spenser indicates that the two 'Heavenly' hymns had been recently composed to 'reforme' the former two which 'one of you two most excellent Ladies' had asked him to 'call in'. The two ladies were sisters, the latter being the widow of Robert's maternal uncle Ambrose Dudley, Earl of Warwick (d. 1590). Lady Warwick figures prominently in Rowland Whyte's correspondence as a staunch supporter of Robert's interests at court during the 1590s.

Ptolemaic universe on the poetic imagination even among those well aware of the Copernican astronomy.[22]

Further detailed echoes of Ficino's Commentary on the *Symposium* will be found cited in the Commentary to the present edition of Robert's poetry, but it must already be clear that Robert was steeped in this central exposition of Neoplatonic love. It may be more than coincidence, therefore, that the books purchased with Robert's donation of £100 to the newly founded Bodleian Library in 1600 include two texts of Ficino's Commentary—that contained in the Greco-Latin edition of Plato published at Lyons in 1591 and that contained in the two-volume edition of Ficino's *Opera* published at Basle in 1576. Ficino's Commentary is thus represented in Robert's donation by both of the only two forms wherein the original Latin text had been published: (1) as part of an edition of Plato, and (2) as part of an edition of Ficino's own collected works.

The letters to Robert from Sir Thomas Bodley among the Sidney papers testify to the friendship between the two men during the 1590s when Bodley was English resident in the United Provinces. On 23 June 1600 Robert's agent Rowland Whyte reported to him that Bodley was then 'at Oxford very busy to sett up his bookes against this Act. Yours is the fairest and greatest gifte that is given; yt hath as I heare the chiefest place in the Library', and six weeks later Whyte again assured his master that 'the bookes are presented, and have a choice place in the Library, which wilbe an everlasting honor to your name' (8 August 1600). The books still stand today on the shelves in Duke Humfrey, many of them clothed in their original bindings distinguished by an elaborate heraldic stamp of Robert's arms.

The section on love in the Fourth Book of Castiglione's *Courtier* is the most influential expression of Neoplatonic philosophy after Ficino himself, from whom it directly descends. A well-known passage from the *Courtier* describes how the lover is to escape torment during absence from his beloved:

and to enjoy beautie without passion, the Courtier by the helpe of reason must full and wholy call backe againe the coveting of the bodie to beautie

[22] For an interesting example of how Robert's poetry may be misunderstood by the modern reader imperfectly acquainted with Neoplatonic doctrine, and conditioned by very different fashions, see G. F. Waller, 'My wants and yowr perfections', *Ariel: a review of International English Literature*, 8 (April 1977), pp. 3–14, where Sonnet 25 is interpreted as 'a seduction argument' and its final couplet as 'an overt sexual demand'.

> alone, and (in what he can) beholde it in it selfe simple and pure, and frame it in his imagination sundered from all matter, and so make it friendly and loving to his soule, and there enjoy it, and have it with him day and night, in every time and place, without mistrust ever to lose it.[23]

Robert's Song 20 is addressed to the poet-lover's senses (i.e. to his eyes and ears) and represents him attempting to console them for being deprived of their only objects during absence from the beloved. In stanza 4 the poet imagines that his senses have *reserved* nothing to themselves of the beauty whereon they had fed until lately, but have entirely transferred that beauty to his *reason* and his *heart*. The poet therefore suggests that his starved senses find out whether his reason and his heart will now *repay* some part of what they had received, only to discover how all that beauty is now permanently lodged in those twin temples. The poet, in fact, has framed beauty in his imagination and made it 'friendly and loving to his soul' so that he can enjoy it there always 'without mistrust ever to lose it'. The conceit embodied in Song 20 is imaginatively evolved from the doctrine expounded by Castiglione and depends for its full understanding on the reader's recognition of its philosophical source.

Astrophil and Stella is a remarkably frank representation of the poet's love and sexual desire for a married lady whose actual identity is hinted at in several poems and whom the poet might earlier have married himself—so Sonnet 33 intimates—and now bitterly regrets his failure to do so.[24] A poignant feature of the sequence consists in Stella's half-suppressed avowals of her own love for Astrophil—avowals made in sighs, looks, and words which are always 'killed before full born' (Sonnet 67) except for her anguished confession in Song viii

> Trust me, while I thee deny
> In myself the smart I try;
> Tyrant honour doth thus use thee,
> Stella's self might not refuse thee.

[23] Quoted from Sir Thomas Hoby's translation, first published in 1561.

[24] Penelope Devereux was born *c.*1562 and was therefore some eight years younger than Philip. *Astrophil and Stella* 33 probably means that when she was offered to him as a bride in 1576 he had refrained from taking advantage of her tender years ('While too much wit (forsooth) so troubled me / That I respects for both our sakes must show'). Penelope's father, who died in Ireland in September 1576, had on his deathbed expressed the wish that 'if God so moved their hearts' Philip Sidney and 'my daughter' might marry. Philip at that time was almost twenty-two, Penelope not more than fourteen.

By contrast, Robert's sequence includes one poem (one only, but the longest) representing a love which is both fully reciprocated and fully avowed by both parties—and the identity of the lady involved in this unique situation is, uniquely, intimated (Song 6: 73–4).

Robert's sequence contains both kinds of love defined by Ficino (II. viii), *simplex amor* 'ubi amatus non amat amantem' (where the beloved does not love the lover) and *mutuus amor* where 'iste in illo, ille in isto vivit' (where each lives in the other). Robert depicts each kind in its extreme or ideal form, while Philip's sequence is poignantly suspended between the two extremes of requited and unrequited love. Both brothers add a dimension to a male-centred genre in the longest poems of their respective sequences—Song viii of *Astrophil and Stella*, Robert's Song 6—both of which give a voice to the woman in love. Yet again, however, the comparison brings out an important difference, for only in Song 6 is the woman able to reveal without constraint that she is as much in love as the man. In creating the purest Neoplatonic sequence in Elizabethan poetry, Robert must have been well aware of how his own portrayal of love differed from the love portrayed in *Astrophil and Stella*.

IDEAL BEAUTY

In the *Arcadia* the shepherd Thyrsis, 'accounted one of the best singers among them', flatly refuses during the Second Eclogues to partner the lovesick Philisides, explaining that 'he should within few days be married to the fair Kala and since he had gotten his desire he would sing no more'. Philisides therefore sings an eclogue by himself, using the echo as his partner. The passage uses the language of pastoral to intimate that poetry arises from unsatisfied and not from fulfilled desire. The relevance of this to the poetry of the two brothers may be partly understood if we remember that at the period when he was composing *Astrophil and Stella*[25] Philip was in his twenty-seventh and twenty-eighth years, was still unmarried and nourishing an adulterous passion, while Robert, on the other hand, some two months before his twenty-first birthday married a young lady who was to prove a loving and devoted wife. The

[25] See Ringler, pp. 439–40 for the evidence that Philip's sequence was mainly composed, and was given its final form, during the summer of 1582.

intimate side of Elizabethan marriage can seldom be glimpsed, and it is pleasant therefore to know that when Barbara was going to join Robert at Flushing in June 1597—in the thirteenth year of their marriage and after a painfully long separation of nearly ten months—she arranged to bring over from England 'a good bed to use upon occasion' (Rowland Whyte to Robert, 2 June 1597).

But Robert's marriage, however happy in itself, could not preserve him from all forms of suffering. His governorship of Flushing often obliged him during the 1590s to endure the pain of absence from his wife and family and from his beloved home in Kent, often forced him to exchange 'sweet Penshurst'[26]—whose soil and air, whose woods and waters, are eulogized by Ben Jonson in his poem *To Penshurst*—for the noisome air of Flushing which each year in the summer months became a plague-spot. As the decade went by he saw his hopes of political advancement gradually fading and came to feel more and more 'forsaken' by the Elizabethan court. The sexual tension which fills Philip's sequence was in Robert's case, we may reasonably assume, alleviated by his happy marriage. Nevertheless, Robert had his own experience of suffering, knew in himself those frustrated desires which in some form or other—or so the *Arcadia* intimates—are a pre-condition for the production of poetry.

Robert's letters from Flushing during the 1590s vividly evoke his daily life there. Sickness is a recurrent theme, and what that actually meant in terms of everyday life is implicit in the laconic references to Robert's best friend among the Dutch who surrounded him during his exile. 'The plague at Midleborrow doth not yet increase', Robert told Barbara on 29 April 1597, 'but it is feared it wil becaws it begins so early. Rowels is not yet dead: both hee and his wyfe had the plague.' The futility of pretending to hope in such a case is demonstrated by the event briefly reported ten days later: 'I have of late lost the best frend I had among the States, Roels the pensionary of Midleborrow: he died this other day of the plague.' (9 May 1597.)

In sending news back to England Robert tried on the one hand to avoid alarming Barbara, and on the other to convince

[26] 'I had much a doe to persuade my Lady to come up [to court], she being so farre in love with sweet Penshurst' (Rowland Whyte to Robert, 3 November 1599).

her of the reality of the dangers which made him reluctant to bring her and the children over, however much they might wish to be together. He wrote to Burghley on 17 October 1596 'heer hath bene great sicknes this end of summer, both of violent Agues, and bloody Fluxes, wherof many are dead, and very many remaine still sick: and now lately the plague is come into one house', and when sending substantially the same report to Barbara sixteen days earlier, though he reassured her 'for myself I ame very well I thanck God and so is all my howshold', he added 'I would not for anything in the world, that I had browght you over with me' and the telling information 'The Commissaries children and Kennels are all sick and generally all children heerabouts.' While thus surrounded at Flushing with disease and death Robert was growing steadily more depressed about his own political career as he repeatedly confided to the Earl of Essex during the first half of 1597. 'Truly My Lord I begin to grow very weary', he wrote in a typical passage on 28 March, 'seing busines increas daily vpon me, and likelihood of more and more troubles: and the longer I goe forwards the less cause to hope for any acknowledgment or requital.'

The words applied in the third stanza of Keats's *Ode to a Nightingale* to life in the real world—'the weariness, the fever, and the fret'—are remarkably apt to the life Robert lived in Flushing during the 1590s. The third stanza of Keats's *Ode* reflects his own experience of life during the year (September 1818-September 1819) which witnessed his greatest creative achievement—and Keats's retrospective verdict on that year was 'Nothing could have in all its circumstances fallen out worse for me than the last year has done' (letter to his brother George, 19 November 1819). Yet it was against this sombre background that Keats realized his finest work, impelled to imagine an ideal beauty beyond the reach of change to set against his daily experience of life's treacherous instability.

At a similarly dark period of his own life Robert was moved to poetry by the same fundamental impulse as moved Keats more than two hundred years later. Love, whose nature it is to intensify the ambivalence inherent in all emotional experience, has itself been viewed in two opposite ways. The antithesis runs through Elizabethan literature, whose poets are sometimes moved by the idea of beauty's evanescence

Beauty decays, love dies, desire doth fly

and sometimes by the idea of a beauty beyond the reach of change

Time wears her not, she doth his chariot guide.

(Both these particular lines reached print anonymously in 1593 in that elegant anthology *The Phoenix Nest*, the Phoenix of whose title refers to Philip Sidney and probably alludes to his rebirth as a poet with the publication of *Astrophil and Stella* in 1591. The former line comes from the poem *A Counterlove*, the latter from the poem beginning 'Praised be Diana's fair and harmless light' generally attributed to Ralegh.)

Robert found the intellectual basis for his own poetry in the Neoplatonic philosophy expounded by Ficino, and through all its changing and conflicting moods his poetry consistently proclaims its allegiance to the imperishable beauty, the beauty which Time cannot wear and which can be perceived and enjoyed only through the kind of love, consciously excluding sexual desire, which Ficino describes in his Commentary on Plato's *Symposium*. One of the great commonplaces of poetry, the lament for beauty's transience, accordingly finds no place in Robert's sequence. When Robert does use the familiar imagery of the soon-fading flowers he uses it of woman's affections, whose mutability is contrasted with the permanence of her beauty that reigns over change:

Flowers chose this day with best show
Tomorrow in dust ranges,
Beauty, queen-like, not alone doth go
But waited on by changes.
(Song 10: 9–12.)

An analogous treatment of the same theme is found in Pastoral 9 where woman's changing affections are equated with the seasonal vicissitudes in the world whose *fair frame* itself—a potent image of permanence—is equated with her beauty:

Thus while the world's fair frame such change approves
She will as false as it be, as as fair.
(Pastoral 9: 17–18.)

Sonnet 35, originally conceived as the finale to the sequence, contains the sequence's strongest clue to the real object of the poet's unattainable love, for beginning 'Time, cruel Time', it builds up to the conclusion that his beloved will outlast Time itself:

> Time, you shall nowhere move
> Where, while you are, you shall not see my love.

The truth of this triumphant assertion can be understood only as we understand the truth of Keats's assertion that the nightingale is outside Time's power—

> Thou wast not born for death, immortal Bird!

Both poets are thinking of the ideal type which outlasts all the type's actual embodiments.

Samuel Daniel also composed a sonnet (first published in 1601) beginning 'Time, cruel Time'. One of the two sonnets might have been directly prompted by the other, but in view of their total divergence after their identical openings, and bearing in mind that during the 1590s Daniel had been a member of the household at Wilton, it seems more likely that both sonnets were composed independently as rival exercises on a set theme. Perhaps the Countess of Pembroke herself challenged both her brother and Daniel to compose sonnets addressing 'Time, cruel Time' in the same way as, over two hundred years later, the members of Leigh Hunt's circle (and one recalls how Keats did not escape) were occasionally set to compose in friendly rivalry on particular themes.

Daniel's sonnet (see Appendix A) starts from the observation that the beloved *seems* to be outside Time's power, and wittily employs that conceit to reproach her for her cruelty. The conceit depends for its force, however, on our recognition that it is *only* a conceit, that in reality the beloved is mortal and the plea for Time to spare her cannot ultimately be granted. Robert's sonnet boldly asserts that the beloved really *is* beyond Time's power, and the notion of pleading with Time to spare her would in his case be inconceivable. Another aspect of this fundamental difference appears in the different attitudes of the two poet-lovers: while Robert's attitude is one of self-abnegation, Daniel reveals his essential self-interest in his elegantly turned conclusion

> She may become more kind to thee or me.

Robert's sonnet was itself probably suggested by Michael Drayton's sonnet 'Stay, stay sweet Time' first published in 1594 and in successively revised versions in 1599, 1602, and 1619 (see Appendix A). The development of the theme in Sonnet 35 certainly shows affinities with Drayton's sonnet rather than with Daniel's. Robert's sonnet like Drayton's is founded on the notion of Time's passage from age to age, and both sonnets are disinterested celebrations of the beloved's heavenly beauty. These resemblances, however, serve in the end to bring out what really distinguishes Robert's sonnet, for Drayton's sonnet—in this respect like Daniel's—finally derives its poignancy from its acknowledgement that the beloved is mortal.

Even passing allusions may incidentally bring out the exceptional purity of Robert's idealism. When he writes

> I through a veil saw glory (Song 10: 14)

he may be echoing Daniel's

> Why then though Delia fade let that not move her,
> Though time do spoil her of the fairest veil
> That ever yet mortality did cover[27]

—and on the surface both poets are certainly using the same Neoplatonic language: Daniel however is thinking of the beloved's mortality under the veil of her outward beauty, while Robert is thinking under that veil of her immortal spirit.

The lover's refrain in *Astrophil and Stella*, song iv

> Take me to thee, and thee to me

is paralleled—perhaps consciously echoed—in the last line of Robert's Song 15 where the lover aspires to hope that

> You will take me unto you.

Yet again the comparison serves to bring out Robert's pure idealism. There is in reality the strongest possible contrast between the respective meanings, in their respective contexts, of these two superficially similar lovers' entreaties—and if Robert is consciously echoing his brother here then that contrast must be what he intended to bring out. The vividly realized setting of Philip's poem—two 'young folks' whispering together in a

[27] First published as Sonnet XXXVII in *Delia* (1592). In 1600 the passage was revised to read (Sonnet XLII)

> And therefore grieve not if thy beauties die,
> Though time do spoil thee of the fairest veil
> That ever yet covered mortality.

moonlit garden, the girl's mother asleep in the house—combines with the reciprocal nature of what the lover asks for to make abundantly clear the sexual urgency behind his repeated request. By contrast, Robert's entreaty comes as the conclusion of a poem which throughout firmly places the beloved in heaven: the vast distance established between beloved and lover combines with the formal phrasing of his prayer to ensure that it is biblical—certainly not sexual—echoes which are awakened (compare, for example, 2 Kings 2: 1 and Psalm 27: 10).

The Religion of Love, a cult which in its origins is entwined with the medieval cult of the Blessed Virgin and which the Renaissance blended with Neoplatonism, permeates Robert's sequence—how deeply may be illustrated from just one more example. Song 5 is a prayer by a lover whose worship of his beloved has been driven underground by her scorn of him. He finally hopes to 'move' her—but not to return his love, simply to acknowledge the truth of his devotion so that he dare once again worship her openly—

> And till the truth your heart do move
> Unheard, unseen, will pray and love.

It will help us to understand the poem aright if we recall how familiar the Elizabethans were with the reality of religious persecution.

The ideal beauty is perceived by a love which has no need of the lower senses (Ficino I. iv: see 'Neoplatonic Love')—a love recalling that imagined by Keats on the Grecian Urn

> All breathing human passion far above.

The sexual purity of Robert's sequence indicates that he practised Neoplatonism as a conscious artistic discipline—though at the same time some striking resemblances to John Keats, whose own 'instinctive Platonism' has been recognized,[28] should tell us that Robert's need to imagine an ideal beauty was rooted deep in his temperament. A poetic kinship between the Nymph and Shepherd of Robert's Pastoral 8 and the marble lovers on Keats's Grecian Urn is disclosed when Keats's lines

> She cannot fade, though thou hast not thy bliss,
> For ever wilt thou love, and she be fair
> (Ode on a Grecian Urn: 19–20)

[28] See Robert Gittings, *John Keats* (1968), p. 152.

are set beside Robert's

> I cannot part from that by which I am,
> Nor grow to be less fond, or you less fair
> (Pastoral 8: 41–2).

On the one occasion when Robert's verse imagines an actual kiss, his line

> I prayed one kiss, might press joy's wine to me
> ('Once to my lips': 4)

seems like an anticipation of Keats's

> Can burst Joy's grape against his palate fine
> (Ode on Melancholy: 28);

and when in a 'night' poem Robert writes of

> Cares which in darkness shine, finding her sight
> Eclipsed which from them is my safeguard best
> (Sonnet 6: 5–6)

we can recognize an emotion similar to that behind Keats's prayer

> Then save me, or the passèd day will shine
> Upon my pillow, breeding many woes
> (To Sleep: 9–10).

Were it possible for Keats to have read Robert's poetry, evidence of direct influence might well have been detected in such resemblances. As it is—while the 'echoes' may well remind us how deeply Keats had imbibed the atmosphere of Elizabethan poetry—we can be sure that both poets are responding independently to the perennial human experience. In a similar way, while Robert's study of the central textbook on Neoplatonic love is manifest in his poetry, in his impulse to imagine an ideal beauty we can recognize a universal human desire preceding the particular philosophy which shaped the expression of that desire for the Renaissance poet.

ROBERT AND BARBARA

The Elizabethan marginalia added to the calendar of the medieval 'Sidney Psalter'[29]—a large fifteenth-century manuscript of

[29] Trinity College, Cambridge, R. 17. 2 (M. R. James 988). The first leaf of the

English workmanship which was owned by the Sidneys in the sixteenth century—record births, marriages, and deaths in the family from 20 July 1529 (the birth of Sir Henry Sidney) to 16 October 1584 (the death, 'being thre yeare old and one daie', of Katherine, eldest daughter of Robert's sister and brother-in-law the Earl and Countess of Pembroke). The amanuensis who compiled this family register recorded Robert's marriage as follows:

> The marriage betweene Robert Sydney esquier, and Barbara Gammage daughter and sole heire to Jhon Gammage of the Castell of Coitie in the Countie of Glamorgan esquier was celebrated in the house of Sr Edward Stradlinge of St Donnets in the same countie on Wenesdaie the three and twentith of September 1584 in the presence of the right honorable Harry Erle of Pembrook, Sr Edward Stradlinge and my Ladie his wife and manie others.

The bride had been left a wealthy heiress on her father's death only fifteen days before (8 September), and the circumstances which culminated in this apparently hasty marriage in the house of her guardians Sir Edward and Lady Stradling may be descried between the lines of letters to the Stradlings from various correspondents—letters which fortunately reached print in the last century. (*Stradling Correspondence: a series of letters written in the reign of Queen Elizabeth*, ed. John Montgomery Traherne, 1840.)

Among the outwardly eligible suitors who had sought Barbara Gamage in marriage during her father's lifetime we can number (1) Herbert Croft, grandson of Sir James Croft (d. 1590), Comptroller of the Queen's Household, (2) Sir James Whitney, Sheriff of Herefordshire, and (3) Thomas, son of Sir Henry Johnes, Sheriff at various times of Carmarthenshire and Brecknockshire. On the news of her father's death, her influential relatives at court grew anxious lest their far-away kinswoman should become the subject of mercenary negotiations. Her father's first cousin, Sir Walter Ralegh, wrote from court on 26 September 1584—evidently unaware of what had already happened at St Donat's—expressing such fears and hoping to prevent their realization by reminding Stradling that the Queen herself 'hath nowe thrise caused letters to be written unto you, that you suffer not my kinsewoman to be boughte and solde in Wales'.

Psalms is a sixteenth-century replacement, and the large *Beatus* initial which begins Psalm 1 is painted with an elaborate representation of the Sidney arms.

The Secretary of State Sir Francis Walsingham—whose daughter had married Philip Sidney the previous year—had indeed written six days before (20 September) informing Stradling of the Queen's latest decision 'that the sayd young gentlewoman bee by yow forthwith brought up hither to the Courte'. Stradling was told to deliver her to another of her father's cousins, Lord Hunsdon, the Lord Chamberlain, and in the interim was to prevent all such access to her 'as wherby shee maye contract or entangle hir selfe for mariage with anye man', and Walsingham's anxiety is shown in his mention of obscure rumours circulating at court to the effect 'that she hath alreadie entangled hir self'. The very next day, however, Walsingham wrote to Stradling in haste revealing that events had begun to move more quickly than anyone, except those immediately connected with Robert and Barbara, had realized. Despite his official letter of the previous day, written at the Queen's command, Walsingham on 21 September frankly encourages the plan which by now he knows is afoot:

> beinge now secreatly geven to understande that for the good will you beare unto the Earl of Pembrooke, you meane to further what yow may younge Mr Robert Sydney, I can not but incorage yow to proceed therin, for that I know her Maiestie will noe waye miselike therof: besyds the Lord Chamberlaine, Mr Rawley, and the rest of the younge gentlewomans kynsfolkes, doe greatly desyre yt.
>
> (Walsingham to Stradling, 21 September 1584.)

As we have seen, the marriage was celebrated in Stradling's house two days later (23 September) and on 27 September Walsingham wrote to reassure Stradling that he will not be blamed for his part in the affair despite the 'blusteringe woords' of one disappointed suitor 'younge Mr Croftes and his frends'. By what can be seen as a happy chance—though it is difficult not to believe that chance was assisted by intelligent anticipation of the danger—the Queen's command to bring Barbara up to court forthwith was carried by a messenger who 'affirmeth' (so Walsingham reports) 'that he came to your howse two howres after the mariadge sollempnised'.

The *Stradling Correspondence* prints letters from Robert's father and brother-in-law which indicate that their acquaintance with Stradling began long before the marriage, and although Sir Henry Sidney was unable to attend the ceremony, he wrote from Wilton six days later (29 September) vowing lifelong gratitude to Stradling for arranging it, and undertaking at the same time to protect him from any ill consequences that might result —'not offendinge the lawes further then the same are transgressed alreadie' (an evident reference to Stradling's apparent thwarting of the Queen's command). The indications that all those closely connected with Robert were delighted at the outcome are confirmed by the letter written to Stradling five days after the marriage by the Countess of Warwick (for whom, see footnote 21 to this Introduction).

When the evidence is pieced together, it is seen not to warrant the assumption recently made that Robert's was an arranged marriage and that 'Barbara Gamage had almost certainly never set eyes on her husband before the wedding day' (Lawrence Stone, *The Crisis of the Aristocracy 1558–1641*, corrected reprint, Clarendon Press, 1979, p. 660). This 'mercenary' view of the marriage might indeed be strengthened if it were true—as Stone states—that Barbara was left 'a very young daughter and heiress'. The Inquisition taken after her father's death, however, shows that Barbara was then aged upwards of twenty-two years (*Stradling Correspondence*, p. 5, footnote 1)—scarcely 'very young' by the standards of the period, and in fact at least a year older than her husband: indeed, it was one of the complaints made in the aftermath of her father's death by another of her over-anxious kinsfolk at court, Charles, Baron Howard (later Lord High Admiral and Earl of Nottingham), that Stradling had taken possession of Coity Castle when it might have been more fitting for Barbara herself to have taken possession of her own 'shee beinge of thos yers she is of' (Howard to Stradling, 26 September 1584). Nothing in what we know warrants the suggestion that Barbara at the age of twenty-two would have consented to marry a man whom she had never met. On the contrary, there is good evidence that any suitor who hoped to win Barbara's hand knew that he must first win her affection: Sir Henry Johnes, father of an earlier aspirant, when soliciting Stradling's support on his son's behalf, particularly asked for 'your friendly assistaunce with my sonne towarde the obtaininge of the gentlewomans goodwill, in whome consistethe the chiefeste succcesse of his suete'.

Barbara had reached the age of twenty-two without 'entangling' herself with any of the apparently eligible suitors who had offered themselves, and she then married—in haste and at some risk of incurring the royal displeasure—the younger son of a knight who, however distinguished in other ways, was not primarily distinguished for possession of this world's riches. The natural explanation is that Robert and Barbara had met and fallen in love—probably while Robert was staying with his father at Ludlow or with his brother-in-law at Cardiff—and had determined to get married before any more powerful rival could interpose.

This romantic explanation certainly fits the sequel, for the marriage proved the prelude to a lifelong romance. Even when not chained in the Low Countries by his post as Governor of Flushing—as he was for much of the 1590s—Robert was often obliged, both by his duties and by family business, to attend the court. He wrote to Barbara frequently during his enforced absences and the many such letters still among the Sidney papers—upwards of 320, spanning almost the whole of their married life—are a surviving witness to the private happiness interwoven with Robert's worldly trials.

The strains of business are an ever-present background, and it is perhaps inevitable that domestic tensions can occasionally be discerned behind letters written in such circumstances. 'Yow wil say I am sure that after mine old fashion as yow call yt I haue broken promis with yow', Robert pleaded in a characteristic passage from an undated letter of the 1590s which concludes 'Farewel sweet hart and do not say now that I haue broken promis since I cannot choose, and loue me stil'. The theme is recurrent and should remind us that letters can never more than hint at the life of such a couple when they are together and have no need for writing. When Robert's faithful agent Rowland Whyte returned from Flushing to England on 2 September 1596 he carried with him a letter for Barbara which suggests how much may lie hidden from us between the lines of the written record:

> Sweet hart. I wrate vnto yow at my landing and caused my letter to bee sent to Ned: Burnham. This is onely, not to let Rol: Whyte kome empty handed. For I haue nothing els to say, but I loue yow (which without writing I ame sure yow would beleeue). . . .

That the romance never really faded may be judged from the letter written from London on 22 July 1618 to tell Barbara that the culmination of their worldly honours had just passed the Great Seal

so as now yowr Ladyship is Countess of Leycester. . . . And sweethart many yeares I pray God may yow enioy this name, to his comfort, whoe will euer bee

yowr most louing husband
Leycester.

Sadly, Barbara lived less than three years to enjoy the new title, dying in the May of 1621 at Penshurst where she lies buried. Perhaps we may see as Robert's final tribute to her the fact that, after waiting nearly four years, in April 1625 he married again. If in this second marriage—to Sarah, widow of his Kentish neighbour Sir Thomas Smythe of Bidborough—Robert hoped to recapture something of his former happiness, the hope was scarcely allowed to fulfil itself for he died little more than a year later (on 13 July 1626). Robert lies buried at Penshurst with Barbara: his widow—whose marriage to Robert had followed shortly after the death of her first husband in 1625—seems to have been much younger than Robert and lived on until 1655; she was buried not at Penshurst but in the village of Sutton-at-Hone where thirty years before she had married Robert.

Barbara does not speak to us with her own voice but must be evoked indirectly (as may already have been noticed) from letters to and about her. Although much correspondence addressed to Robert both at Flushing and elsewhere has been preserved, and although Barbara preserved the letters she received from Robert, no letters at all from her to him are known to survive. In fact, only two documents containing Barbara's handwriting are preserved among the Sidney papers, and in each case she has simply signed her name to a text penned by an amanuensis. The earlier document (21 April 1602) is a formal receipt signed *Bar: Sydney* for the allowance which was paid her out of her husband's rents through the agency of Thomas Golding, steward at Penshurst. The later document (23 April 1607) consists of a letter to Golding concerning her allowance and, at the foot of the same page, a formal receipt for the latest instalment thereof: both letter and receipt are signed *B: Lisle* (Robert had been created Viscount Lisle on 4 May 1605). The individual letters composing her name are separately formed in each of the three signatures, all of which are in effect drawn rather than written. The conclusion

Robert to Barbara, 9 May 1597 (Courtesy of Viscount De L'Isle, VC, KG)

seems inescapable that Barbara never achieved fluency with the pen, and the (lost) letters from her occasionally mentioned in the Sidney papers must have been penned on her behalf by an amanuensis. It is a reasonable deduction that Barbara could not read fluently either, and when letters arrived for her we may guess that Rowland Whyte would be called on when necessary to assist in the task of deciphering them. We can at the same time more clearly understand why Whyte often included re-assurances about Barbara and the family when writing himself from England to Flushing during the 1590s. We cannot know whether Barbara ever wrote to Robert with her own hand, but if so it would probably have been merely to add a few affectionate words to a letter whose 'business' part had been set down by an amanuensis. The conspicuous gap in the family papers represented by the absence of any letters to Robert from his wife suggests that he considered her letters in some way too personal for any eyes but his own: a reluctance to expose Barbara's illiteracy may have been what persuaded her husband not to allow her letters to survive.[30]

Behind several passages in Robert's correspondence we can discern his anxiety lest his growing family should suffer as a result of their beloved mother's lack of education. The disrespect shown towards the lady of the house by the children's schoolmaster Mr Bird created for a time a somewhat embarrassing situation, reported to Robert by Rowland Whyte in a way which should bring home to us what Barbara's illiteracy could mean in terms of domestic life:

Touching Mr Bird. I doe not know what cause he hath of discontentment, but seing my lady troubled at what you wryte of hym, I can witnes that her ladyship doth vse hym as well as no man of his place can desire more, there is nothing in your house denied hym or to deere for hym . . . my lady complaines that she hath suffred at his hands more contempt then was fitt for hym to vse, in laying before her the want of educacion in her self, and therfore cold not iudge of yt in others. Yt became hym not to say

[30] In the Introduction to Volume Two of the HMC *Report on the MSS of Lord De L'Isle & Dudley* (1934), William A. Shaw described what he took to be Barbara's letters to Robert—'she almost invariably writes to him as "Dear Hart", and on both sides there is an equal mixture of frankness and tenderness' (p. vi). Dr Shaw must have been confusing Barbara with Dorothy, wife of the second Earl. The Sidney papers include over forty letters from Dorothy to her husband, most of which begin *My dearest hart* and are signed *D Leycester*: one can see how the flourished D of the signature might be misread as *B*.

> yt, nether wold my lady now haue remembred yt but that she sees hym goe about to wryte and cause others to wryte vnto you they know not what. Your lordship may doe well to wryte vnto hym, to continue his paines and wonted care towards your children, or els to giue a reasonable warning before he depart, that you may provide another. (Rowland Whyte to Robert, 24 January 1599/1600.)

Barbara's innocence of literature suggests a personal reason why Robert should have conceived his tribute to their mutual love in a form which might be sung to a native ballad tune: Song 6 could come alive for Barbara herself if she heard it sung to the popular tune of 'Walsingham' in her own family circle, where—as we may learn from the letters of Rowland Whyte quoted above (see 'Robert and Music')—music was frequently performed.

In England, Barbara dutifully attended the court to promote Robert's interests there whenever friends advised that it might be expedient for her to do so, and she was always ready to join her husband in Flushing whenever an opportunity arose. These considerations apart, however, she was happiest at home surrounded by her growing family. Robert's love for her blended naturally with his love for his home and garden to form the image of happiness which became during the 1590s his private refuge from the worldly disappointments he experienced ever more acutely as the decade wore on.

When deprived in Flushing of Barbara's company Robert was often, in the intervals of official business, dreaming of home and forming plans. 'Sweethart. I pray yow remember to send to Jacques the gardner to come to Penshurst against Alhalowtyde and to bring yellow peaches, apricots, cherry and plum trees to set along the wall towards the church' (Flushing, 25 September 1595) runs a typical passage, and he naturally associated Barbara with his plans—'I ame glad to heare my garden goes so wel forwards: and as much for yowr sake is yt as mine own that I bestow the charge. I wil send ouer some trees from hence' (Flushing, 2 October 1596). Emblems of their love remain on the fabric of Penshurst. The Long Gallery completed in 1607 was Robert's own addition to the house: the initials BS flank the Welsh dragon above the arch leading into the nether gallery at the far end, while outside on the Gallery's garden face are to be seen on either side of the central bay the Sidney porcupine with the initials RS (on the left) and the Welsh dragon with the initials BS (on the right). Those who arrive on foot at Penshurst's main entrance may still observe, set into the great oak doors dating from Robert's time, a modest postern carved in homely style with the initials RS–BS.

Rowland Whyte understood Barbara's reluctance to exchange her country home for the court. 'I had much a doe to persuade my Lady to come up', he reported from London on 3 November 1599, 'she being so farre in love with sweet Penshurst.' It is entirely appropriate that the one positive clue to Barbara's identity which Robert's verse contains should take the form of a covert allusion to Penshurst (Song 6: 73–4).

Under the guise of a transparent fiction Song 6 portrays the frequent separation of Robert and Barbara during the 1590s, with Barbara at home in Penshurst and Robert chained by duty almost due East of her in Flushing. While Song 1 is not—as is Song 6—an avowed celebration of mutual love, it nevertheless represents a situation (the leave-taking) as inevitably familiar to the couple in real life as the separated existence which followed each parting. The generalized language of Song 1 is punctuated in lines 13–15 by two more specific details, and comparison of these with Robert's letters from Flushing strengthens the impression that Song 1 closely reflects aspects of Robert's real life. The *heavy loss Of friend* (lines 13–14) seems to echo the actual loss of Robert's friend Roels. (See above, 'Ideal Beauty'.) During this same spring of 1597 Robert's attempts to obtain home leave were being thwarted by jealous rivals at court who preferred him out of the way while such prizes as the Wardenship of the Cinque Ports (for which Robert proved an ultimately unsuccessful candidate) were being contended for. 'I wil therefore resolue that I must stay heer', Robert wrote from Flushing to the Earl of Essex on 12 April 1597, 'as long as such whoe haue a wil to cross me haue power to do it.' This supplies a convincing gloss on line 15

Or care to see how some my fortunes cross.

The key word of Song 1 is *delights*, the word which in this poem represents what the beloved means to her lover (see lines 9, 19, 29). How closely this corresponds with the language which Robert used in real life to express his love for Barbara may be judged from a letter he wrote her on 6 January 1593/4 from Dover, where he was awaiting a fair wind to take him across the Channel. He had tried to get across country to take ship at Rye—which would have been within striking distance of Penshurst should an opportunity arise—but had been prevented. 'Yet if I had bin at Ry I would haue made sometimes a start vnto yow, but heer I ame far from all delight.'

But it is Song 1's kinship with Song 6 in thought and imagery which might finally persuade the reader to recognize Barbara as the inspiration of the former poem as the text itself covertly acknowledges her to be of the latter. Both poems are founded on the image of absence as a kind of death, and the reader attuned to the poet's language will recognize that as the lover departs from his beloved in Song 1 the *living burial* towards which he is being led (stanza 4), the *unjust decay* towards which he is going (stanza 6), have actually taken place in Song 6, where the Knight speaks of himself as already a *carcass* and *buried* in the *joyless grave* which the world itself has become in the absence of his Lady (Song 6: 97–100). Both poems employ the antithesis between *feigned* and *true* (Song 1: 35–6 and Song 6: 79–80)—an antithesis not expressed in those precise terms elsewhere in the sequence. The antithesis in Song 1 between the truth of the poet's love and the *feignèd fires* of other men is balanced in Song 6 by the corresponding antithesis between the truth of the Lady's worth and the worth which men *feign* to find in other women. The links between Song 1 and Song 6 are the first example of those connections between different poems which indicate that there is a controlling design behind Robert's sequence (see 'Robert's Use of the Sequence as a Form').

The 'missed meeting' in Sonnet 22 exemplifies a stock theme of the Renaissance love sequence. (*Astrophil and Stella* 105 presents a variant of the same theme, where the lover is cheated of his ardent hope merely to see the beloved as she passes by.) The primary function of Robert's Sonnet 22 is to represent an aspect of the lover's experience which would otherwise be lacking in his sequence, but what distinguishes his 'missed meeting' is the fact that it had been arranged for the eve of the lover's departure—when he was

Even now to leave your light, my life's delight.

This reference to impending departure links with Song 1 and suggests that Barbara may be the inspiration behind Sonnet 22 also. It is incidentally worth noticing that the setting of Sonnet 22—the *low shady room* where the lover waits expectantly as daylight fades—is more precisely imagined than is usual with Robert.

Neither Song 1 nor Sonnet 22 contains any suggestion that the lady is permanently unattainable, which is the dominant view of the beloved in the sequence as a whole, though in another important respect—in their view of the beloved as an image of heaven—both these poems, and Song 6, are in full accord with the main emphasis of the sequence. The inclusion of Song 1 and Sonnet 22 illustrates the flexibility appropriate to a genre whose essential purpose was to portray the variety of the lover's experience. In the typical Renaissance sequence, however, love is seen exclusively from the male point of view. In Song 6 Robert does what his elder brother had done in Song viii of *Astrophil and Stella*: he adds a new dimension to the sequence by giving a voice to the woman in love—and in Song 6 not only does the woman reveal that she is as much in love as the man, she does so openly and free from the constraints which inhibit Philip's Stella.

ROBERT AND OTHER WOMEN

Barbara was the abiding love of Robert's life, but we will falsify our picture of the man if we ignore the evidence that he was also interested in other women, while other women could be fond of him. This evidence survives in letters to Robert among the Sidney papers from both Rowland Whyte and Thomas Edmondes—letters which must be viewed in context to be properly understood: when the relevant passages are then put together they disclose a man who was both attracted by and attractive to the opposite sex.

In 1597-8, during probably the most difficult period of Robert's life, feminine affection for him shines through passages in Whyte's letters. During the spring of 1597 Robert's candidature for the Wardenship of the Cinque Ports was being opposed by the (ultimately successful) Lord Cobham and his supporters, who thwarted Robert's attempts to obtain home leave since it was obviously more convenient that the opposition candidate should be tied in Flushing for as long as possible. In March, Whyte reported how difficult it had proved to find at court a suitable person who would be prepared to hand to the Queen a letter which Robert had written her on his candidature. The reluctance Whyte encountered indicates that most people at court had no wish to be associated with what they must have sensed was a losing cause—even Lady Warwick, that staunch supporter of her late husband's nephew, evaded this challenge and replied that she would have delivered the letter with all her heart but was about to leave for her home in Hertfordshire. When Whyte eventually fell into conversation with the beautiful Lady Rich he realized that her heart was in the right place, so he took the letter from his pocket and asked her to deliver it. 'She kissed yt and tooke yt and told me that you had never a frend in Court would be more ready then her self to doe you any pleasure. I besought her in the loue I found she bore you', Whyte goes on, 'to take some tyme this night to doe yt. And without asking anything at all of the contents of yt, she put yt in her bosome and assured me, that this night or tomorrow morning yt wold be reade and byd me attend her.' (19 March 1596/7.) Tact may have prompted Whyte to make a point of suggesting that Lady Rich knew nothing of the letter's contents, for she was evidently well aware of the general state of affairs. Rather more than a month later Whyte informed Robert how she had 'told me that your last letter was so full of kindnes that she cold not tell how to answer yt and saies that 200 [Robert Cecil] doth greatly labour 1500 [the Queen] for 30 [Lord Cobham] but yet yt doth little good. She wishes yt may neuer haue other success' (30 April 1597). The *kindnes* which Lady Rich felt unable to answer was presumably contained in Robert's letter of thanks for her support, a letter which may well have mingled gratitude with amorous compliment. That is what Whyte's report of her coy reaction suggests, and the suggestion is somewhat confirmed by a surviving letter to her from Robert, written from Flushing in October 1596, whose rather formal tone may partly reflect the fact that on this occasion he was agreeing to act merely as an intermediary for Count Lewis of Nassau:[31]

when I parted from him hee demanded that trust of me, that I would procure the letters hee should send vnto me to be safely deliuered and if any answer kame to bee in like sort sent vnto him. It may bee hee is in earnest

[31] Hatfield House, Cecil Papers 46/23. The two letters from Count Lewis which Robert mentions as *adioined* are no longer present.

and so I haue some cawse to imagin: it may bee it is but gallantary. Howsoeuer, I besech yow Madame let him know of the receipt of his letters. For hee is a fine yong gentleman, and of a great hows, and one that eccedingly honors My Lord yowr brother and yowrself. This is all that your faier eyes shall bee troubled withall at this time: sauing onely that I ame promised My Lord Riches Arras shall bee heer very speedily so as I dout not but yow shall haue yt before Christmas. I do very humbly kiss yowr hands and rest

Yowr most humble creature
and seruant
R: Sydney.

In the following year (1597) Lady Rich's brother the Earl of Essex publicly backed Robert's candidature for the disputed Wardenship of the Cinque Ports, but by then it had become painfully evident that under pressure Essex was prepared to sacrifice his friends in the interests of his own unbridled ambition. Rowland Whyte reported to Robert how Essex had leagued himself with the powerful Robert Cecil, 'they are often and priuat together, they consult how to bring this and that to pass . . . and yet I see in them both no agreeing to giue you contentment' (4 May 1597), and although Essex's friends united in their protests against his recent behaviour, 'he answers you all with silence' (2 June 1597). Lady Rich's support for Robert at this critical juncture goes beyond what can reasonably be attributed to sisterly loyalty and attests her warm affection for Robert himself.

When at the beginning of March 1598 Robert's long-awaited leave was finally granted—months after Lord Cobham had won the Wardenship—the news that another rival for favour and advancement was about to return home was not greeted with unmixed pleasure at an envious and suspicious court. 'I was at Court of purpose to enquire what is sayd of this vnexpected leaue. I heare that it is mused at.' The same letter from Rowland Whyte (4 March 1597/8) which reports this cold reaction also describes Lady Essex's immediate response when Whyte told her the news —'she told me that nobody had greater cause to be gladde of yt then herself, and I well found yt by her countenance. You were euer beholding vnto her.' The affection for Robert spontaneously evinced by both Essex's sister and Essex's wife at this dark period contrasts vividly with the guarded attitude of those courtiers absorbed in the ceaseless game of 'who loses, and who wins'.

In the previous decade Lady Rich and Lady Essex had been the two loves in the life of Robert's elder brother. It was probably in 1581–2 (cf. p. 62) that Philip commemorated his love for Lady Rich in *Astrophil and Stella*, while Lady Essex had been the girl whom Philip married in 1583 when he was in his twenty-ninth year and she in her sixteenth. In 1597, the dark period of Robert's life when (as we have seen) both ladies revealed their fondness for him, Lady Rich was thirty-five years old and Lady Essex was thirty.

During his embassy to France to negotiate with Henri IV on behalf of the Huguenots—a visit which occupied the early months (9 January–8 April) of 1594—Robert made what can be regarded as his most glamorous 'conquest', and the lady in question was not more than twenty-one at the time. Whatever the political difficulties attendant on his mission, during its course Robert won for himself the personal affection not only of Henri IV but also of Gabrielle d'Estrées (1573–99), the king's beloved mistress whom he hoped to marry and who, since he had honoured her, was known simply as *Madame*. For the first hint of this we are again indebted to Rowland Whyte, reporting how Sir Roger Williams fresh from France had visited Nonesuch the previous day and 'byds me tell you that the King of France in very great kindnes asked hym for you, and gaue at his table many good words of you, and willed him to put you in mynd of the howndes you promised hym: Madame in like sort asked very graciously where you were; he thincks you shall doe well to wryte to the King and to her as occasion serues' (4 October 1595). The English diplomatic agent to Henri IV, when writing to Robert from Paris some three years later, reveals for us something of the affection which must have lain behind Madame's 'gracious' enquiry of Sir Roger Williams:

> Your letter to Madame was exceedinglie welcome, And I must needes saye that her Contynuall professions to your Lordship geiue testimonie rather of loue than of frendshipp. She doth often enquyre of me whether your Lordship will not come againe into France, and tould me last, that she would be gladd some occasion might bring your Lordship ouer, that she might see you after she shalbe marryed. (Thomas Edmondes to Robert, *Paris*, 15 July 1598.)

The same theme reappears in another letter five months later:

> It maie please your Lordship I haue delyuered your Lordships letter and present to Madame the which it was not needfull to accompanie with anie

Complements as your Lordship requyred me, she hauing long since better conceiptes of your Lordship then my witt is able to Intymatt vnto her. Your Lordships present was verie welcome vnto her, and she sayth she will requyte your Lordship with some remembrance of her parte. (Thomas Edmondes to Robert, *Paris*, 12 December 1598.)

Against the background which Edmondes's letters supply we can realize the point of the court gossip retailed by the faithful Rowland Whyte only two days after he had reported the visit of Sir Roger Williams to Nonesuch with gracious messages for Robert from Henri IV and Madame. 'Yt was told me that some lady of the priuy chamber demanded of John Simmons what Madam did, he answered she was well when he saw her, and deliuered vnto her certain perfumed skins from Sir Robert Sydney, and this hath bene told the queen' (6 October 1595). Elizabeth's quickness to resent any hint of amorous involvement on the part of her courtiers was notorious: the incident recounted to Whyte suggests that the friendship between Robert and Gabrielle d'Estrées had become talked about at the English court and that there were some who—in a spirit of mischief or jealousy—were prepared to use that glamorous friendship to injure Robert in the queen's eyes.

There are other occasions also when Whyte can be seen trying to warn Robert of the threat to his career which his behaviour might involve. On the eve of his return in March 1598 from his longest period in Flushing 'some doe ymagin that you shalbe vicechamberlen, yet they say you are to younge, and to amorous to be conuersant with and amongest the ladies' (4 March 1597/8). Since Robert was now in his thirty-fifth year it is evident that *younge* was not being used in a purely literal sense, and the same sort of allusion can be recognized again in a conversation reported by Whyte two years later when he told Robert that both the Earl of Nottingham and Lady Warwick

did assure me that they neuer found her Maiesty haue a better opinion of you than at this present. And that she shuld say, that now all your youthful toyes were out of your brain you wold proue an honest man. My lord I obserue that the lest Toy is here made powerfull to hynder any mans preferment and therefore you and all that stand for aduancements here ought to auoyd & shun euery small occasion that may hurt. (21 February 1599/1600.)

It should by now come as no surprise to learn that Robert was not blind to the most obvious chance for amorous excitement which Elizabeth's court offered—the band of well-born and nubile young ladies, dressed all in white to symbolize their (officially) virgin state, who constituted the royal Maids of Honour. The occasional references in Whyte's letters to Robert's interest in *the presence chamber* have been interpreted as allusions to his 'ambition' (*History Today*, xv, 1965, p. 187)—though in fact they always concern behaviour which Whyte warns Robert will damage his career. When these passages are put together and seen in context it becomes clear that they refer to Robert's amorous interests: the (to us enigmatic) *presence chamber* allusions would have been transparent to any Elizabethan who knew the court, for it was in the Presence Chamber that the Maids of Honour paraded when on duty. Whyte's description of the formal reception accorded to Verreicken, envoy to Elizabeth from the Archduke Albert, incidentally illustrates this: '. . . and soe he entered the presence chamber full of great ladies, and the faire Maides attired all in whyte excellently braue.' (24 February 1599/1600.)

The first of these 'sensitive' *presence chamber* allusions occurs in a passage whose second paragraph makes clear the nature of what is being talked about:

> You haue hard of my lord Essex keeping his chamber by my former lettres during which tyme he ofte sent to the queen about diuers buisnes, diuers persons. He that he sent to satisfie her Maiesty with the weaknes of your direction for the stay of the ships, told me that the queen vsed very many good speaches of you, that you were a very fine gentleman and had many good parts but that your mynd was to much addicted to the presence chamber. For the discharge of the duty I owe you, I doe with all humblenes signify vnto you what I heare.
>
> Yesterday a principall follower of my lord of Essex told me that he saw two letters of yours sealed with gold and the broad arrow head, directed to two of the maydes, and that a knight who was too open, had the charge to deliuer them. I thincke yt was told me of purpose because I shuld take notice of yt. (27 February 1596/7.)

(Whyte's reference here to the *broad arrow head* of the Sidney arms may recall to us the conclusion of *Astrophil and Stella* 65 which turns on the conceit that Cupid's arms bear love's arrow while Philip's bear the arrowhead.) Two weeks later, in a letter concerning the disputed Wardenship, Whyte unfolded his anxiety in a way which disarmingly reveals his own embarrassment:

I haue indeed too often troubled you with the presence chamber, but to giue you satisfaction yt was my Lady Warwick and Sir ed: dier that in their loue to you did wish your ennemies had not had that only way to hurt you in her Maiesties favor who speakes often of yt. and lately Sir gilly meirick who professes to loue you did tell me he was sorry to hear of some courses you held that harmed greatly your reputacion. I neither was nor am inquisitiue to know of hym any particulars, yt is not my lord the report of any base fellow that shuld haue moued me to take the boldnes to wryte vnto you of such matters, for I know they doe not beseeme a seruant to doe, but hearing of yt from these kind of persons I cold not chuse in dischardge of my duty, but to aduertise yt, for Sir Edw dier in plaine termes told me that he hard the Queen had such an Impression of yt grownded in her as she thought you to young for any place about her. (16 March 1596/7.)

Some light is shed on Robert's reputation outside his own circle by a passage in a news-letter[32] dated from London on 29 December 1601 by Dudley Carleton to John Chamberlain at Knebworth:

The Queen dined this day priuatly at my Lord Chamberlains. I came euen now from the black friers where I saw her at the play with all her candidae auditrices. Mistress Neuill who played her prises and bore the bell away in the P. d'amours reuells was sworne maide of honor before Christmas, and Sr Rob: Sidney hath her allready in chase to make her forsweare both mayde and honor.

In spicing his budget with scandal the news-letter writer was catering to the same taste as today's gossip columnist, and his reports should be treated with similar caution. The true value of Carleton's paragraph lies in its revelation of how Robert was sometimes regarded in fashionable circles—though we do not really know whether his amours ever went beyond courtly 'gallantry'. His *youthful toyes* never resulted in open scandal, nor have we any reason to suspect that his marriage was ever threatened.

The typical Renaissance sequence depicts a love relationship outside marriage: Robert's Song 6 stands out in bold contrast within a sequence whose dominant emphasis is on an unattainable love. Although we share Rowland Whyte's ignorance concerning the 'particulars' of Robert's amours, we can recognize that his relations with other women imply the existence of amorous aspirations beyond what could be fulfilled within even

[32] Public Record Office, State Papers Domestic (Elizabeth), CCLXXXII/48.

a happy marriage, and these must have been an element in that complex of unsatisfied desires under whose combined pressure he turned for an outlet to poetry.

THE BELOVED PORTRAYED IN THE SEQUENCE

Astrophil and Stella, the most influential of Elizabethan sonnet sequences, is remarkable among them for its bold representation of an adulterous passion, and for its deliberately planted clues to the actual identity of the poet's beloved (see in particular Sonnets 24 and 37). The manuscript miscellany compiled during the second half of the sixteenth century by the Harington family[33] tells us something of how Philip's sequence was viewed by a slightly younger contemporary who was himself a poet, courtier, scholar, and soldier (and a friend, moreover, of Philip's brother and sister[34]). The opening sonnet of *Astrophil and Stella* is transcribed on fo. 155 of the miscellany in the hand of Sir John Harington himself (1560–1612), who has also supplied the heading 'Sonnetts of Sr Phillip Sydneys [vppon *deleted*] to ye Lady Ritch' (a heading evidently intended for the sequence though in the event only the first sonnet was actually copied). Some insight into an Elizabethan poet's view of such matters may be obtained if we compare Harington's direct naming of the lady on fo. 155 with the identification he appended to the only other *Astrophil and Stella* poem in his miscellany. The poem in question is Song x, though it is untitled in this manuscript: it occurs on an earlier page (fo. 36^v^) and is also copied by Harington himself, whose subscription reads 'Sr Phillip Syd: to the bewty of the worlde'. Although Song x is charged with sexual desire, Harington's subscribed phrase—'the beauty of the world' had been used by Philip himself of Philoclea in the original version of the *Arcadia*—points to an idealized love: the beauty of the world reflects the beauty of heaven, which is the ultimate object of all Platonic love. It is however the poet's nature, when he wishes, to find the universal beauty embodied in his own particular lady, and it is as a reminder of this that we may value Harington's two (distinct but reconcilable) 'identifications' of the beloved portrayed in *Astrophil and Stella.*

33 The miscellany is now in the library of the Duke of Norfolk at Arundel Castle.

34 See the letter from Robert Sidney to Harington, first printed in *Nugae Antiquae* (1769), pp. 120–3.

Spenser's sequence *Amoretti*, the form of whose original publication implicitly suggests that the sonnets concern the lady whom the poet eventually marries (see 'Robert's Use of the Sequence as a Form'), can be seen as a counterbalance to the adulterous *Astrophil and Stella*. In the typical Elizabethan sequence, however, the beloved is a shadowy figure who eludes precise identification and concerning whose actual bodily existence there usually remains a doubt. At this point we may usefully recall Giles Fletcher the elder (1546–1611) whose sequence *Licia*, published in 1593, has been regarded as an especially representative example of its genre (cf. *Elizabethan Sonnets*, ed. Maurice Evans, 1977, p. 221). Fletcher prefaced his sequence with discursive preliminary matter cast in the form of (1) a dedicatory epistle to Lady Molineux, and (2) an address To the Reader. In a teasing passage of the latter, wherein we may detect allusions to Fletcher's own academic background (he had been Fellow of King's, 1568-81, and Deputy Public Orator of Cambridge University, 1577-81), he thus deals with the question of his beloved's identity:

If thou muse what my LICIA *is, take her to be some* Diana, *at the least chaste, or some* Minerva, *no* Venus, *fairer farre; it may be shee is Learnings image, or some heavenlie woonder, which the precisest may not mislike: perhaps under that name I have shadowed* Discipline. *It may be, I meane that kinde courtesie which I found at the Patronesse of these Poems; it may bee some Colledge; it may bee my conceit, and portende nothing: whatsoever it be, if thou like it, take it, and thanke the worthie Ladie* MOLLINEUX, *for whose sake thou hast it.*

A poet directly challenged to 'explain' usually makes this kind of deliberately evasive response as a way of hinting that the only real 'explanation' is contained in the poetry itself, though that explanation may be discovered only by those able to understand the inner meaning of the poet's language.

Fletcher obliquely warns his reader against a simple identification of Lady Molineux with the Licia of his sequence. Similarly, the sister to whom Robert formally inscribed his poems on the first page of the notebook is manifestly not in herself the subject of his verse. That Robert if challenged to 'explain' would have made the kind of response indicated above may be deduced from his sequence, which contains within itself two carefully positioned and complementary clues to its inner meaning—one pointing to the unattainable love which occupies the greater part of the sequence, the other pointing to the wholly attained love represented in Song 6. In the final couplet of the final sonnet, itself originally conceived as the finale to the whole sequence, Robert intimates that the object of his *simplex amor* is an ideal, and is not ultimately to be identified with any actual person (Sonnet 35: 13–14—see 'Ideal Beauty'). In the heart of Song 6, itself positioned at the heart of the sequence which was to conclude with Sonnet 35, he tells us that the Lady whose reciprocated love for her Knight is depicted as a perfect example of *mutuus amor* is the Lady who dwells on the banks of the Medway (Song 6: 73–4)—intimating that she is in reality his own wife, dwelling at Penshurst while duty holds her Knight away from her to the East in Flushing.

'LYSA' AND 'CHARYS'

The typical Elizabethan sequence bears a title which commemorates the poet's beloved and at the same time masks her actual identity—and indeed evades the question as to her real bodily existence—under a manifestly allegorical guise. While Robert's sequence, unusually for the genre, possesses neither title nor dedication (beyond the impersonal *For the Countess of Pembroke* inscribed on the first page), his beloved is given a name in five of his poems: she figures as *Lysa* at Pastoral 7: 1 and at Sonnet 28: 8 (original version) and as *Charys* at Sonnet 28: 8 (revised version), at Elegy 16: 3, at Song 20: 9, and at Song 21: 2–3, 6–7, 9, and 19–20. Both names represent aspects of the ideal beauty which the climax of Sonnet 35 may tell us is the ultimate object of the poet's unrequited love.

In the original version of the sequence—the version which concluded with Sonnet 35—the beloved appeared only as *Lysa*. The allusion contained in the name itself, the allusion to the fleur-de-lys (the type of unsullied purity), is brought out in the sequence by the fact that Pastoral 7 and Sonnet 28 are the only two poems which explicitly evoke a garden in springtime, and the progression from 'April' in Pastoral 7, where the cold wind still blows, to 'May' in Sonnet 28, where the air plays softly among the leaves, confirms that the two *Lysa* poems were consciously associated in the poet's mind. In Pastoral 7 *Lysa* figures in company with her shepherd-lover *Rosis*, a name which appears only in this poem. While *Rosis* evidently alludes to

*Ro*bertus *Si*dneius (on the analogy of his elder brother's pastoral persona *Philisides*), the name in itself evokes the *rose*, and the poem activates the inherent allusion by the way *Rosis* at the start of stanza 2 symmetrically balances *Lysa* at the start of stanza 1: the reader attuned to the patterned language of Elizabethan verse will recognize here the conventional pairing of the *lily* and the *rose*, the former signifying purity and the latter signifying passion (we may compare the balancing of *Beauty/blest you* and *love/Wretch me* in the chiasmally patterned final couplet of Song 22: see p. 28). Two reasons have already been suggested (p. 15) why Robert should eventually have replaced *Lysa* with *Charys* in Sonnet 28 and a further motive may now be suggested—to confine the former name to Pastoral 7 where *Lysa* figures with her counterpart *Rosis*.

The introduction of *Charys* into Sonnet 28 points to a late stage of revision, after Robert had decided to continue the sequence beyond Sonnet 35, for *Charys* does not otherwise appear until we reach Elegy 16, the poem which terminates the first stage of the expanded sequence. *Charys* alludes both to the Greek χάρις = 'grace' and to the English *care* = 'object of tender concern' (cf. Shakespeare's Sonnet 48: 'Thou best of dearest, and mine only care'). Both these inherent senses are activated by verbal plays in Robert's verse—at Elegy 16: 3 'Charys cares of the heavens', and at Song 21: 9 'Grace only is what's Charys' grace'.

It has been suggested that the name *Lysa* points to an actual lady called Elizabeth (*British Library Journal*, i, 1975, pp. 122, 139), where the suggestion is linked with an interpretation of Sonnet 12 (Sonnet 2 of the Crown) which takes the first three lines of the sestet to mean that the beloved bears the same name as the saint whose feast was celebrated on Robert's birthday. Since that day (19 November) was in fact dedicated to St Elizabeth of Hungary, the suggestion that Robert's beloved was named Elizabeth appears to gain credibility: before accepting the idea, however, Sonnet 12 must be set in context in order to establish its true meaning.

Sonnet 12 is the first poem in the sequence explicitly to treat the theme of Predestination, a theme which continues through the rest of the unfinished Crown and which underlies much Renaissance love poetry. Robert may have received the idea directly from his elder brother's *Arcadia* where in the Fourth

Eclogues Philisides confesses about Mira 'I began to persuade myself in my nativity I was allotted unto her', but how ingrained the idea was is revealed in such casually light-hearted references as Katharine's 'And Longaville was for my service born' (*Love's Labour's Lost*, V. ii. 284). Spenser's *Hymne in Honour of Beautie* represents the most influential statement in English of the Neoplatonic doctrine of love, and Spenser's *Hymne* extends the theory of Predestination to include the idea that true love is a recollection of a former life in 'heavenly bowres' where the lovers had originally met and recognized that they were destined to love each other after they had descended here on earth (lines 197–203). Although this theory of pre-existence is not explicit in Robert's verse, it is found attributed to Plato himself in the sonnet by William Drummond beginning 'That learned Grecian who did so excell'—a sonnet whose final couplet

> No wonder now I feel so fair a flame,
> Sith I her loved ere on this earth she came

reads like an echo of Robert's

> For ere on earth in you true beauty came,
> My first breath I had drawn upon the day
> Sacred to you, blessèd in your fair name
> (Sonnet 12: 9–11).

When Robert's lines are set in their proper literary/philosophical context it should become clear that no saint other than the poet's own beloved is involved: the poet's birthday is *sacred* to her simply because on that day was born the man predestined to love her.

It is strictly unnecessary, therefore, to ask whether a committed Protestant such as Robert would have alluded in such a way to an actual saint of the Catholic church (a saint not commemorated in the *Anglican Prayer Book*). We might fruitfully speculate, however, on the fact that St Elizabeth of Hungary does not happen to be commemorated in the medieval Psalter which belonged in the sixteenth century to the Sidneys, who used the ample margins of its liturgical calendar as a family register of births, marriages, and deaths (see 'Robert and Barbara'). The details of Robert's birth are duly recorded in the margin of the November page, where the blank in the text itself is emphasized by the fact that the empty space is sandwiched between entries for the octave of St Martin (18 November) and the feast of St Edmund, king and martyr (20 November). It is misguided to seek the explanation of Robert's Sonnet 12 in the Catholic church calendar, but we may agreeably wonder whether the conspicuous blankness of 19 November in the pre-Reformation calendar of the family Psalter might not have encouraged Robert to dedicate his own birthday to the unattainable beloved celebrated in his poetry. That the conceit would, in any case, have been readily understood by the Elizabethan reader may be gathered from the satirist Joseph Hall's description of the modishly lovesick sonneteer who aspires to place his beloved among the stars

> or if not there,
> Sure will he saint her in his Calendar.
> (*Virgidemiarum* (1597), I. i.)

The wish to discover an actual lady, other than Robert's own wife, as the inspiration behind his sequence has prompted the suggestion that the 'clues' here examined point to Elizabeth Carey, only child of Sir George Carey and his wife Elizabeth, dedicatee of Spenser's *Muiopotmos* (1590). In this connection, attention was drawn to the proposal—a proposal in which, it was stated, Robert 'evidently took great interest'—to marry the young Elizabeth Carey to Robert's nephew, the fifteen-year-old William Herbert, future Earl of Pembroke (see *British Library Journal*, i, 1975, pp. 122–4). What was there implied concerning Robert's interest in the affair is not, however, borne out by an examination of the Sidney papers, where the only references to the young Elizabeth Carey occur in letters from Rowland Whyte during the brief period (September–December 1595) when the marriage was being proposed. Whyte was naturally anxious to report whatever he might learn about a matter of such potential interest to the Sidney family, but his letters reveal how he had to put his ear to the ground to catch such rumours as he could concerning the progress of the affair. Whyte's first reference occurs on 25 September when he reports that Lady Carey and her daughter had gone to the Isle of Wight: 'Great preparacion was made for them at Wilton, but they came not their, I know not the occasion.' Two weeks later Whyte had gained a little more insight: he reported that the Earl of Pembroke and his son had come up to see the queen 'and (as I heare) to deale in the matter of a marriage with Sir George Careys daughter' (8 October). A week after this Whyte makes his longest reference to the affair:

> As for my Lady Careys not going to Wilton, I am informed that she expected at Court a dispatch in her sute for certain lands that shuld discend to her daughter, by being next of kinn unto her Maiestie by the mothers syde: and lest the speach of marriage might overthrow it, twas thought best to put yt off till another tyme. My lord Harbert likewise being a suter for certain parkes and reversions, tis feared if the marriage were spoken of yt might bring hindrance unto yt. And therefore here is the place chosen fittest for the two younge ones to have an enterview, where without suspicion they may oft meete in secret, and to that end coms my lord of Pembroke up upon Monday next. I heare that yt is a motion very pleasing to both sydes: this is all that I can as yet learn. (*London*, 15 October 1595.)

Two weeks later the tenor of the rumours was changing: 'Theire hath been an enterview between the parties, and as I heare 9000 [Lord Herbert] wilbe hardly brought to affect pp.qq. [Elizabeth Carey]' (29 October), and the gloomy forecast was confirmed on 22 November when Whyte reported 'The speach of marriage between 9000 and qq. is quite broke off, by his not liking. And I feare me their is like to grow great unkindnes between 1000 [Essex] and 2000 [Pembroke]. When I know the true cause I will advertise your lordship.' The affair disappears from Robert's correspondence after 5 December, when Whyte reported that 'Sir George Carey takes it unkindly that Lord Pembroke broke off the match between Lord Harbert and his daughter.'

From the tone of these references we may doubt whether Elizabeth Carey was at all personally known to Robert at this period: we certainly gather that Robert was not himself involved in the negotiations, and that his interest in them was simply that which any Elizabethan in Robert's position would naturally take in the marriage prospects of a nephew who was heir to an earldom.

The lady does not altogether drop out of Robert's life after this episode. On 19 February 1595/6—very shortly after the breakdown of the Herbert match, and while the bride was still in her twentieth year—Elizabeth Carey married Sir Thomas Berkeley (heir to the Berkeley barony though destined never to inherit, since he died in 1611 two years before his father). Through what turned out to be an unhappy marriage to a spendthrift husband Elizabeth Berkeley became personally involved in the ancient litigation between the Berkeleys and the Dudleys for the Berkeley lands in Gloucestershire—litigation the Dudley side of which Robert had inherited through his mother's brother. In a letter[35] concerning this complex legal dispute, written to her steward Thomas Smyth on 5 February 1609, Elizabeth Berkeley expresses her readiness

> to give seven thowsand pownds, but not a iott more, of which one thowsand I will freely give out of my poore stock to pourchass peace, the rather for that notwithstanding theyse differences I have ever fownd a noble respect towards mee from the Lord Lisle, and would be glad to bee an actor in the ending of theis expensive suites with an adversarie of whom I must ever holde an honorable opinion.

We may deduce from this, if we wish, that Elizabeth Berkeley and Robert had met by this time and that she had been charmed —a view which would certainly accord with indications elsewhere of how other women responded to Robert (see 'Robert and Other Women'). The theory that the two may once have had 'a special relationship' (*British Library Journal*, i, 1975, p. 124) is, however, quite unwarranted by the known evidence.

While there is evidence pointing to Robert's having nourished amorous aspirations outside marriage, there are no solid grounds for suspecting that his love was ever seriously focused on any woman other than his wife (see 'Robert and Other Women'). The search for an actual woman behind the unreciprocated love portrayed in the sequence may obscure the intimations contained in the poetry itself that the object of the poet's *simplex amor* is not finally to be identified with any particular embodiment. To obscure these intimations is at the same time to obscure the central contrast round which Robert's sequence is constructed —the contrast between the unattainable love which occupies most of the sequence and the wholly reciprocated love for the real woman who is celebrated in Song 6.

THE BETRAYAL THEME

The genre to which Robert's sequence belongs exists to show the reader 'what it is to love', and this essential purpose is realized in Robert's portrayal of the eternal idealist as he experiences what

[35] British Library, Add MS 33588, fo. 54.

is at once the most powerful, and the most fluctuating in its moods, of all human emotions. Of the variegated themes which Robert weaves into the total picture, the theme of the beloved's desertion or betrayal—the theme introduced in Song 3—receives particularly intense expression as his sequence develops.

There are three sonnets—16, 27, and 29—which revolve entirely around the betrayal motif, and while all three are direct addresses they are arranged within the sequence to form collectively a graduated progression culminating in direct accusation. Sonnet 16 proclaims the beloved's betrayal but still addresses her formally as *Most fair*, she remains for the poet *a piece of heaven*, he does not *dare* accuse her but reproaches instead his own *fond mind* for having discovered her treachery. Sonnet 27 is not addressed to the beloved but to Falsehood itself: the poet admits that his lovesickness had blinded him to treachery, but this sonnet's reproach is directed neither against himself nor against the beloved, but against Falsehood for having corrupted her *beauties* and her *fair mind*. In Sonnet 29 such pretences are finally dropped, the poet is *innocent* and the beloved herself is directly and bitterly reproached. In a sequence whose dominant view of the beloved is as an image of heaven, Sonnet 29 is remarkable for its presentation of her as a sinful woman who confesses faults, promises amendment, and then breaks her promise.

The 'betrayal' Sonnets 27 and 29 belong to the group of bitter Sonnets—a group also including nos. 17, 21, 24, and 31—whose relationship to passages in Robert's letters suggests that the deep sense of betrayal which finds expression in the sequence was rooted in the frustrations he experienced in his political career during the second half of the 1590s. While tied to his post in Flushing he saw rivals who were less experienced but better placed for recognition being advanced ahead of him, and was provoked to exclaim 'I kannot choose but see, the extreeme inequalitee is held between others and me' (Robert to Barbara, 20 March 1596/7). Eight days later, in the course of a long letter to the Earl of Essex wherein he unburdens himself of his pent-up feelings, he enlarges on the theme:

I kan not bee so blind but I must see the great inequalitee held between me and others: neither is there any man of my profession, which hath had commandment, but one way or other hath had somewhat added vnto him. I have serued heer now a full prentiship: besides the time I spent before in her Maiesties court and wars and kan truly say that yet I know not what it is to haue credit or proffit bestowed vpon me . . . and now I must bee contented to see a nomber in the opinion of the world farr gotten before me. . . . (Robert to Essex, 28 March 1597.)

In a retrospect of the decade Robert is still harping on the same string:

I cold also say for my self that hauing bene there gouernor now almost ten yeares and nothing added vnto me either in reputacion or profitt, but rather diuers thinges taken from me, whereas all of myne own rancke haue bene preferred, and such as were farr behind me made equall vnto mee, and some sett before mee. . . . (Robert to Cecil, 26 April 1599.)

Comparison between such passages in Robert's letters and the culminating accusation in Sonnet 27 (*labours new / Reap of long faith the hire*) suggests an intimate link between the 'bitter' love sonnets and Robert's public career.

The second quatrain of Sonnet 29

> Your wrongs made me with losses bide content
> And now a safe though homely rest prepare,
> And as hopes had left me, I leaving care
> Work on the breaches of time fondly spent

needs the real-life background which Robert's letters supply for its full understanding. The *safe though homely rest* which the poet prepares for himself in the sonnet can be recognized again in the self-counsel contained in a letter already quoted from Robert to his wife:

If my fortune bee not good now, I hope it wil bee better one day. In the meane time wee must make the best of our own, and make much one of another, and care only for them that deserue wel of vs: and God I trust one day wil send better fortune. . . . (Robert to Barbara, 20 March 1596/7.)

The curious image in the last line of the quatrain becomes intelligible when we recognize in it an allusion to the fortifications of Flushing, which throughout the 1590s were a cause of major concern to Robert as Governor. A *breach* in a fortification is normally the result of enemy battery: the metaphorical *breaches* in Sonnet 29 are the result of neglect—of *time fondly spent*—and the same is literally true of the decayed condition of the Flushing fortifications at this period. Typical of a recurrent theme in Robert's official correspondence is his request that the Queen should 'haue respect of the fortifications, which ar exceedingly out of order, and must be wrought vpon while we ar at quiet' (Robert to Cecil, 13 October 1595). This provides a precise literal gloss on the metaphor in Sonnet 29 about working, during a period of *rest*, to repair the *breaches* caused by neglect.

Sonnet 17: 7–11 contains a striking image of the hapless poet-lover

> on whom a storm of losses blows
> And tides of errors run: yet sail on still
>
> While my corrupted sense doth think it sees
> The long sought land of rest, and while to bliss
> I think there is a way, though yet I miss.

The imagery in these lines strongly recalls a passage in another of the many letters which Robert wrote to Essex from Flushing in 1597 about the difficulties of his Governorship:

> I kan not saile against wind and tyde: nether hath the Queen power heer to command. I wil do as the barck that when it is guided makes way according to the sufficiency of her building. For wiser then I ame I wil not make my self nor promis to make a better viage then they which haue run the cours before me. (Robert to Essex, 9 January 1596/7.)

The general impression that Robert's verse and Robert's prose are here directly related is reinforced by a textual detail of Sonnet 17—the fact that *way* in line 11 was actually substituted during revision for the original *cours*: both words, it will be noticed, are used in the relevant passage of the letter.

As he unravelled his political frustrations to Essex on 28 March 1597 Robert was driven to confess 'I must thinck there is some secret Canker in my fortune to which no medicin wil bee fownd.' The sentence not only evokes the general mood of the bitter sonnets: it is precisely paralleled at Sonnet 21: 10–11

> a canker (think) unseen
> The apple's heart, though sound without, doth eat.

In another passage of the same letter Robert indignantly repudiates the rumour being circulated at the English court that he was enriching himself out in Flushing:

> But the Queen is made beleeue, how great a place this gouerment is, and that therfore I kannot do that seruice in it, but that by it, already I ame sufficiently rewarded. So good a place it is, as if I were but as I was when I first kame vnto it, I should thinck it a very vnlucky hower wherin I

vndertook it: and whosoeuer hee bee that hath it, and deales as hee should do in it, wil earne his wages as deerly as hee that cuts wood for the Queens kitchin: and, from yt, wil haue less mony in his purse, at the yeares end then the other wil haue. (Robert to Essex, 28 March 1597.)

When this passage is set beside the dramatic opening of Sonnet 21

> Alas why say you I am rich? when I
> Do beg, and begging scant a life sustain

a literal dimension is disclosed behind what on the surface is a metaphor referring to the condition of the lover deprived of his lady's favour.

It was a stock Renaissance device to address occasional sonnets of a love sequence to an unsympathizing friend (cf. *Astrophil and Stella* 14, 21, and 51) and Robert is employing that device in Sonnet 21. Comparison with Sonnet 24—the only other sonnet of the sequence which directly addresses an individual other than the beloved—indicates that while the former sonnet addresses a type the latter addresses a real person, who is addressed as *thou* (contrast *you* in Sonnet 21) and whose own particular experience is evoked in the first quatrain and paralleled with that of the poet-lover in the second quatrain. The sonnet begins

> Canst thou turn from the haven of thy rest
> For bitter storms that beat thee from the shore?
> Canst thou forsake the mine whose golden store
> Must make thee rich, with labours lost distressed?

The specific references here would have enabled any well-informed courtier in 1595-6 to recognize that the person being addressed is Sir Walter Ralegh, who had performed his celebrated voyage to Guiana in 1595 and who published his narrative of it at London in 1596 as *The Discoverie of the large, rich, and bewtiful Empyre of Guiana, with a relation of the great and Golden Citie of Manoa (which the Spanyards call El Dorado)*. When published Ralegh's narrative was dedicated, not to the Queen as seems to have been his original intention (cf. the letter from Rowland Whyte quoted below, p. 100), but to his kinsman Charles, Baron Howard, Lord Admiral, and to Sir Robert Cecil. In the dedicatory epistle Ralegh declares that his devotion to the Queen's service had caused him to turn away from the untold wealth of the region and return to England:

From my selfe I haue deserued no thankes, for I am returned a beggar, and withered, but that I might haue bettred my poore estate, it shall appeare by the following discourse, if I had not onely respected her Maiesties future Honor, and riches. . . . But I have chosen rather to beare the burthen of pouerty, then reproch. . . .

On pages 89–90 of the published narrative Ralegh vividly describes the bitter storm which arose as he and his companions were about to set sail from the American mainland on their homeward journey (see Commentary).

Both Ralegh and Charles Howard had earlier figured in Robert's life among those influential cousins of Barbara Gamage who in 1584 had concerned themselves about her marriage prospects (see 'Robert and Barbara'). Ralegh appears frequently in Rowland Whyte's letters to Robert during the 1590s, and shortly after the return from Guiana, Whyte reports:

Sir Walter Rawleis frendes doe tell her Maiestie what great service he hath donne unto her by his late voiage, in discovering the way to bring home the wealth of India, and in making knowen to that nation, her vertues, her Iustice. He hath brought hither a supposed prince, and lefte hostages in his place. The Queen gives good eare unto them. I am promised for you his own discours to the Queen of his iorney. (Rowland Whyte to Robert, 27 September 1595.)

Ralegh's own letters to Cecil towards the end of 1595 reveal how quickly the hopes with which he had returned from Guiana were betrayed, and his bitterness was still festering a year later when Rowland Whyte told Robert how '24 [Ralegh] is not pleased that the Queen doth not esteme his services worth thankes, and protestes he wil goe to the plough, and never harken after imploiements any more' (22 September 1596). Ralegh's Guiana voyage was the most conspicuous case during the 1590s of an arduous service performed by a member of the Elizabethan court but not properly appreciated by the Queen. It was natural for Robert to sense a parallel between his own experience and the disillusion experienced in 1595–6 by his wife's glamorous kinsman.

The thinly veiled reference to the Guiana voyage in Sonnet 24 represents the only identifiable allusion to a public event which Robert's verse contains. That allusion occurs in the last of three sonnets (22–4) all of which start from an image of a shore and a storm-beaten mariner. This image, which recalls Ralegh's narrative, is the thread connecting three consecutive but otherwise unrelated sonnets.

Yet another passage is relevant here from the long letter written at Flushing wherein Robert unburdens himself of his pent-up frustrations:

> Truly My Lord I begin to grow very weary seing busines increas daily vpon me, and likelihood of more and more troubles: and the longer I goe forwards the less cause to hope for any acknowledgment or requital. (Robert to Essex, 28 March 1597.)

Mood and expression here are closely similar to the second quatrain of Sonnet 24:

> Ah when do I, from troubles in my breast
> See peace or truce? or with limbs faint and sore
> Leave off the lovèd chase, which more and more
> Flies from before me, when I follow best.

It is significant that behind both prose and verse can be discerned the well-known adage *Follow love and it will flee.*

When in May of 1597 the Earl of Essex was in England engaged in preparing his expedition to the Azores, Robert wrote from Flushing regretting his own inability to join a venture which—though it was to prove a failure in the event—was attended in advance with high hopes and promised opportunities to win recognition. Robert acknowledged, however, the futility of his regrets, 'since I see Flushing must bee the graue of my yowth and I feare of my fortune' (Robert to Essex, 24 May 1597). The remark epitomizes the close link between Robert's private and public lives, for although its immediate context is political Robert here envisages Flushing as representing a twofold death. In the twofold light of his poems and his correspondence the remark can be seen as referring to (1) the 'death' of absence from all he loves (*the grave of my youth*)—the death foreshadowed in Song 1 and realized in Song 6, and (2) the 'death' of his hopes for worldly advancement (*the grave I feare of my fortune*)—the death alluded to in 1598 by the Earl of Essex who 'takes all oportunity to put her Maiestie in mynd what a worthy servant she hath of you, and what pitty yt is you shuld be buried as you are' (as reported to Robert on

1 February 1597/8 by Rowland Whyte, who was himself reporting what Lady Warwick had told him).

In the winter of 1595 an episode in Robert's career as Governor of Flushing culminated in a way which may throw light on the importance of the betrayal theme in his verse. The fugitive Irish priest Patrick Segrave alias Fitzjames had originally approached Robert in 1590–1 with an involved story about delivering Antwerp to the English in exchange for money payments and promises of Catholic toleration. Robert soon sensed that Segrave was more likely to betray England to Spain than Spain to England, and he reported the matter to the Queen and Lord Burghley. The suspect negotiations lapsed in 1592 and when Segrave approached Robert again in the autumn of 1595 in an attempt to renew them, Robert forwarded the priest's letter to Burghley on 12 September remarking that 'hee intends nothing but naughtines'. The Queen and Burghley wanted Robert to promise Segrave safe conduct to and from Flushing but to seize him once he was inside the town and put him to the rack in order to extract a full confession. Robert declined to give a promise with the deliberate intention of breaking it, and in the course of a long and courageous protest he told Burghley

> but I trust her Maiestie wil not command me to do that which wil bee a perpetual blott vnto me, and wil make me less able herafter to do her seruice in greater matters, in breaking my faith with so slender a person. For how bad soeuer hee bee, he cannot bee worse after he hath bin with me, then I know him to bee already and therfore either I should not giue my word vnto him or hauing giuen yt should not breake yt. For (as they say) how worthy soeuer hee may bee to haue promis broken with him, I thinck my self vnworthy to do yt.

Near the end of the letter Robert apologizes for troubling Burghley with such an extended discourse on what the writer acknowledges is essentially a personal matter:

> But I trouble your Lordship to long with this matter: since it may seeme indeed especially to concern myself: I wil therfore onely beseech your Lordship that yow wil deliuer my humble sute vnto her Maiestie that it wil please her to giue me leaue to bee careful of the small reputation I haue hetherunto maintained, but that theyr shall bee no man whoe wil more freely giue his lyfe and all that he hath vnto her seruice. . . . (Robert to Burghley, *Flushing*, 10 December 1595.)

Robert recurs to the matter in the course of writing to Burghley a week later:

By this time also I hope your Lordship hath receiued mine of the tenth of this month wherin I set down my knowledg of patric Segraue or Fithiames according as your Lordship had required by your last vnto me, as also by your Lordship I besowght her Maiestie that if he came vnto me I might not bee forced to breake my word with him, which I do now also again. . . . (Robert to Burghley, *Flushing*, 18 December 1595.)[36]

Burghley's replies to these particular letters, like almost all his letters to Robert, have disappeared: there seems in fact to be no further reference to the affair in the surviving correspondence, and Robert's involvement with Segrave apparently came finally to a halt with the end of the year 1595.

It was from 1595, however, that Robert's hopes of advancement began perceptibly to fade. In the first half of the 1590s Flushing could be thought of as the place where Robert was serving his apprenticeship in the royal service, but his being left stranded there through the second half of the decade while younger men in England were advanced ahead of him was a serious set-back. While there may be no surviving proof to link the 'crosses' in Robert's fortunes after 1595 with his conduct in December of that year, he obviously cared deeply about the issue of principle involved in the Segrave affair and it is natural to suppose that the episode and its bleak aftermath contributed to the sense of betrayal so strongly felt throughout the sequence.

The abnormally deep sense of betrayal which Robert's love poetry reveals is illuminated when that poetry is seen against the dual background of (1) the Neoplatonic cult of the beloved as a reflection of the deity, and (2) the special version of that cult which focused on Queen Elizabeth. The latter flourished in England during the late sixteenth century, when it became the fashion for Elizabethan courtiers to profess to be 'in love' with their Queen. While Robert did not publicly adopt this pose, as both Essex and Ralegh conspicuously did, the blending of Neoplatonism with the 'establishment' cult of Queen Elizabeth nevertheless helps explain how frustrations which were political rather than amorous in origin could yet be included in the complex of unsatisfied desires which finds an outlet in his sequence.

[36] Public Record Office, State Papers, Foreign: Holland. SP 84/51: fos. 272–3 (10 Dec.) and fos. 290–1 (18 Dec.).

ROBERT'S USE OF THE SEQUENCE AS A FORM

Robert's system of numbering the poems in his main sequence in two parallel series is related to an overall metrical design, as explained above (see 'The Formal Aspects of the Poetry'). The seven unnumbered poems reveal, by their positions in the notebook, something about the way the numbered sequence itself evolved and at the same time underline the unity of that sequence by providing for comparison poems which manifestly fall outside it.

The unnumbered poems are entered in two groups, four of them following Sonnet 35 and three of them following Elegy 16, and this confirms that Sonnet 35 and Elegy 16 each represented the conclusion of the sequence at successive stages of its evolution. Sonnet 35 is the last of the sonnets and is manifestly climactic, while Elegy 16 with its circular celebration of the beloved makes another appropriate finale (see 'Formal Aspects': 'Patterns'). There were therefore two stages during the whole time that Robert was using the notebook—namely, after entering Sonnet 35 and again after entering Elegy 16—when (for a brief period in each case) he felt free to use the volume for material unconnected with the sequence.

It can be shown from their metrical forms alone that the unnumbered poems do not belong to the sequence: two (*Upon a Snuffkin* and *In another place*) are in octosyllabic couplets, two ('From fairest breast' and 'Once to my lips') are in the *ottava rima* also used in Pastoral 9, one (*Translated out of Seneca*) is in the heroic couplets also used in Elegy 16, one (*Translated out of Spanish*) is in quatrains identical in form with those used in Song 21, while only one ('I would be blind') uses a stanza form found nowhere else in the notebook. Within the sequence itself, every poem not a sonnet is metrically differentiated from every other.

The artistic integrity of the sequence, however, resides not merely in its formal design but more deeply in its pervading unity of tone, image, and vocabulary. This unity of style arises from the subject-matter which fills the entire sequence—a love which comes close to fulfilling the ideals outlined by Marsilio Ficino in his Commentary on Plato's *Symposium*. It is when viewed in this light—as portraying a love which transcends the body and is the source of all grief and all joy—that Song 6 can be seen as an integral member of the sequence. By including Song 6 in the sequence, however, Robert is making an original use of the genre—to provide a unified context within which the profound contrast between requited and unrequited love can stand out. From within the dominant Petrarchan convention which he is using, Robert makes his own implicit comment on that convention. He is in complete accord with the Petrarchan exaltation of love as an absolute value, he recognizes the special nobility of loving without hope of a return, but at the same time he demonstrates that an exclusive preoccupation with hopeless love shuts out a whole dimension of human experience.

From this point of view, Robert's sequence may be compared to Edmund Spenser's, first published in 1595. The little volume wherein *Amoretti* originally appeared culminates in *Epithalamion*, Spenser's song in celebration of his own marriage. While the pains of love are part of Spenser's theme, however, and while several sonnets portray his beloved as the cold-hearted goddess of Petrarchan convention, the emphasis which progressively develops through the *Amoretti* is on a love born to be reciprocated: the reader progressively senses that the beloved, after a due period of 'sweet reluctant amorous delay', will eventually reward her lover. The *Epithalamion*, which triumphantly fulfils the hope foreshadowed in the *Amoretti*, is a richly sensuous hymn to sexual love glorified and made holy by religious ceremony. By contrast, the strict Neoplatonic decorum of Robert's sequence excludes all dwelling on the sexual aspect of love: while we need not doubt that Robert's marriage had in real life its physical side (see 'Ideal Beauty', p. 63), Song 6 poetically depicts that marriage as a perfect example of *mutuus amor*—a concept which, as Ficino defines it, has no need of sex. Song 6 is in spirit akin to Shakespeare's *The Phoenix and Turtle* rather than to Spenser's *Epithalamion*. Spenser's sequence seen as a whole does not really illustrate the rigid distinction made by Ficino between *simplex amor* and *mutuus amor*: considered from one viewpoint, Robert's sequence might almost have been written precisely in order to embody the theory of love expounded by Ficino.

Neither a wholly reciprocated nor a wholly unreciprocated love admits in itself of chronological development. Certain recurrent situations can indeed be recognized in Robert's sequence—the beloved has forsaken him for another (Song 3 and *passim*), she is legally another's (Pastoral 8; Song 11, stanza 3), she had earlier encouraged him (Sonnet 16; Song 10, stanza 4), he had been in love with other women before meeting her or before recognizing her as his true beloved (Sonnets 9, 13–14, and Pastoral 8)—and there occasionally occur such specific events as that he is forced to depart (Song 1), she writes him a letter (Sonnet 10), or fails to keep an appointment (Sonnet 22). All the situations and events, however, are traditional, they belong to the genre—to the poetic medium which Robert is using—and it would be rash to read them literally as autobiography and to seek a straightforward narrative thread running through them. The Elizabethan sonnet sequence—and in this respect Robert's is a pure example of the genre—exists not to tell a story but to portray the perennial experience of the lover in a series of sometimes meditative, sometimes dramatic monologues. Robert was following his elder brother's example when he interspersed among these first-person monologues occasional poems where the lover is presented in the third person as a shepherd, sometimes heard soliloquizing (Song 3, Pastoral 9), sometimes engaged in dialogue (Pastorals 2, 8, and 14). Philip's own brief but revealing comment on the psychology behind this characteristically Sidneian use of the third person is contained in the Third Eclogues of the *Arcadia* where the lovesick Philisides (Philip's pastoral persona), being invited to sing a song, 'began to utter that, wherewith his thoughts were then (as always) most busied: and to show what a stranger he was to himself, spake of himself as of a third person, in this sort'—then follows the poem which begins *The lad Philisides*. The most obvious comparison is with Robert's introduction of himself as *Rosis, poor shepherd lad* in Pastoral 7, but the paradox implicit in Philip's comment may also help us to understand one of the unique features of Robert's Song 6, namely its presentation of the male lover at two removes as the Knight whose speech is reported by the Pilgrim. This could suggest that in this poem, the most deeply personal in the sequence, the poet's grief for his absent love has made him doubly a stranger to himself, while at the same time Song 6's unique portrayal of a wholly mutual love is set in a different perspective from the rest of the sequence.

Love was known to the Elizabethans as not only 'the most puissant and passionate' of all human affections, but also the most 'variable' and 'inconstant' in its moods.[37] The lover's unstable and contradictory moods had been recognized as the primary symptoms of his malady since at least the time of Galen, but here we need only refer once more to the central Renaissance textbook on Neoplatonic love. Ficino in his Commentary on the *Symposium* thus describes the lover's condition:

Fit etiam ut amore illaqueati vicissim suspirent et gaudeant. . . . Calent quoque vicissim et frigent instar eorum quos tertiana febris invadit. . . . Ideo timidi quoque vicissim et audaces apparent. Ebetissimi praeterea quique acutiores amando redduntur. (II. vi.)

Shakespeare's most complete study of the condition is embodied in the character of Duke Orsino. Having in the opening speech of *Twelfth Night* struck the keynote of his own character, Orsino unfolds it more fully in the central scene (II. iv) where he invites Viola–Cesario

if ever thou shalt love
In the sweet pangs of it remember me:
For such as I am, all true lovers are,
Unstaid and skittish in all motions else
Save in the constant image of the creature
That is beloved

and where he then proceeds to demonstrate his own inconsistency by first asserting the superiority of woman's love over man's

For boy, however we do praise ourselves,
Our fancies are more giddy and unfirm,
More longing, wavering, sooner lost and won,
Than women's are

and shortly afterwards—thinking now solely of his own love for Olivia—asserting the direct opposite:

Alas, their love may be called appetite,
No motion of the liver, but the palate,
That suffer surfeit, cloyment, and revolt;
But mine is all as hungry as the sea,
And can digest as much. Make no compare
Between that love a woman can bear me
And that I owe Olivia.

[37] See George Puttenham, *The Arte of English Poesie* (1589), Lib. I, chap. XXII 'In what forme of Poesie the amorous affections and allurements were uttered'.

Orsino's general demeanour provokes the detached and ironic Feste to comment 'Now the melancholy god protect thee, and the tailor make thy doublet of changeable taffeta, for thy mind is a very opal.' Feste's mockery is aimed at the lover who is in love with love itself and who luxuriates in his own melancholy. Sebastian's successful wooing of Olivia arouses Orsino from his introversion to recognize and reciprocate Viola's love for himself. Shakespeare's implicit comment in *Twelfth Night* on the Petrarchan cult of hopeless love is comparable to the comment which Robert Sidney makes by including Song 6 within his sequence.

The universal recognition that varying and contradictory moods are intrinsic to the lover's experience explains how the sonnet sequence, which by convention depicts an outwardly static situation (the lover permanently in love with a permanently unattainable lady), can yet as a genre admit of endless variation. The poet could permit himself considerable freedom when arranging his poems to form a sequence whose purpose was to reflect the true nature of love. His material might consist of individual poems composed on separate occasions but he could move freely among them, bringing together poems whose juxtaposition would point up the paradox of love's contrariety or, with a more purely aesthetic motive, balancing light and shade, the sombre mood against the joyful, in the same spirit as a painter disposing colours on his canvas or a composer creating a symphony.

That such were Robert's motives in arranging his own poems is revealed in many aspects of the sequence. Thus Song 11 is immediately followed by Song 12: both poems concern the beloved's desertion of the poet, but in the former he asks to be shielded from the painful truth and allowed the comfort of false hope which in the latter he refuses. The paradox is emphasized by the fact that each poem contains the word *betray* in its last line, the poet in the conclusion of Song 11 cynically inviting his thoughts to deceive him

> My pains will seem redressèd
> While your rest doth betray me

and in the conclusion of Song 12 decisively rejecting such fallacious comfort

> You never more shall lead me, flattering delight,
> You shall not betray me once again.

In Sonnets 32 and 33 the poet rejoices in the celebration of his beloved's beauty: these are the two most purely joyful poems in the sequence and that Robert regarded them as companion pieces[38] is indicated by his having brought them together and sandwiched them between the particularly sombre Sonnets 31 and 34.

Pastorals 8 and 9 are also to be viewed as companion pieces—but in this case as deliberately *contrasted* companion pieces. Both are of exactly equal length and in iambic pentameters throughout, the eight six-line stanzas of Pastoral 8 matched by the six eight-line stanzas of Pastoral 9 (i.e. each poem contains forty-eight lines = 480 syllables), and each symmetrically balances the other on either side of the longest uninterrupted run of Sonnets (18–26) in the sequence. In Pastoral 8 the shepherd endures a series of more and more decisive rejections without flinching from his adoration: in Pastoral 9 the beloved's treachery drives the shepherd to curse the world of nature and finally to renounce his love.

In *As You Like It* (V. ii) the faithful shepherd Silvius is commanded by his scornful beloved Phebe to 'tell this youth [Rosalind-Ganymede] what 'tis to love' and his reply includes a definition which neatly epitomizes the paradox of the lover's condition—'It is to be . . . all patience, and impatience.' The shepherd in Robert's Pastoral 8 is 'all patience' while the shepherd in Pastoral 9 is 'all impatience', firstly resenting his beloved's falsehood and finally rejecting his bondage to her. Pastoral 9 is immediately followed by Song 10 which provides a different kind of contrast, treating the same theme of woman's falsehood and the lover's rejection of his bondage but in a very different tone—a tone of buoyant disengagement. The same theme similarly treated reappears in Song 12, whose buoyant cynicism immediately follows the bitter cynicism of Song 11. Personal resentment of the beloved's treachery reaches a climax within the diversified series in Pastoral 9, which can be seen as the counterpart of Sonnet 29 within the sonnet series—and these two poems are linked by their direct mention of the beloved's *faults* and *sin* (Pastoral 9: 42, 47, and Sonnet 29: 4, 9).

[38] It is significant that Robert headed *both* poems 'Son: 32' (cf. 'This Edition').

In constructing the sequence, Robert used relationships between different poems in various ways—to bring out affinities, contrasts, emotional progressions, and emotional ambivalences. This Introduction has already commented on the affinities between Song 1 and Song 6 (see 'Robert and Barbara'), on the progression from April to May in the two 'garden' poems Pastoral 7 and Sonnet 28 (see ' "Lysa" and "Charys" ') and on the very different progression, beginning in self-reproach and culminating in direct reproach of the beloved, which is revealed in the 'betrayal' Sonnets 16, 27, and 29 when these three separated poems are brought together in the reader's mind and viewed collectively (see 'The Betrayal Theme'). Yet another kind of connection can be recognized between the three poems addressed to Absence: Sonnet 23 (*Absence what floods of plaints 'gainst thee would rise*), Sonnet 30 (*Absence I cannot say thou hid'st my light*), and Song 24 (*Absence I fled to thee*). When these three poems are viewed collectively they recall the then fashionable academic exercise which required students to argue on every side of a set theme. The theme which connects all three 'absence' poems may be defined *Whether the presence or the absence of the beloved is more painful to the unrequited lover.* Sonnet 23 concludes that presence is more painful than absence, Sonnet 30 concludes that presence and absence are equally painful, Song 24—whose imagery echoes that of Sonnet 23—finally decides in favour of presence. All three theoretically possible answers to the set question are successively propounded—though the paradox is disguised by the fact that the three poems concerned are set wide apart from each other in the sequence.

It was evidently part of Robert's general plan of arrangement to conceal such relationships between different poems below the surface of his sequence, where they may suggest an intellectual design underlying the whole work. The presence of such an underlying design seems implicit in the central contrast-within unity revealed when the longest poem (Song 6) is seen in relation to the rest of the sequence. Robert has arranged the items composing the sequence so as to ensure that the details of th underlying design will not be fully disclosed on a first readin but will gradually emerge as closer acquaintance develops.

We have already seen that the love portrayed in the sequenc is a pure Neoplatonic love which needs only the two highe senses of sight and hearing—the two senses which operate at a distance from their objects. The lower triad of smell, taste, touch (the three interlinked senses which depend on physical contact with their objects) are carefully excluded—with one notable exception. It must be by deliberate design that Robert inserted Sonnet 28—the one poem which, in contrast to the rest of the sequence, appeals to the lower triad and virtually excludes sight and hearing (though see Pastoral 7: 18 and note). Sonnet 28 gains its value largely from its special role within the sequence. The controlling image of the air mediating between the poet and his beloved preserves decorum by avoiding any suggestion of direct physical contact, while the poem appeals to all three lower senses simultaneously. The *thirsting sense* of line 12 is identified as *taste* at the end of line 14 though the garden fragrance which the poem evokes might seem primarily to involve the sense of smell. The implied fusion of the lower senses would have been readily understood by the educated reader: taste was ranked in the middle of the triad, being closely linked with both smell and touch (respectively above and below) and having been actually called a form of touch in Aristotle's *De Sensu*. In revising the text Robert eliminated *roses* and *violets* and substituted *myrrh* and *amber*, thus heightening and refining (by reducing the poem's visual suggestions) the appeal to the sense of smell. In the revised version it is only the references to *rosy May* (line 4) and to Charys' lips (described as *ruby* in line 8 and as *cherries* in line 9) which carry any visual suggestions, and these are completely conventional. The dominant image of the beloved in the sequence as a whole is of her radiant beauty, which shines especially in her eyes. In Sonnet 28 the beloved is evoked solely through her red lips, and those lips are not regarded in this poem as the source of speech but simply as the source of fragrance and as the recipients of the chaste kiss of the air. The sonnet is inserted where its springtime freshness provides a relief between two 'poisonous' sonnets on the beloved's treachery. The artistry of Sonnet 28 can be properly appreciated only when it is viewed in the context of the whole sequence by a reader acquainted with the traditional doctrines concerning the five senses.

We need to bear in mind when considering the sequence that we probably do not possess it in a form which Robert himself would have considered final. In particular, some at least of the eleven numbered poems in diversified metres (Pastoral 14–Song 24) which follow Sonnet 35 in the notebook would probably have been inserted at various points before the last sonnet in any completed scheme. While acknowledging the provisional status of the only text we possess we should at the same time recognize that to look for a 'final' order in any sequence designed to portray the shifting moods of love may be to pursue a mirage. The relevance of this in Robert's case is brought home by the fact that he has assigned alternative numbers in the upper margins to thirteen of the first fifteen items in the notebook. The system used in this alternative numbering differs from that used in the main numbering in the following respects: (1) the alternative numbering does not distinguish between sonnets and 'diversified' poems but includes both kinds in one consecutive series, (2) the *Crown of sonnets* is counted as a single item, (3) Sonnets 7 and 8 of the main sequence are omitted. Taken together, these differences show that Robert was not rearranging poems *within* the main sequence; he was constructing another sequence out of material selected from the main sequence. The numbers assigned in the main sequence to the poems selected for the alternative sequence remain undeleted, as do Sonnets 7 and 8. This confirms that the selective and reordered arrangement was not intended to supersede the main sequence but was designed rather as another way of presenting the lover's experience.

On page 124 is printed a Table of the alternative sequence, indicating the relationship between the order of the items therein and the order of the same items in the main sequence. It will be noticed that the *Crown* is the last item in the notebook to be assigned an alternative number, that the alternative sequence consists of thirteen items in all, and that the unfinished *Crown*—which Robert's appended note tells us was itself meant to consist of thirteen sonnets—is positioned within that sequence as the centre-piece (i.e. as item 7). All the indications are that Robert deliberately constructed the alternative sequence round the number 13, in allusion to its unluckiness in popular belief (see pp. 26–7; cf. also the headnote to Song 13 in the Commentary).

In bringing together in the alternative sequence items 8 and 9 (respectively Sonnet 6 and Sonnet 2 of the main sequence) Robert has created another pairing which points up love's contrariety. The sestet of item 8 begins

They are not flames of love but fires of pain
That burn so fair

which is countered in the opening of item 9

The pains which I uncessantly sustain,
Burning in hottest flames of love most pure,
Are joys, not griefs. . . .

Item 8 is the one thoroughly despondent sonnet in the alternative sequence, and Robert has positioned it where it is immediately counteracted by the next item. We can probably deduce from this the reason why Robert omitted from the alternative sequence Sonnets 7 and 8 of the main sequence: both are despondent sonnets whose inclusion might have upset the emotional balance of a sequence which—while its overall design symbolizes the luckless condition of the unrequited lover—was nevertheless intended to be positive in its ultimate emphasis. This intention is reflected in the choice of a concluding poem (item 13 = Sonnet 5 of the main sequence) that oscillates between the two opposite emotions of joy and grief which between them compose the lover's experience. Precisely the same oscillation is found in the sonnet which concludes *Astrophil and Stella*, but while Philip symmetrically balances the two emotions in his final lines

So strangely (alas) thy works in me prevail
   That in my woes for thee thou art my joy
   And in my joys for thee my only annoy

the corresponding lines of Robert's alternative sequence more positively emphasize in their conclusion the joyful aspect of love:

Heavy with grief, till I mine eyes do heave
Unto her face, whence all joys I receive,
And think all nothing that for her I prove.

What we learn of Robert's fundamental artistic intentions from the alternative sequence confirms what we learn from considering the main sequence. He is not unfolding a story with a beginning and an end: he is interested in formal design and in aesthetic effect, but fundamentally he is concerned to portray the emotional life of the perennial lover who alternately grieves and rejoices at being destined to go 'round and round in the narrow theme of love'.[39]

[39] Cf. W. B. Yeats, 'Solomon to Sheba'.

THIS EDITION

Since in normal circumstances no Elizabethan printer or amanuensis cared about accurately reproducing the accidentals of his exemplar—the layout, punctuation, and spelling of what he copied—a special evidential value attaches to Robert's notebook, which contains the largest body of original verse to have survived from the Elizabethan period in a text entirely set down by the poet himself. The left-hand (verso) pages in the body of this edition contain a transcript of Robert's manuscript as faithful to the original as I have been able to make it and as the medium of modern print allows. Material deleted by Robert is enclosed within square brackets in the transcript, and his interlinear revisions are printed in smaller type than that used for the text as originally set down. In parallel with the transcript, on the facing (recto) pages, is printed a modernized text of Robert's final version (i.e. silently omitting deleted material and silently incorporating revisions into the main text). Some comment on Robert's practice with regard to accidentals may help elucidate the principles underlying the modernization. The reader may examine for himself the operation of those principles by comparing the modernized text with the facing transcript.

LAYOUT

This is an aspect of presentation which the Elizabethan reader may have seen as significant in ways which his modern counterpart might miss. In this respect the features most worth calling to the reader's attention are (1) the way the sestets of the sonnets are spaced *either* in groups of 3 + 3 *or* in groups of 4 + 2 according to the sense pattern which each embodies, and (2) the way the quatrains of Song 6 are (exceptionally) not separated by regular spaces, this undivided layout reflecting the manner in which it is natural to suppose that a popular ballad was sung —straight through, without strong pauses between the stanzas. (See pp. 37 and 53.)

PUNCTUATION

The scene which, it is generally agreed, Shakespeare contributed in his own hand to the play of *Sir Thomas More* (British Library, MS Harley 7368) is sparsely punctuated and the author was evidently relying in the main on situation and context to tell the actors how to speak his words. Compare this with the self-conscious use of punctuation in the episode of Quince's 'tangled' Prologue and the fastidiously articulated comments of the courtly audience on its bungled delivery (*A Midsummer Night's Dream,* V. i). The contrast brought out by the comparison may itself be compared to the contrast involved in the transition from the unpunctuated second quatrain of Robert's Sonnet 25 to the scrupulously punctuated third quatrain. Thus the Elizabethan who could use punctuation deliberately for calculated rhetorical effects might rely in general on the rhythms inherent in his verse and prose to articulate his meaning. The verbal patterns do not primarily depend on grammatical signals for their recognition and could in fact be obscured or distorted by the attempt to introduce a rigorously 'logical' punctuation of the kind required for expository prose. Thus in the chiasmally patterned final couplet of Song 22

> Beauty and love, which only true
> Wretch are in me, and in blest you

the line-end pause after *true*, and the two commas which divide each line into equal halves, are all that is required to bring out the structure (analysed above, 'Formal Aspects: Patterns')—and in particular to indicate that the centrally placed *true* governs every element in the pattern.

We should bear in mind, however, that Robert in the notebook was not writing for the public eye and possibly envisaged no audience beyond himself and some amanuensis whom he may have intended to entrust with the task of preparing a formal presentation manuscript for the Countess of Pembroke (see 'Provenance')—and such an amanuensis would normally be expected to impose his own habits of spelling and punctuation[1] in much the same way as a modern printer is expected to impose

[1] A case in point is Ralph Crane, scribe to the King's Players in the early seventeenth century, for whose graphic habits see W. W. Greg, *The Editorial Problem in Shakespeare*, second edition, 1951.

Sonnet 26 from Robert's notebook (British Library, Add. MS 58435)

his own 'house style' on any text entrusted to him. In the circumstances, we can understand a certain casualness or insouciance on Robert's part about the details of presentation: this is reflected both in the various blots and smudges, and in the occasional presence of marks about which it may be impossible to decide in any given case whether what we see is a deliberate comma signifying a rhetorical pause, a momentary rest of the pen, or a sheer accident. (Marks which seem to be purely accidental have of course been ignored in the transcript.) Robert's own punctuation has always been taken into account, but the presence on the facing pages of a transcript which aims to be exact has been held to authorize a reasonable liberty in adapting the punctuation of the modernized text for today's non-specialist reader, whose expectations in this matter have of course been differently conditioned from those of his Elizabethan counterpart. Quotation marks have been supplied where the modern convention calls for them (e.g. Song 1: 35–6 and Sonnet 22: 10–11) and have been employed to signal a characteristic usage which Robert himself signals by distinctive spellings in the two places where it occurs, namely Song 3: 24–6 and Song 10: 41–2. In the former place the word *ever* occurs twice, in the latter place the word *never* occurs twice, each word on its second appearance becoming a noun as Robert notifies with an initial capital. The distinction is best conveyed to the modern reader by quotation marks, but it is in any case worth noting that to ignore the significance of Robert's capital at Song 10: 42 results in reading as a negative and reflexive construction what was intended as a positive and active one (i.e. understanding as *never bound herself even to one hour* what was intended to mean *bound her 'never' to one hour*).

SPELLING

Robert's own spelling reflects the two pronunciations of 'flattering' described above ('Formal Aspects': 'Pronunciation')—*flattering* in Song 12 and *flattring* elsewhere—but in general he makes no attempt in his spellings to distinguish variant pronunciations or to establish exact syllabic values. Thus *hower* (= hour), *sower* (= sour), *shower, flower*, and *euen* are usually or invariably so spelt, while 'fair' is variously rendered *fayre, faier,* and *fayer*, though every one of the words here enumerated is always counted as a monosyllable in the metrical scheme. The failure of the spelling consistently to indicate elisions is conveniently illustrated in the second stanza of Pastoral 7, where in line 2 we find *flowry*

that thowght a flowry feeld

though we find *liuery* in the corresponding position in line 5

in Aprils liuery fayre.

The poet's own spelling is not even a reliable guide to the pronunciation of words ending in *ed*: sometimes the *e* is omitted where it is not syllabic, e.g.

Loue not whoe haue not lou'd (Song 3: refrain)

Now turnd to raine and winde (Song 3: 47)

But scornd, repulst, hartbroken I remoue (Sonnet 7: 12)

Sommond by so greate truth, I must confes (Sonnet 8: 9);

sometimes non-syllabic *e* is included in the spelling, e.g.

vnto yowr loue ordained, a free bownd slaue (Sonnet 12: 6)

woords not beleeued, were better lett alone (Pastoral 8: 14)

Shee whome I loued, and loue shall still
(Translated out of Spanish: 1)

when shee had borrowed Charys light (Song 21: 6).

At Song 22: 38 and 40, and at Song 23: 14 and 16, the rhyme words are respectively spelt *beleeued/greeued* and *restored/stored* which might mislead the unwary into reading them as feminine rhymes though the stanzaic patterns in both poems require masculine rhyme in these places and prove that the final *ed* is not syllabic.

Robert relies on the strict syllabic structure of his verse to tell the reader in each case how words of variable phonetic value are to be sounded, and no reader who pays due attention to that structure need be misled on the matter. In refraining from any systematic attempt to incorporate guides to the metre in his spelling Robert implicitly recognizes that the actual pronunciations of such 'hypermonosyllables' as *power, heaven, fair, prayer*—or the sounds 'heard' internally by the silent reader—never exactly conform to the theoretical pronunciations required by the metre. The responsibility for hearing the verse in the right way is left to the individual reader, as in the end it always must be.

The modernized text distinguishes words ending in *ed* whose forms might otherwise mislead by accenting the termination where it is syllabic (e.g. *conceivèd*, Song 10: 20). I have also supplied apostrophes of elision between unstressed open vowels in two lines, namely:

> I wait to'adore, in rays as sweet as bright (Sonnet 22: 7)
>
> The sun shines when he'is like her eyes (Song 21: 11).

The omission of the elision marks in these two places was presumably inadvertence on Robert's part since he has supplied them in two analogous cases elsewhere, in 'I would be blind': 8, and Song 19: 12 (in the latter case Robert's spelling omits the elided vowel itself). Ben Jonson defines this use of the apostrophe in *The Second Book of English Grammar*: '*Apostrophus* is the rejecting of a vowel from the beginning or end of a word. The note whereof, though it many times through the negligence of writers and printers is quite omitted, yet by right . . . hath his mark, which is such a semicircle (') placed in the top.'

Apart from the cases just mentioned I have not attempted in the modernized text to supply guidance which Robert himself, whether deliberately or through negligence, omitted to provide. The editing would otherwise have become, in my judgement, unduly officious. If (for example) the two pronunciations contained in the line which Robert set down

> All power is vnder heauyer power sett
> (Translated out of Seneca: 6)

were editorially distinguished in the modernized text by printing

> All pow'r is under heavier power set

consistency would require that the line which Robert set down

> powers of first blowing, ripening powers (Song 22: 12)

should be rendered

> Pow'rs of first blowing, rip'ning pow'rs

and I can only hope the reader will agree that such a procedure would finally have proved more fussy than helpful.

Two irregularities in Robert's headings are silently normalized in the modernized text—first, the numbering of two consecutive sonnets as 32 (and the consequential numbering of Sonnets 34 and 35 as 33 and 34) and second, the failure to supply a heading to Song 24. As regards the first, the apparent slip contains a clue to Robert's design when constructing the sequence (see 'Robert's Use of the Sequence as a Form' and head-notes in the Commentary to Sonnet 33 and Song 21): the two sonnets involved might best be thought of as Sonnet 32A and Sonnet 32B respectively.

Every poem in the numbered sequence begins on a new page in the notebook except (1) the Sonnets which compose the unfinished Crown, and (2) Song 17, the shortest poem in the sequence, which directly follows the last of the unnumbered poems. This edition reproduces the text of the notebook page for page and uses *fleurons* to represent the freely drawn terminal flourishes which Robert normally made below each completed poem. Robert omitted the terminal flourish below Song 5—an inadvertent omission, it seems clear, and probably attributable to the fact that Song 5 fills the one page which it occupies in the notebook: in the modernized text given here the standard *fleuron* has been supplied below Song 5.

The order of the poems should remind us of the provisional status of the only text we possess, since it can hardly represent the poet's final intention that the seven unnumbered poems—four of them following Sonnet 35 and three of them following Elegy 16—should thus intrude into the numbered sequence.

Robert's notebook shows that he had constructed a different arrangement of poems selected from the main sequence—at a comparatively early stage, it would seem, of that sequence's development—as an alternative way of presenting the lover's experience (cf. 'Robert's Use of the Sequence as a Form'). Robert indicated the rearranged selection by means of numbers added in the upper margins of the pages containing the poems concerned, except for the first item in the selection (Sonnet 4 of the main sequence) where—conscious perhaps that the figure 1 might be mistaken for an accidental pen stroke—he has spelt out *This showld bee first*. This alternative numbering is not represented in the body of this edition, but the items composing the alternative sequence itself are listed on page 124 below.

Robert's irregular numbering of the notebook's leaves[2] would be unintelligible if transferred to another setting and is accordingly not represented in this edition, which also ignores the ticks in the upper margins that Robert presumably made when checking the poems either against his own rough drafts or against a fair copy intended for presentation (see p. 4).

[2] Robert's numbering begins as a pagination though rectos only are actually numbered, i.e. fos. 2–26 are numbered on their rectos from 1 to 49. The numbering changes without warning to a foliation on the next seven leaves, i.e. fos. 27–33 are numbered on their rectos from 50 to 56. Robert discontinues his numbering after this but his foliation has been continued in nineteenth-century pencil (i.e. fos. 34–46 are numbered on their rectos from 57 to 69).

THE ALTERNATIVE SEQUENCE

The design of the alternative sequence is discussed above (pp. 112–13) where will be found an explanation of the differences between the system used in numbering the alternative sequence and the system used in numbering the main sequence. The items in the alternative sequence are listed below in order: after each item is an indication of its heading in the main sequence (e.g. Sonnet 4) followed by an indication of its overall position within that sequence (e.g. item 5).

1. These purest flames, kindled by beauties rare [Sonnet 4: item 5]
2. Oft had I passed the joys and griefs in love [Sonnet 9: item 12]
3. Beauties born of the heavens, my soul's delight [Sonnet 3: item 4]
4. You purest stars, whose never-dying fires [Sonnet 1: item 1]
5. My soul in purest fire [Song 4: item 13]
6. She whom I serve to write did not despise [Sonnet 10: item 14]
7. *A Crown of sonnets, but unfinished.* [Sonnets 11–14: item 15]
8. When rest locks up the treasures of delight [Sonnet 6: item 9]
9. The pains which I uncessantly sustain [Sonnet 2: item 3]
10. Shepherd, i'faith, now say how well [Pastoral 2: item 6]
11. O eyes, O lights divine [Song 1: item 2]
12. Love not who have not loved [Song 3: item 7]
13. Of travails past oft when I thinking am [Sonnet 5: item 8]

THE POEMS

For the Countess of
Pembroke.

[Song *altered to*] Sonnet 1.

Yow purest stars, whose neuer dijng fyres
deck heauenly spheres, and rule the world belowe
grudg not if I in yowr cleer beauties know
[a *altered to*] the faier maides eies, the stars of my desires

harts
To earthly [minds] yowr light wch not expires
makes known the matchless place wherin yow goe
and they the mind, wch throw thē shines doe show
whose cleerest beames, my sowle as heauen admires

Yow shine stil one, and alter not yowr race
at sute of those, wch most yowr lights adore
for wel yow know yow shine for heauens grace

And they in whome all eyes on earthe are blest
thogh then the heauēly lights I loue thē more
shine to the worlde, and mee but wth the rest

Sonnet 1

You purest stars, whose never-dying fires
Deck heavenly spheres, and rule the world below,
Grudge not if I in your clear beauties know
The fair maid's eyes, the stars of my desires.

To earthly hearts your light which not expires
Makes known the matchless place wherein you go;
And they the mind which through them shines do show,
Whose clearest beams my soul as heaven admires.

You shine still one, and alter not your race
At suit of those which most your lights adore,
For well you know you shine for heaven's grace:

And they, in whom all eyes on earth are blest,
Though than the heavenly lights I love them more,
Shine to the world, and me but with the rest.

Songe. .1.

O eyes, o lights deuine
wch in vnmatched face
like twoe fayre suns, in cleerest heauē do shine
and from so glorious place
voutsafe yowr beames to moue
on humble mee to raise my thowghts to loue

2

Yow are my dearest lights
my Suns, my cleerest day
the sfeares wch moue my ioies, and liues delights:
O bee content to stay
yowr heauenly beames on mee
and see and know the greefes, wch in mee bee

3

It is no heauy loss
of frende wch I doe rue
or care to see how some my fortunes cross
It is and must bee yow
from whome I now must part
Alas I liue to say I doe depart.

4

To all delights quite dead
I liue to woe and care
an Anchorite, to liuing burial lead

But yet

Song 1

O eyes, O lights divine,
Which in unmatchèd face
Like two fair suns in clearest heaven do shine,
And from so glorious place
Vouchsafe your beams to move
On humble me to raise my thoughts to love:

2

You are my dearest lights,
My suns, my clearest day,
The spheres which move my joys, and life's delights:
O be content to stay
Your heavenly beams on me,
And see and know the griefs, which in me be.

3

It is no heavy loss
Of friend which I do rue,
Or care to see how some my fortunes cross;
It is and must be you
From whom I now must part,
Alas I live to say 'I do depart.'

4

To all delights quite dead
I live to woe and care,
An anchorite to living burial led:

But yet before yow are
deer eyes eclipst from mee
see this, and let not this forgotten bee

5

See one whoe but by yow
for yow and to yow liues
and loues his lyfe becaus to yow tis true
see one whoe parting giues
to all delights farewel
beare wth him
and leauing yow, doth [thinck, his lyfe] his hel

6

And when that gon I ame
to mine vniust decay
and that yowr beauties other harts inflame
O heauenly eyes then say
Ah smokes of fained fyres
Hee is not heer, that burns in true desires.

But yet before you are,
Dear eyes, eclipsed from me,
See this, and let not this forgotten be.

5

See one who but by you,
For you and to you lives,
And loves his life because to you 'tis true:
See one who parting gives
To all delights farewell,
And leaving you, doth bear with him his hell.

6

And when that gone I am
To mine unjust decay
And that your beauties other hearts inflame,
O heavenly eyes then say
'Ah smokes of feignèd fires,
He is not here, that burns in true desires.'

Sonnet. 2.

The paines wch I vncessantly susteine,
burning in hottest flames, of loue most pure
are ioies, not greefs, since each of them are sure
witnes, that faith not wil, in mee doth raine

vaine may their hopes all proue, their ioies more vain
whome sence of pleasure, doth to loue allure:
Blest in my bands, rather may I endure
for yow, then toild wth ioies, loue elswhere gaine

Heauenly yow$^{r}_{\wedge}$ beauties are, and may there bee,
mutual bands, to ty earthe to the skyes:
showld I
yow I adore, and [I hope to see] hope to see
one fyre embrace, both saint and sacrifise

No no most fayre, for yow I end and cry
Ioyful I liu'd to yow, ioyful I dy.

Sonnet 2

The pains which I uncessantly sustain,
Burning in hottest flames of love most pure,
Are joys, not griefs, since each of them are sure
Witness that faith, not will, in me doth reign.

Vain may their hopes all prove, their joys more vain,
Whom sense of pleasure doth to love allure:
Blest in my bands, rather may I endure
For you, than toiled with joys love elsewhere gain.

Heavenly your beauties are, and may there be
Mutual bands to tie earth to the skies?
You I adore, and should I hope to see
One fire embrace both saint and sacrifice?

No no, most fair, for you I end and cry
'Joyful I lived to you, joyful I die.'

Sonnet. 3.

Beauties born of the heauens, my sowles delight
care
the onely cause, for wch I ioye to see
yow in my hart let no darcke sorrows bee
yow from mine eyes banish, all shew of night

wth purest beames, yow lightē to my sight,
of yowr deuiness in the Maiestee
yow in my hart from shrine of deitee
shine in all glory, by loues fairest light

Blest bee mine eyes, by whome my hart was browght
my
to vowe to yow all [his] deuotions
Blest bee my hart, by whome myne eyes were taught
onely to ioye in yowr perfections

to
O onely fayre [in] yow I liue and moue
yow for yowrself, myself for yow I loue

Sonnet 3

Beauties born of the heavens, my soul's delight,
The only cause for which I care to see,
You in my heart let no dark sorrows be,
You from mine eyes banish all show of night:

With purest beams you lighten to my sight,
Of your divinesse in the majesty;
You in my heart from shrine of deity
Shine in all glory, by love's fairest light.

Blest be mine eyes, by whom my heart was brought
To vow to you all my devotions;
Blest be my heart, by whom mine eyes were taught
Only to joy in your perfections:

O only fair, to you I live and move;
You for yourself, myself for you I love.

Sonnet. 4

These purest flames kindled by beauties rare
strengthned by loue, assured by destiny
in whome I liue, wch in mee kannot dy
wch are what I ame, and I what they are

True vestale like, wch wth most holy care
preserue the sacred fyres, relligiously
I doe mantein, and that no end they try
subiect
of my best parts their [fuel] I prepare

And wth a minde free from all fals desires
vntoucht of other[s] loues, of vowes vntrue
I worship her that shineth in these fyres

Thincking it shame, nay sinne, if that in mee
those fairest beames, of heauē the image true
wth powers of meaner worthe, showld matched bee

Sonnet 4

These purest flames, kindled by beauties rare,
Strengthened by love, assured by destiny,
In whom I live, which in me cannot die,
Which are what I am, and I what they are,

True-vestal-like, which with most holy care
Preserve the sacred fires, religiously
I do maintain, and that no end they try
Of my best parts their subject I prepare:

And with a mind free from all false desires,
Untouched of other loves, of vows untrue,
I worship her that shineth in these fires:

Thinking it shame, nay sin, if that in me
Those fairest beams, of heaven the image true,
With powers of meaner worth should matchèd be.

Pastoral. 2 Shepheard, Nymphe.

N. Shepheard iffaith now say how wel
thow doest loue me
S. Wonder and ioye kan onely tel
how I loue thee
N. Tel mee how much?
S. O neuer such
heauenly fayre mayde owr feelds did bless
nor euer wil,
O to me vnkind Shepherdess
but O deer stil.

2

N. These are but words, I must proue thee
Now doe not mocke
Whether doest thow loue better mee
or thy good flocke
S My sheep alas
my loue once was
Now my best wool growes on thy care
thow art my stocke
thy rosy cheekes, my ritch feelds are
thine eyes, my flocke

Ye retchless

Pastoral 2: Shepherd, Nymph.

Nymph Shepherd, i'faith, now say how well
Thou dost love me.
Shepherd Wonder and joy can only tell
How I love thee.
Nymph Tell me how much!
Shepherd O never such
Heavenly fair maid our fields did bless
Nor ever will:
O to me unkind shepherdess,
But O, dear still.

2

Nymph These are but words, I must prove thee:
Now do not mock—
Whether dost thou love better me
Or thy good flock?
Shepherd My sheep, alas,
My love once was;
Now my best wool grows on thy care,
Thou art my stock:
Thy rosy cheeks my rich fields are,
Thine eyes, my flock.

3

N Ye retchless felloes often doe
their goods despyse
But mee doest thow beare more loue to
or to thine eyes
S. Mine eyes to mee
no pleasure bee
Since that they kannot thee stil see
wealth of my sight
or that they kan, astraide from thee
see other light.

4

N. Thine eyes perhaps thow doest reproue
for their bad choice
but in thy lyfe more or thy loue
doest thow reioice
S. My lyfe is that
I least ioye at
Since all the time I lou'd not thee
as lost I holde
and what remains few howers wil bee
thee to beholde.

What's past

3

Nymph Ye retchless fellows often do
Their goods despise.
But me dost thou bear more love to
Or to thine eyes?
Shepherd Mine eyes to me
No pleasure be
Since that they cannot thee still see,
Wealth of my sight,
Or that they can, astrayed from thee,
See other light.

4

Nymph Thine eyes, perhaps, thou dost reprove
For their bad choice.
But in thy life more or thy love
Dost thou rejoice?
Shepherd My life is that
I least joy at,
Since all the time I loved not thee
As lost I hold,
And what remains few hours will be
Thee to behold.

5

N. What's past thow hast forgot, nor now
Knowst what wil bee
but at this time more louest thow
thyself or me
S. Myself I nere
shall loue I feare
Thy cares are mine, thow art my wil
I loue wth thee
myself I shall not loue vntil
thow louest mee

6

N. Tush these fine words do no whit please
make known thy loue
for if thow car'st for none of these
what kanst thow loue
S. My cares are one
for thee alone
N. Like what then doest thow loue, tel this
thow weariest mee
S Like thyself like nothing els is
my loue to thee

Like mee

5

Nymph What's past thou hast forgot, nor now
Know'st what will be;
But at this time more lovest thou
Thyself or me?
Shepherd Myself I ne'er
Shall love I fear;
Thy cares are mine, thou art my will,
I love with thee:
Myself I shall not love until
Thou lovest me.

6

Nymph Tush, these fine words do no whit please,
Make known thy love,
For if thou car'st for none of these
What canst thou love?
Shepherd My cares are one—
For thee alone.
Nymph Like what then dost thou love? Tell this,
Thou weariest me.
Shepherd Like thyself, like nothing else, is
My love to thee.

7

N. Like me how's that. Sh: fayre as Sunbeames
louely as day
sweet as fresh flowers, fine as cleer streames
ioyful as May.
lips of cherries
hands of lillies
Eyes stars of fyre, brest fram'd in snow
hart (ah) heauen hy
Blessed Nymphe shepheards thus thee know
and thus loue I.

7

Nymph Like me, how's that? (*Shepherd*) Fair as
Lovely as day, [sunbeams,
Sweet as fresh flowers, fine as clear streams,
Joyful as May.
Lips of cherries,
Hands of lilies,
Eyes stars of fire, breast framed in snow,
Heart (ah) heaven-high:
Blessèd Nymph, shepherds thus thee know,
And thus love I.

Songe. 3.

Loue not whoe haue not lou'd
and whoe doe loue, loue no more

1.

Winter is kome at last
cold winter, darck and sad
and on the world, hath cast
his mantle fowle and bad.
Delights departed are
labours doe onely tary
Diuorst from pleasures mary
hencefourth wee doe wth care
Loue not whoe haue not lou'd
and whoe doe loue, loue no more.

2

Nothing is as it was
what hath had birth doth change
This day acquainted has
what yesterday held strange
Thus whyle wee doe secure,
owr smiling seasons cherish,
before owr eyes they perish
when most wee thinck them sure
Loue not whoe haue not lou'd
and whoe doe loue, loue no more

The springe

Song 3

Love not who have not loved,
And who do love, love no more.

1

Winter is come at last,
Cold winter, dark and sad,
And on the world hath cast
His mantle foul and bad.
Delights departed are,
Labours do only tarry:
Divorced from pleasures, marry
Henceforth we do with care.
Love not who have not loved,
And who do love, love no more.

2

Nothing is as it was,
What hath had birth doth change,
This day acquainted has
What yesterday held strange.
Thus while we do, secure,
Our smiling seasons cherish,
Before our eyes they perish
When most we think them sure.
Love not who have not loved,
And who do love, love no more.

3

The spring that promist, his
delights showld euer last
Shews in how few howers is
owr [euer *altered to*] Euer kome and past
Where now of leaues thy store
where is of flowers thy glory
Ah thow art now a story
of that w[ch] is no more.
Loue not whoe haue
and whoe doe etc

4

The Sun whoe ful of ioye
did loue and was belou'd
in whome wee did inioye
the light owr sowles best lou'd
Now turneth from vs, as
if hee no more did know vs
and giues light but to show vs
what wee are, what hee was.
Loue not whoe
and whoe doe

The ayre

3

The spring, that promised his
Delights should ever last,
Shows in how few hours is
Our 'ever' come and past.
Where now of leaves thy store?
Where is of flowers thy glory?
Ah, thou art now a story
Of that which is no more.
Love not who have not loved,
And who do love, love no more.

4

The sun, who full of joy
Did love and was beloved,
In whom we did enjoy
The light our souls best loved,
Now turneth from us, as
If he no more did know us,
And gives light but to show us
What we are, what he was.
Love not who have not loved,
And who do love, love no more.

5.

The ayre whose body sweet
on rosy wings did moue
and kissing where it hit
inspired lyfe and loue
Now turnd to raine and winde
vs wth his blowes hath beaten,
wch most sharpe, yet doe threaten
there are more harms behinde.
Loue not whoe
and whoe doe etc

6.

Meddows feelds, forrests, hils,
wth face defaced strange
proue nothing so soon kils
the lyfe as vnkind change
I now poor, sad, alone
did once possess a treasure
but loose did wealth and pleasure
by vniust change of one
Loue not whoe
and whoe doe etc

Thus sayd

5

The air, whose body sweet
On rosy wings did move
And kissing where it hit
Inspirèd life and love,
Now turned to rain and wind
Us with his blows hath beaten,
Which most sharp, yet do threaten
There are more harms behind.
Love not who have not loved,
And who do love, love no more.

6

Meadows, fields, forests, hills,
With face defacèd strange,
Prove nothing so soon kills
The life as unkind change.
I now poor, sad, alone,
Did once possess a treasure,
But lose did wealth and pleasure
By unjust change of one.
Love not who have not loved,
And who do love, love no more.

7

Thus sayd a shepheard, once
wth weights of change opprest
For hee had lost atonce
what euer hee lou'd best
And saw whyle hee did mourn
[But seeing left to mourn]
the worlds fayre lookes renewed
whyle hee a state past rewed
wch neuer would retourn.
Loue not whoe haue not lou'd
and whoe doe loue, loue no more.

7

Thus said a shepherd, once
With weights of change oppressed,
For he had lost at once
What ever he loved best;
And saw, while he did mourn,
The world's fair looks renewèd
While he a state past ruèd
Which never would return.
Love not who have not loved,
And who do love, love no more.

Sonnet. 5.

Of trauailes past oft when I thincking ame
of daies in sorrowes spent, of easles nights
as they wch shew deepe scars of bluddy fights
glory to me of my loues wounds I frame

Thus on my ruins doe I builde my fame
thus doe my miseries appeer delights
hurts
Til some new [blowes] make my benommed sprites
feele that loues blowes, [is *altered to*] are no so pleasant
[game

Then ful of paine my to fond wil I curse
and cry at her, as then a tigre wurse.
and doe forsweare all bondage more to loue

Heauy wth greef til I mine eyes do heaue
vnto her face, whence all ioies I receaue
and thinck all nothing, that for her I proue

Sonnet 5

Of travails past oft when I thinking am,
Of days in sorrows spent, of easeless nights,
As they which show deep scars of bloody fights
Glory to me of my love's wounds I frame.

Thus on my ruins do I build my fame,
Thus do my miseries appear delights,
Till some new hurts make my benumbèd sprites
Feel that love's blows are no so pleasant game.

Then full of pain, my too fond will I curse,
And cry at her as than a tiger worse,
And do forswear all bondage more to love;

Heavy with grief, till I mine eyes do heave
Unto her face, whence all joys I receive,
And think all nothing that for her I prove.

Sonnet. 6.

When rest locks vp the treasures of delight
that face, those eyes, that voice, those hands, that brest
not in them nor the Sun, sad earth now blest
comfort
and no power left, that [conquer] may the night.

Cares wch in darcknes shine, finding her sight
eclipst, wch from them is, my safegarde best
reuiue my secret flames, and wthout rest
shew me vnto myself, in a trew light.

They are not flames of loue, but fyres of paine
that burn so fayre; loue far from me is fled
whoe all loue giue and no loue haue againe.
[Refusals *altered to*] Repulses and the thowsand formed head
of scorn I see, while vniust night from me
her beauty hides, and shews her crueltee.

Sonnet 6

When rest locks up the treasures of delight—
That face, those eyes, that voice, those hands, that breast—
Not in them nor the sun sad earth now blest,
And no power left, that comfort may the night;

Cares which in darkness shine, finding her sight
Eclipsed which from them is my safeguard best,
Revive my secret flames, and without rest
Show me unto myself in a true light.

They are not flames of love but fires of pain
That burn so fair; love far from me is fled,
Who all love give and no love have again.
Repulses and the thousand-formèd head
Of scorn I see, while unjust night from me
Her beauty hides, and shows her cruelty.

Sonnet. 7.

The hardy Captein vnusde to retyre
turns and returns to the to wel kept place
where wound to wound disgrace vpon disgrace
hee takes, while wil and power gainst him conspire

Scorn of repuls, of loss the stinging fyre
his hart wth greefe doth fill, wth shame his face
But no force finding way, wth heauy pace
forsake hee doth, his il blest fayre desyre

W^th^ equal care, but wth an ende more hy
I sowght to win the kingdome seate of loue,
Beauties best treasure, praise of victory
But scornd, repulst, hartbroken I remoue
reaping loss for desert, for loue contempt
and greef and shame, for so deer foild attempt.

Sonnet 7

The hardy captain, unused to retire,
Turns and returns to the too-well-kept place
Where wound to wound, disgrace upon disgrace
He takes, while will and power 'gainst him conspire:

Scorn of repulse, of loss the stinging fire,
His heart with grief doth fill, with shame his face;
But no force finding way, with heavy pace
Forsake he doth his ill-blest fair desire.

With equal care, but with an end more high,
I sought to win the kingdom seat of love,
Beauty's best treasure, praise of victory:
But scorned, repulsed, heartbroken I remove,
Reaping loss for desert, for love contempt,
And grief and shame for so dear foiled attempt.

Sonnet. 8

If that her worth I kowld as wel forget
as of my loue the haples lott I know
then to my wounded sowl, a meane might grow
wch if not health, yet some ease would beget

But when I thinck I haue my quiet met
and that loue foild yealds to his ouerthrow
the Idol of her beauties prowd doth show
in
vnto my thowghts, [w^{th}] beames wch neuer set

Sommond by so greate truth, I must confes
that all what fayr, what good, what parfet is
all is in her, nothing in her doth miss.

And now greef takes the place, loue did possess
hopes
and all [loue] dead, I liue, to feel this sore
More that shee worthy is, my loss the more.

Sonnet 8

If that her worth I could as well forget
As of my love the hapless lot I know,
Then to my wounded soul a mean might grow
Which if not health, yet some ease would beget.

But when I think I have my quiet met
And that love foiled yields to his overthrow,
The idol of her beauties proud doth show
Unto my thoughts, in beams which never set.

Summoned by so great truth, I must confess
That all what fair, what good, what perfect is,
All is in her, nothing in her doth miss:

And now grief takes the place love did possess
And all hopes dead, I live to feel this sore—
More that she worthy is, my loss the more.

Sonnet 9.

Oft had I past the ioies and greefes in loue
and weary of them both was layde to rest
and now desyre as an vnworthy ghest
wch doth oppress his frend, I did remoue

Noe womans force, I thowght showld euer moue
my sowle kome home againe to new vnrest
or
when yow [and] in yowr shape an Angel drest
caled out my quiet thowghts once more to loue

Streight my prowd wil did vnto praiers tur̄e
for whoe in yow, not cause of loue doth finde
or blinde hee is of eyes, or blinde of minde

I yealde, I loue, to yow, thē erst, I burn
more hott, more pure, like wood oft warme before
But to yow burnt to dust, kan burn no more.

Sonnet 9

Oft had I passed the joys and griefs in love
And weary of them both was laid to rest,
And now desire, as an unworthy guest
Which doth oppress his friend, I did remove:

No woman's force, I thought, should ever move
My soul come home again to new unrest,
When you, or in your shape an Angel dressed,
Called out my quiet thoughts once more to love:

Straight my proud will did unto prayers turn,
For who in you, not cause of love doth find
Or blind he is of eyes, or blind of mind.

I yield, I love: to you, than erst, I burn
More hot, more pure; like wood oft warm before,
But to you burnt to dust, can burn no more.

Songe. 4.

My sowle in purest fyre
doth not aspyre
to rewarde of my paine
True pleasure is in loue
onely to loue
and not seeke to obtaine.

2

Common loue euer bends
to his own ends
to preuaile to inioye
my loues end is to serue
not to deserue
More I loue, more I ioie.

3

Cast by loue yet I see
an ende of mee
grace
if of [loue] I doe miss
But for yow if I ende
I haue mine ende
are
And mans ends [is] his bliss

4

Yet this grace yowr fayre eies
doe not despyse
sweetest beames to imparte

O fayre

Song 4

My soul in purest fire
Doth not aspire
To reward of my pain:
True pleasure is in love
Only to love
And not seek to obtain.

2

Common love ever bends
To his own ends,
To prevail, to enjoy:
My love's end is to serve
Not to deserve,
More I love, more I joy.

3

Cast by love, yet I see
An end of me
If of grace I do miss;
But for you if I end
I have mine end
And man's ends are his bliss.

4

Yet this grace your fair eyes
Do not despise—
Sweetest beams to impart:

O fayre lights, in yow lies
the lyfe of eyes
but the deathe of the harte

5

whoe kan see, and not see
yowr face to bee
beauties sphere, throne of loue
O face a paradise
yow seeme of eies
but the sowles hel doe proue

6

Must my harms then in mee,
stil nourisht bee?
and I liue by my harms?
Harms wch nor phisicks skil
nor time helpe wil
nor praiers, nor gifts, nor charms?

7

Dearest wounds, sweetest bands
in whose truth stands
perfet proof of my loue
They
[yow] I know from my harte
wil not departe
nor from them I remoue

But in

O fair lights, in you lies
The life of eyes
But the death of the heart.

5

Who can see, and not see
Your face to be
Beauty's sphere, throne of love:
O face, a paradise
You seem of eyes
But the soul's hell do prove.

6

Must my harms then in me
Still nourished be?
And I live by my harms?
Harms which nor physic's skill
Nor time help will,
Nor prayers, nor gifts, nor charms?

7

Dearest wounds, sweetest bands,
In whose truth stands
Perfect proof of my love;
They, I know, from my heart
Will not depart,
Nor from them I remove.

8

But in them and my fyres
my sowle aspires
to the Suns of yowr eyes
ful of ioye ful of pryde
by noe lawe tyde
myself to sacryfyse.

9

O fayre eies, O deer lights
O my delights
hart and eies I doe turne
and in yow and my fyres
wth pure desyres
phenixlike ioye and burne.

~

8

But in them and my fires
My soul aspires
To the suns of your eyes,
Full of joy, full of pride,
By no law tied,
Myself to sacrifice.

9

O fair eyes, O dear lights,
O my delights,
Heart and eyes I do turn
And in you and my fires
With pure desires
Phoenixlike joy and burn.

Sonnet 10

Shee whōe I serue to wryte did not despyse
few words but wch wth wonder filde my spryte
how from darck incke as from springs of delight
beawtie, sweetnes, grace, ioye and loue showld ryse

Til I remembred, that those fairest eyes
whose beames are ioies and loue did lend their light
that happy hand, those blessed words did wryte
wch where it towcheth, marcks of beawtie ties

Those ruby lips ful of Nectar diuine
a rosy breath did on the words bestowe
that heauenly face did on the paper shine
from whose least motion thowsand graces flowe

And that faier minde the subiect did approue
wch is it self, all other prais aboue

Sonnet 10

She whom I serve to write did not despise—
Few words, but which with wonder filled my sprite
How from dark ink, as from springs of delight,
Beauty, sweetness, grace, joy and love should rise;

Till I remembered, that those fairest eyes
Whose beams are joys and love did lend their light,
That happy hand, those blessèd words did write
Which where it toucheth, marks of beauty ties;

Those ruby lips, full of nectar divine,
A rosy breath did on the words bestow,
That heavenly face did on the paper shine
From whose least motion thousand graces flow,

And that fair mind the subject did approve,
Which is itself, all other praise above.

A Crown of sonnets, but vnfinished.

11.

Thogh the most parfet stile kannot attaine
the praise, to praise enowgh the meanest parte
of yow, the ornament of natures arte
worth of this worlde, of all ioies the Souueraine

And thogh I know, I labour shall in vaine
to painte in words, the deadly wounds, the darte
of yowr faier eyes doth giue, since mine own hart
knowes not the measure, of my loue and paine

yet since yowr wil the charge on mee doth lay
yowr wil the law I onely reuerence
Skilles, and praisles I doe yow obey

Nor merit seekc, but pitty if thus I
doe folly shew, to proue obedience
who giues himself, may il his words deny

2 Sonnet. 12

Whoe giues himself may il his words deny
my words gaue mee to yow, my worde I gaue
stil to bee yowrs, yow speech and speaker haue
mee to my worde, my worde to yow I ty

Long ere

A crown of sonnets, but unfinished.

11

Though the most perfect style cannot attain
The praise to praise enough the meanest part
Of you, the ornament of Nature's art,
Worth of this world, of all joys the sovereign;

And though I know I labour shall in vain
To paint in words the deadly wounds the dart
Of your fair eyes doth give, since mine own heart
Knows not the measure of my love and pain:

Yet since your will the charge on me doth lay,
Your will, the law I only reverence,
Skill-less and praise-less I do you obey;

Nor merit seek, but pity, if thus I
Do folly show to prove obedience;
Who gives himself, may ill his words deny.

12

Who gives himself, may ill his words deny;
My words gave me to you, my word I gave
Still to be yours, you speech and speaker have:
Me to my word, my word to you I tie.

Long ere I was, I was by destiny
vnto yowr loue ordained, a free bownd slaue
chois
Destiny wch mee to mine own [liking] draue
and to my ends, made mee my wil apply

For ere on earthe in yow trew beauty kame
my first breath I had drawn, vpon the day
Sacred to yow, blessed in yowr faire name

And all the daies and howers I since do spend
time
are but the fatall, wished [hower] to slay
to seale the bands of seruice wthout end.

3 Sonnet 13

To seale the bands of seruice wthout ende
in wch myself I from myself doe giue
no force but yowrs, my thowghts kould euer driue
for in my chois, loue did yowr right defend

I know there are wch title doe pretend
as in their seruice hauing vowed to liue
But reason fatall faults, wils to forgiue
Loue gaue mee not to thē hee did but lend

Not but

Long ere I was, I was by Destiny
Unto your love ordained, a free-bound slave;
Destiny, which me to mine own choice drave
And to my ends made me my will apply:

For ere on earth in you true beauty came,
My first breath I had drawn upon the day
Sacred to you, blessèd in your fair name;

And all the days and hours I since do spend
Are but the fatal, wishèd time to slay,
To seal the bands of service without end.

13

To seal the bands of service without end,
In which myself I from myself do give,
No force but yours my thoughts could ever drive,
For in my choice, love did your right defend.

I know there are which title do pretend,
As in their service having vowed to live;
But reason fatal faults wills to forgive—
Love gave me not to them, he did but lend.

of power
Not but their beawties, were [enowgh] to moue
the prowdest hart, to fall down at their feet
or that I was so ennimy to loue

But those faier lights, wch doe all for the best
and rule owr worcks below, thowght it most meet
that so greate loue to yow showld bee adrest.

4 Son: 14

That so greate loue to yow showld bee adrest
then wch the Sun nothing doth see more pure
yowr matchles worth, yowr iudgmēt may assure
since rarest beauties, like faith haue possest

yet would on mee, no note of chang did rest
wch in yowr sight, my truths light may obscure
Ah let not mee, for changing blamc indure
whoe onely changd, by chang to finde the best

For now in yow I rest, in yow I finde
iustice
Destinies foresight, loues [strength, my], [wils *altered to*] Wils end,
trew
Beauties [great] wonders, ioy and rest of mind

Let mee

Not but their beauties were of power to move
The proudest heart to fall down at their feet,
Or that I was so enemy to love;

But those fair lights, which do all for the best
And rule our works below, thought it most meet
That so great love to you should be addressed.

14

That so great love to you should be addressed—
Than which the sun nothing doth see more pure—
Your matchless worth your judgement may assure,
Since rarest beauties, like faith have possessed:

Yet would on me no note of change did rest
Which in your sight my truth's light may obscure;
Ah let not me for changing blame endure,
Who only changed, by change to find the best:

For now in you I rest, in you I find
Destiny's foresight, Love's justice, Will's end,
Beauty's true wonders, joy and rest of mind.

Let mee bee then to yow accounted true
Defend yow them, whoe for yow doe offend
whoe for yow is vniust is iust to yow.

5 Son:

Whoe for yow is vniust, is iust to yow
O yow the fayre excuse of faults in loue
ers
who for yow [errs], his errors praises proue
O yow to mee honor, wisdome, vertue.

The rest of the 13 sonnets
doth want.

Let me be then to you accounted true,
Defend you them who for you do offend;
Who for you is unjust, is just to you.

5

Who for you is unjust, is just to you.
O you, the fair excuse of faults in love,
Who for you errs, his errors praises prove;
O you to me honour, wisdom, virtue.

The rest of the 13 sonnets
doth want.

Songe. 5.

1 If those deuotions now noe more
(Most fayre) appeer, late shewd so prowd
whyle eyes admire, hands did adore
lips sang yowr praise, knees to yow bowde
know persecutions rage doth drive
faith thogh vnchangd, vnknow̄ to liue

2 And know yowr wil makes loue not dare
to doe the rytes of zeale stil borne
and yow yowrself the Tirant are
that martires loue in fyre of scorne
yet truth in mee stil feruent knows
my wonted vowes, thogh now new shows.

3 Nor could yowr torments make mee swerue
from yow whoe truth of beauty bee
Nor I the pleasurc leaue to serue
wrongs
for [paines] in yow, or paines in mee
But I whoe haue but yow noe end
Since please can not, wil not offend

4 And now yowr cruel wil I know
I silent doe darcke offrings giue
And doe shut vp, but not orethrow
the temple where yowr fyres doe liue
and til the truth yowr hart doe moue
vnharde, vnseen, wil pray and loue

Song 5

1 If those devotions now no more
(Most fair) appear, late showed so proud,
While eyes admire, hands did adore,
Lips sang your praise, knees to you bowed,
Know, persecution's rage doth drive
Faith, though unchanged, unknown to live:

2 And know, your will makes love not dare
To do the rites of zeal still-born,
And you yourself the tyrant are
That martyrs love in fire of scorn,
Yet truth in me still fervent knows
My wonted vows, though now new shows.

3 Nor could your torments make me swerve
From you, who truth of beauty be,
Nor I the pleasure leave to serve
For wrongs in you, or pains in me,
But I, who have but you no end,
Since please can not, will not offend.

4 And now your cruel will I know
I silent do dark offerings give,
And do shut up, but not o'erthrow,
The temple where your fires do live,
And till the truth your heart do move
Unheard, unseen, will pray and love.

Song. 6.

Lady. Pilgrim.

L. Yonder comes a sad pilgrim
from the East hee returns
I wil aske if hee saw him
whoe for mee absent mourns.
Aged father so to thee
thy trauuail worcke thy rest
Say if thy happ were to see
the knight that loues mee best.
P: Many one see wee lady
as wee come as wee goe
by what tokens how showld I
yowr
this knight from others know.
L. Pilgrim hee is wel to know
these marcks hee euer beares
Clad in russet hee doth goe
his face greefs liuerie weares
To the west hee turns his eyes
where loue fast holds his hart
Duty there the body ties
his sowl hence cannot part.
P. Such a one I saw lady
I once saw such a one
But him no more see shall I
Hee is now dead and gon. Onely

Song 6

Lady. Pilgrim.

Lady Yonder comes a sad pilgrim,
From the East he returns,
I will ask if he saw him
Who for me absent mourns.
Agèd father, so to thee
Thy travail work thy rest,
Say if thy hap were to see
The knight that loves me best.
Pilgrim Many one see we lady,
As we come, as we go:
By what tokens, how should I
Your knight from others know?
Lady Pilgrim, he is well to know,
These marks he ever bears:
Clad in russet he doth go,
His face grief's livery wears.
To the West he turns his eyes
Where love fast holds his heart;
Duty there the body ties,
His soul hence cannot part.
Pilgrim Such a one I saw lady,
I once saw such a one,
But him no more see shall I,
He is now dead and gone.

Onely loue to him gaue breath
   loue gaue him sence to moue
Absence draue him to his death
   that helde him from his loue.
L. O thow cruel, lijng Spryte
   to tempt mee come from hel
many harms may on thee light
   for the tale thow doest tel.
For to him since I lyfe giue
   and in him liue doe I
how can hee dy and I liue
   or I liue and hee dy.
P. Lady know truth, truth to bee
   and leaue fond flattring toies
loue no perpetuitee
   graunts of daies or of ioies
What the morning sweet appeers
   loue turns ere night to sower:
what is winning many yeares
   loue looseth in an hower
Spirits in him all spent bee
   All ioies in him end haue
heauen no more behold doth hee
   hee lies deep in darcke graue.

Farewel

Only love to him gave breath
  Love gave him sense to move,
Absence drave him to his death
  That held him from his love.

Lady O thou cruel, lying sprite
  To tempt me come from hell,
Many harms may on thee light
  For the tale thou dost tell.
For to him since I life give
  And in him live do I,
How can he die and I live
  Or I live and he die?

Pilgrim Lady know truth, truth to be,
  And leave fond flatt'ring toys:
Love no perpetuity
  Grants of days or of joys.
What the morning sweet appears
  Love turns ere night to sour:
What is winning many years
  Love loseth in an hour.
Spirits in him all spent be,
  All joys in him end have,
Heaven no more behold doth he,
  He lies deep in dark grave.

was

L. Farewel then whatere [what] true:
Gon is ioy and pleasure:
parfet loue, and care adieu:
[gon] Farewel my lifes treasure
of his death then let mee heare
Death now fayr name doth proue
lyfe for mee I held not deer
I lovd lyfe for my loue.
of my lyfe the limmits weare
the ioies his loue did lend
wil not forbeare
wch since death [from mee doth teare]
desyre of lyfe doth end.
Faithles lyfe true death, by thee
owr vowes in one shall liue
lyfe him could not keep wth mee
death mee to him shall giue.

P. Neer vnto the sea this knight
was browght to his last wil
present cares were his delight
absent ioies did him kil.
On a sand hil as hee lay
pilgrim sayd hee to mee
of good pity I thee pray
doe this last deed for mee

Tel the

Lady Farewell then whate'er was true:
Gone is joy and pleasure:
Perfect love and care adieu:
Farewell my life's treasure.
Of his death then let me hear—
Death now fair name doth prove:
Life for me I held not dear,
I loved life for my love.
Of my life the limits were
The joys his love did lend,
Which since death will not forbear
Desire of life doth end.
Faithless life, true death! by thee
Our vows in one shall live:
Life him could not keep with me,
Death me to him shall give.

Pilgrim Near unto the sea this knight
Was brought to his last will;
Present cares were his delight,
Absent joys did him kill.
On a sandhill as he lay
'Pilgrim,' said he to me,
'Of good pity I thee pray
Do this last deed for me:

Tel the lady that doth rest
        Medwayes
  neer [ritch Tons] sandy bed
Hee that in her sight livd blest
  Absent accurst is dead.
        wil bee small paine
To finde her [bee not afrayd]
                err
  See, and thow canst not [miss]
            men faine
What worth of all els [is sayd]
    is all provd   in
  [All is sayd] true [of] her.
What is good from her mind growes
  what rare is, is her grace
Nothing fayr is that not flowes
  in her heauen opning face
In her fayr gray eyes, loue showes
  Sweetnes wth Maiestee
        marck well
Ah poor man [beware] theyr blowes
  ioies or wownds theyr beames bee.
Her breath my lyfe nursing ayre
  on her deer words I fed:
wth the want of food so fayre
            are
  famisht my powers [ly] dead.
No sun knew I but her eyes
  by theyr warmth I did liue
Dead and colde what I ame [is *altered to*] lies
  now theyr flames no heate giue
Buried deep in ioyles graue
  this carcas is of mine

For the

Tell the lady that doth rest
   Near Medway's sandy bed
He that in her sight lived blest
   Absent, accursed is dead.
To find her will be small pain—
   See, and thou canst not err:
What worth of all else men feign
   Is all proved true in her.
What is good from her mind grows,
   What rare is, is her grace;
Nothing fair is that not flows
   In her heaven-opening face.
In her fair grey eyes love shows
   Sweetness with majesty:
Ah poor man, mark well their blows,
   Joys or wounds their beams be.
Her breath my life-nursing air,
   On her dear words I fed:
With the want of food so fair
   Famished my powers are dead.
No sun knew I but her eyes,
   By their warmth I did live;
Dead and cold what I am lies
   Now their flames no heat give.
Buried deep in joyless grave
   This carcass is of mine,

For the world is a darck caue
    where her lights doe not shine.
This one gift of her I pray
    my sole and last request
that shee mee herself wil lay
    where neer her I may rest.
L. what hee askes performd shall bee
    to please him dead I craue
hee whoe liuing livd in mee
            there his tombe shall
    dead [shall his burial] haue
They wch once hee loued best
    and were his liues delights
that hee may ly more at rest
    fulfil shall his last rytes.
These arms wch lockt and desplayd
    the glories of his hart
his beer shall bee, til hee layd
    bee, whence hee shall not part.
My heare whose fayre store hee thowght
    Best kings crownes to desgrace
shall him winde, when hee is browght
    to his last resting place
Mine eyes late, his ioyful day
    whyle day came to his eyes
Torches shall bee, him the way
    to shew where his rest lies.

These lips

For the world is a dark cave
   Where her lights do not shine.
This one gift of her I pray,
   My sole and last request,
That she me herself will lay
   Where near her I may rest.'
Lady What he asks performed shall be,
   To please him dead I crave:
He who living lived in me
   Dead there his tomb shall have.
They which once he lovèd best
   And were his life's delights,
That he may lie more at rest
   Fulfil shall his last rites.
These arms, which locked and displayed
   The glories of his heart,
His bier shall be, till he laid
   Be whence he shall not part.
My hair, whose fair store he thought
   Best kings' crowns to disgrace,
Shall him wind, when he is brought
   To his last resting place.
Mine eyes, late his joyful day
   While day came to his eyes,
Torches shall be, him the way
   To show where his rest lies.

These lips but wch none power had
ease
him [rest] of minde to bring
(stung wth doutes wth longings mad)
his Requiem shall sing.
In my brest his tombe shall stand
to him best Marble whyte
where loue wth truthes stedfast hand
this Epitaf shall wryte
The most louing, most belou'd
to death by absence prest
by no time to bee removd
At ful ioies heer doth rest.

These lips, but which none power had
   Him ease of mind to bring
(Stung with doubts, with longings mad)
   His requiem shall sing.
In my breast his tomb shall stand,
   To him best marble white,
Where love with truth's steadfast hand
   This epitaph shall write:
The most loving, most beloved,
   To death by absence pressed,
By no time to be removed
   At full joys here doth rest.

Soñet. 15.

Yow that haue power to kil, haue wil to saue
O yow, fayr leader of the hoast of loue
from [con]yealding hands, desarmed praiers approue
wch ioies nor wealth, but lyfe of Captiue craue.

weake
Noe [small] or foe or force, mee vanquisht gaue
that faint defence showld scorne, not pity moue:
vertue, fortune, skil, to my ayde I proue
All by yow broken, mee forsaken haue.

Yowr face, the feelde where beauties orders shine
yowr
what can resist? [Those] eyes, loues Canons strong,
The braue directions of yowr lips deuine!

wounded I try to scape? In garde along
legions of worthe and graces I descry.
then to wth stand
what meanes [for mee to stryue], what way to fly?

Sonnet 15

You that have power to kill, have will to save:
O you, fair leader of the host of love,
From yielding hands disarmèd prayers approve
Which joys nor wealth, but life of captive crave.

No weak or foe or force me vanquished gave
That faint defence should scorn, not pity move:
Virtue, fortune, skill, to my aid I prove;
All by you broken, me forsaken have.

Your face, the field where beauty's orders shine,
What can resist? Your eyes, love's cannons strong,
The brave directions of your lips divine!

Wounded I try to 'scape: in guard along
Legions of worth and graces I descry.
What means then to withstand, what way to fly?

Pastoral. 7.

sweet
1 Lysa [fayr] Nymph did sit
where an vngentle winde
to her fayr face an open way did finde
As her the ayre did hit
her smiling beames shee threw
as if her eyes would warme the colde that blew.

2 Rosis poor shepheard lad
that thowght a flowry feeld
hee saw to rage of winters blasts to yeald
Or els a garden clad
in Aprils liuery fayre
haue daintiest coulers nipt wth frosty ayre

best
3 Sat where hee thowght hee [might]
might
[best] keepe away the colde
deer
and wth glad arms her body [sweet] did fold
where whyle into his brest
thowsand contentments sancke
and wth broad eyes hee thowsand beauties dranck

Pastoral 7

1 Lysa, sweet nymph, did sit
Where an ungentle wind
To her fair face an open way did find:
As her the air did hit
Her smiling beams she threw
As if her eyes would warm the cold that blew.

2 Rosis, poor shepherd lad,
That thought a flowery field
He saw to rage of winter's blasts to yield,
Or else a garden, clad
In April's livery fair,
Have daintiest colours nipped with frosty air,

3 Sat where he thought he best
Might keep away the cold,
And with glad arms her body dear did fold;
Where, while into his breast
Thousand contentments sank
And with broad eyes he thousand beauties drank,

4 The flames of those fayre eyes
wch no colde ere can slake
in his close brest, a hot fyre soon did make
wch when hee felt to ryse
lookes rage
wth [eys] where [sparcks] did swarme
and wth hot sighs hee sowght the Nymph to warme

5 But shee complaining stil
of colde; the lad gan cry
[Ah *altered to*] Alas why doe [not] the fyres in wch I fry
the cold in her not kil.
or els why quencheth not
the colde in her my fyres wch burn so hott.

4 The flames of those fair eyes—
Which no cold e'er can slake—
In his close breast a hot fire soon did make;
Which when he felt to rise,
With looks where rage did swarm
And with hot sighs, he sought the nymph to warm:

5 But she complaining still
Of cold, the lad gan cry
'Alas, why do the fires in which I fry
The cold in her not kill?
Or else, why quencheth not
The cold in her my fires which burn so hot?'

Sonnet. 16.

Most fayre when first wth pleasd but cursed eyes
ou
I did behold that peece of heauen in y[ow]
O that I had as to deuines due
onely of vowes and praiers don sacrifize

And blessed so, in so contented wyse
from passions free enioied pleasures true
when yow yowrself (I would I sayd vntrue)
kindled the sparckes whence loue and rage did ryse

Yet on those hopes thogh fals would I had stayd
proue
but I in searching owt yowr truth did [finde]
my true mishaps in yowr betraijng loue

Cruel I loue yow stil thogh thus betrayd
on
nor [can *altered to*] dare lay blame [to] yow: but my [fond minde
doe curse, wch made such hast yowr faults to finde.

Sonnet 16

Most fair, when first with pleased but cursèd eyes
I did behold that piece of heaven in you,
O that I had, as to divinesse due,
Only of vows and prayers done sacrifice;

And blessèd so, in so contented wise,
From passions free enjoyèd pleasures true;
When you yourself (I would I said untrue)
Kindled the sparks whence love and rage did rise.

Yet on those hopes though false would I had stayed,
But I in searching out your truth did prove
My true mishaps in your betraying love.

Cruel, I love you still though thus betrayed,
Nor dare lay blame on you: but my fond mind
Do curse, which made such haste your faults to find.

Sonnet. 17.

The endless Alchymist, wth blinded will
that feedes his thowghts wth hopes, his hopes on showes
and more his worck proues vaine more eagre growes
whyle dreames of golde, his head wth shadowes fill

Feeles not more sure the scourg of flattring skill
when in fals trust of wealth true need hee knowes
then I, on whome, a storme of losses blowes
and tydes of errors run̄: yet sail on still

whyle my corrupted sense, doth thinck it sees
the long sowght land of rest: and whyle to bliss
way
I thinck there is a [cours], thogh yet I miss.

shun̄ing
Thus [fearing] to haue lost, I still doe lees
and hope and want: and striue and faile: and proue
wth ioies [cares] from cares
Nor end [from] [paines], nor end [wth ioies] in loue

Sonnet 17

The endless alchemist, with blinded will,
That feeds his thoughts with hopes, his hopes on shows,
And more his work proves vain more eager grows
While dreams of gold his head with shadows fill,

Feels not more sure the scourge of flatt'ring skill,
When in false trust of wealth true need he knows,
Than I, on whom a storm of losses blows
And tides of errors run: yet sail on still

While my corrupted sense doth think it sees
The long sought land of rest, and while to bliss
I think there is a way, though yet I miss.

Thus shunning to have lost, I still do leese,
And hope and want: and strive and fail: and prove
Nor end with joys, nor end from cares in love.

Pastoral 8

Nymph: Shepheard

1

N.   Shepheard, why doest thow so looke still on mee
from whence doe these new humors grow in thee?
Sh: Best Nymph, heer saw I first wth comfort greete
the fayrest day, that ere spredd beames of gold
ledd hence astray, benighted since and colde
I come to yow (my Sun) for light and heate.

2

thee thy
N.   From them that ledd [yow] hence [yowr] help must ryse
bestow theyr beames on better
Mine eyes [are looked on, by deerer] eyes.
Sh: Nor can the Moon thogh faier, the yeer renewe
nor can the stars giue day, thogh cleer and bright
Dead are all other flames, grown dim̄ each light
I must liue cold and darck, or looke on yow.

3

talke vn
N.   Thow wearst as good to [say this] to a stone
woords not beleeued, were better lett alone
Sh: Soon as the spring cold winter doth remoue
from stocks wch lyfe none shewd, leaues in store ryse
The time that mee restores, moues in yowr eyes
and I that from yow freezd: heer burn in loue

4

N.   what bootes beleef, where no regard is born?
Thee and thy loue, and vowes and othes I scorn!
Sh: In earth, on naught the Sun, worth him, doth shyne
drest in his beames, yet shee his glory shewes
In mee, els little worth, yowr beauties knowes
the temple where they are adored in shryne

Perhaps

Pastoral 8

Nymph. Shepherd.

1

Nymph Shepherd, why dost thou so look still on me,
From whence do these new humours grow in thee?
Shepherd Best Nymph, here saw I first, with comfort greet,
The fairest day that e'er spread beams of gold:
Led hence astray, benighted since and cold,
I come to you (my sun) for light and heat.

2

Nymph From them that led thee hence thy help must rise,
Mine eyes bestow their beams on better eyes.
Shepherd Nor can the moon though fair, the year renew,
Nor can the stars give day, though clear and bright:
Dead are all other flames, grown dim each light—
I must live cold and dark, or look on you.

3

Nymph Thou wer'st as good to talk unto a stone:
Words not believed were better let alone.
Shepherd Soon as the spring cold winter doth remove,
From stocks which life none showed leaves in store rise.
The time that me restores moves in your eyes,
And I that from you freezed, here burn in love.

4

Nymph What boots belief where no regard is born?
Thee and thy love, and vows and oaths I scorn.
Shepherd In earth, on naught the sun worth him doth shine,
Dressed in his beams yet she his glory shows.
In me, else little worth, your beauties knows
The temple where they are adored in shrine.

5

N. Perhaps thow thinckst, desert will scorn abate
but I hate thee and in thee, loue doe hate.
Sh: To drown the feelds the angry brookes, do moue
theyr streames, yet euen in that, growes the feelds pryde
On stone of wrongs, loues truth is parfet tryde.
louing all is in yow, yowr hate I loue

6

N. If scorn nor hate will serue, let this thee moue
that there is one that liues prowd in my loue
Sh: The humble shrubb, whose welfare heauē neglects
lookes yet to heauen as well as fauored pine
loue whome yow list: please yor own choice, not mine
My sowl to loue and looke: naught els affects.

7

N. what may I more to giue thee answer, say
showld
but that I now [doe] bidd thee goe away
Sh: wth his fayre beames, the Sun would cleer the ayre
of clowdes: yet are the clowdes drawē by the same
I cannot part from that, by wch I ame:
Nor grow to bee less fond, or yow less fayre

8

N. Then I will goe: Shepheard bee heer alone
vnlookt on loue: vnthowght on, make thy mone
Sh: Till in the heauens, the Moon her face shews nue
streames
in theyr dead [fluds], the seas her absence mourn
liue fayrest still: (best Nymph) soon to retourn
I colde and darck, will wast, till I see you.

5

Nymph Perhaps thou think'st desert will scorn abate,
But I hate thee, and in thee love do hate.
Shepherd To drown the fields the angry brooks do move
Their streams, yet even in that grows the field's pride.
On stone of wrongs, love's truth is perfect tried;
Loving all is in you, your hate I love.

6

Nymph If scorn nor hate will serve, let this thee move—
That there is one that lives proud in my love.
Shepherd The humble shrub whose welfare heaven neglects
Looks yet to heaven as well as favoured pine.
Love whom you list: please your own choice, not mine.
My soul to love and look: naught else affects.

7

Nymph What may I more to give thee answer say
But that I now should bid thee go away?
Shepherd With his fair beams the sun would clear the air
Of clouds, yet are the clouds drawn by the same.
I cannot part from that by which I am,
Nor grow to be less fond, or you less fair.

8

Nymph Then I will go:—shepherd, be here alone,
Unlooked on love, unthought on make thy moan.
Shepherd Till in the heavens the moon her face shows new
In their dead streams the seas her absence mourn.
Live fairest still, best Nymph, soon to return:
I cold and dark, will waste till I see you.

Sonnet. 18

Most faier: [the *altered to*] The feeld is yowrs: now stay y^{or} hands
No power is left to stryue: less to rebell.
I pleasure take, that at yowr blowes I fell
and lawrell weare, in Triumph of my bands

yowr
Ah how, [those] eyes, the ioies of peace, seem brands
to wast, what conquest hath, assured so well
yowr prowd
How [those] lawgiuing lips, in [pure] redd swell
whyle my captiued sowl, at mercy stands.

O best: O onely faier: suffer these eyes
to liue, wch wayte yowr will, humble and true
These knees wch from yowr feet do neuer ryse
These hands, wch still held vp, sweare faith to you

O saue: doe not destroy what is yowr own
[A *altered to*] Iust prince to spoile himself, was neuer know̄

Sonnet 18

Most fair: the field is yours—now stay your hands;
No power is left to strive, less to rebel.
I pleasure take that at your blows I fell,
And laurel wear in triumph of my bands.

Ah how your eyes, the joys of peace, seem brands
To waste what conquest hath assured so well;
How your lawgiving lips in proud red swell,
While my captivèd soul at mercy stands.

O best, O only fair: suffer these eyes
To live, which wait your will humble and true;
These knees, which from your feet do never rise,
These hands, which still held up swear faith to you,

O save: do not destroy what is your own.
Just prince to spoil himself was never known.

Sonnet. 19

When other creatures all each in theyr kinde
comfort of light, quiet from darcknes featch
of wretched monsters, I most monstrous wreatch
nor day from paines, nor night wth rest can finde

But as the slaue, whome storme, or Sun or winde
all day doth beate: in whose syde bloody breach
the scourge doth leaue: whoe on the oare doth stretch
his lims all day, all night his wownds doth binde

Cheynd to those beauties, whence I cannot fly
I know no day so long, wherin each hower
showes not new labours lost: and wherin I
take not new wounds, from theyr vnsparing power

night
Nor longest [day], is long enowgh for mee
to tell my wounds, w[ch] restless bleeding bee

Sonnet 19

When other creatures all, each in their kind,
Comfort of light, quiet from darkness fetch,
Of wretched monsters, I most monstrous wretch
Nor day from pains, nor night with rest can find;

But as the slave, whom storm or sun or wind
All day doth beat, in whose side bloody breach
The scourge doth leave, who on the oar doth stretch
His limbs all day, all night his wounds doth bind,

Chained to those beauties whence I cannot fly
I know no day so long, wherein each hour
Shows not new labours lost, and wherein I
Take not new wounds from their unsparing power:

Nor longest night is long enough for me
To tell my wounds, which restless bleeding be.

Sonnet. 20.

Shine on fayre stars: giue comfort to these eyes
wch know no light but yowrs: no lyfe but you:
shyne that theyr loue, yowr worth, may haue your due
whyle ioyes to them, glory to yow doth ryse

But vpon mee, amid yowr beames there lies
a blacker night then euer forrest knue:
mourning
whoe by yowr light, discern the [darcknes] true
husband-Suns loss
of widow sky, wch [Suns departure] tries.

the bee
Raine now alone: in yow [bee this] night blest
my wants, anothers store grudg not to see
But ere long will a Sun ryse from the East
in whose cleer flames, yowr sparcks obscurd will bee

Till then in Spryte, those hid beames I adore
and know more stars I see my night the more.

Sonnet 20

Shine on fair stars, give comfort to these eyes
Which know no light but yours, no life but you;
Shine that their love, your worth, may have your due
While joys to them, glory to you doth rise.

But upon me amid your beams there lies
A blacker night than ever forest knew,
Who by your light discern the mourning true
Of widow sky, which husband-sun's loss tries.

Reign now alone, in you the night be blest,
My wants, another's store, grudge not to see;
But ere long will a sun rise from the East
In whose clear flames your sparks obscured will be:

Till then, in sprite those hid beams I adore
And know more stars I see, my night the more.

Sonnet. 21.

Alas why say yow I ame ritch? when I
doe begg, and begging scant a lyfe sustaine:
why doe yow say that I ame well? when paine
lowder then on the rack, [on *altered to*] in mee doth cry.

O let mee know myself! my pouerty
wth whitening rotten [walles *altered to*] walls, no stay doth gaine.
keep
and these small hopes yow tell, [stay] but in vaine
lyfe wth hott drincks, in one layd down to dy.

If in my face, my wants and sores, so greate
doe not appeer: A canker (thinck) vnseen
the apples hart thogh sownd wthout doth eate.

Or if on mee from my fayre heauē are seen,
some scattred beames: Know sutch heate giues theyr light
as frosty mornings Sun: as Moonshyne night.

Sonnet 21

Alas why say you I am rich? when I
Do beg, and begging scant a life sustain:
Why do you say that I am well?—when pain
Louder than on the rack, in me doth cry.

O let me know myself! My poverty
With whitening rotten walls no stay doth gain,
And these small hopes you tell, keep but in vain
Life with hot drinks, in one laid down to die.

If in my face my wants and sores so great
Do not appear, a canker (think) unseen
The apple's heart, though sound without, doth eat:

Or if on me from my fair heaven are seen
Some scattered beams—know such heat gives their light
As frosty morning's sun, as moonshine night.

Sonnet. 22.

a
On vnknown shore, wth wether hard destrest
the fainting Mariner so feares the night
as I whoe in the dayes declining light
doe read the story of my wrack of rest.

Blest in yowr sight: and but in sight yet blest
euen now to leaue yowr light, my lifes delight
I wayte to adore, in rayes, as sweet as bright
the Sun lodg'd in yowr eys, heauēs in y^{or} brest

O of mans hopes the vaine condition!
whyle I ame saijng, thow lowe shady roome
straight shalt a match to highest spheares becoom.

Sad night to bee more darck y^{or} stay puts on.
and in yowr fayling paints, her black aspect,
yet sees a minde more darck, for y^{or} neglect.

Sonnet 22

On unknown shore, with weather hard distressed,
The fainting mariner so fears the night
As I, who in the day's declining light
Do read the story of my wrack of rest.

Blest in your sight, and but in sight yet blest,
Even now to leave your light, my life's delight,
I wait to'adore, in rays as sweet as bright,
The sun lodged in your eyes, heavens in your breast.

O of man's hopes the vain condition!
While I am saying 'Thou low shady room
Straight shalt a match to highest spheres become'

Sad night, to be more dark, your stay puts on,
And in your failing paints her black aspect;
Yet sees a mind more dark for your neglect.

Sonnet. 23.

Absence what floods of plaints gainst thee would ryse
wch euen the hellish wants doest make mee tast
If perisht barck on shore by tempest cast
wch late praide for the land, now on it dyes

Did not paint out my lyfe, wch fetterd lyes
and famisht, darck, in prison, cold doth wast
till when my lifes Queen present shines at last
a medcin worse then greef it self it tries.

For as the condemnd man from dungeon ledd
whoe wth first light hee sees, ends his last breath
when I see her, I see scorns banner spredd
each word refuses, each refuse giues death

Thē thee sad absence I no longer curse
as present paine, then absent ioy is wurse.

Sonnet 23

Absence, what floods of plaints 'gainst thee would rise—
Which even the hellish wants dost make me taste—
If perished bark on shore by tempest cast,
Which late prayed for the land, now on it dies,

Did not paint out my life, which fettered lies
And famished, dark, in prison, cold doth waste;
Till, when my life's queen present shines at last,
A medicine worse than grief itself it tries.

For—as the condemned man from dungeon led
Who with first light he sees, ends his last breath—
When I see her, I see scorn's banner spread,
Each word refuses, each refuse gives death.

Then thee sad absence I no longer curse,
As present pain, than absent joy, is worse.

Son: 24.

Canst thow turn from the hauē of thy rest
for bitter storms, that beate thee from the shore?
Canst thow forsake, the mine whose golden store
must make thee ritch, wth labours lost distrest?

Ah when doe I, from troubles in my brest
see peace or truce? or wth lims faint and sore
leaue of the loued chace, wch more and more
flies from before mee, when I follow best.

Nor now doth hope aspyre more to the bliss
wch once it fram'd so fayre: enowgh it is
if loue doe liue, thogh liue in cares and feares

Like him whoe from a steep rock hedlong cast
on bough or stone, his grasping hands sets fast
and falling dies, and holding torment beares.

Sonnet 24

Canst thou turn from the haven of thy rest
For bitter storms that beat thee from the shore?
Canst thou forsake the mine whose golden store
Must make thee rich, with labours lost distressed?

Ah when do I, from troubles in my breast
See peace or truce? or with limbs faint and sore
Leave off the lovèd chase, which more and more
Flies from before me, when I follow best?

Nor now doth hope aspire more to the bliss
Which once it framed so fair; enough it is
If love do live, though live in cares and fears:

Like him who from a steep rock headlong cast,
On bough or stone his grasping hands sets fast,
And falling dies, and holding torment bears.

Son: 25.

Yow that take pleasure in yowr cruelty,
and place yowr health in my infections:
yow that add sorrowes to afflictions
[and Triumphs leade in my captiuity]
and thinck yowr wealth shines in my pouerty

Since that there is all inequality
between my wants and yowr perfections
between yowr scorns and my affections
between my bands and yowr soueranity

O loue your self: bee yow yowrself yowr care:
Ioy in those acts, in wch yowr making stood:
made, these
Fayre, louely, good: of these [composd] yow are:
pity is fayre, grace louely, mercy good.
Sunn
And when [heauē] like, yow in yowrself yow show
Let mee the point bee, about wch yow goe.

Sonnet 25

You that take pleasure in your cruelty
And place your health in my infections,
You that add sorrows to afflictions
And think your wealth shines in my poverty,

Since that there is all inequality
Between my wants and your perfections,
Between your scorns and my affections,
Between my bands and your sov'ranity—

O love yourself: be you yourself your care:
Joy in those acts, in which your making stood:
Fair, lovely, good—of these made, these you are;
Pity is fair, grace lovely, mercy good.

And when sun-like, you in yourself you show,
Let me the point be about which you go.

Son: 26.

Ah deerest lims my lifes best ioy and stay
how must I thus let yow bee cutt from mee
and loosing yow myself vnusfull see
and keeping yow, cast lyfe and all away

Full of dead Gangreins doth the sickman say
whose [loss] of part [ra] of the rest must bee
  (death above [loss]; health above [ra])
Alas my loue from no infections free
like law doth giue of it or my decay

My loue more deer to mee then [hand *altered to*] hands or [eye *altered to*] eys
neerer to mee, then what wth mee was borne
delaied, betraied, cast vnder chang and scorn

Sick past all help or hope, or kils or dyes
[Endures all paines that feares and wants can try]
blood it sheades
whyle all the [sores loue beares] my hart doth bleed
Cancres
and wth my bowels I his [vultures] feed.

Sonnet 26

'Ah dearest limbs, my life's best joy and stay,
How must I thus let you be cut from me,
And losing you, myself unuseful see,
And keeping you, cast life and all away'

Full of dead gangrenes doth the sickman say
Whose death of part, health of the rest must be;
Alas my love, from no infections free,
Like law doth give of it or my decay.

My love, more dear to me than hands or eyes,
Nearer to me than what with me was born,
Delayed, betrayed, cast under change and scorn,

Sick past all help or hope, or kills or dies;
While all the blood it sheds my heart doth bleed
And with my bowels I his cancers feed.

Pastoral. 9

1

Day wch so bright didst shyne, how darck art thow?
Ayre euen now sweet, how doe mists in thee growe?
Sea late so calme, how high wrowght are yow now?
thee
Brooke once so cleer, how doth sand in [yow] flowe?
Trees so full blowen, how bare now is each bow?
Feelds how doe weeds, yowr ritch corn ouergrowe?
  Day, ayre, sea, brooke, trees, feelds: say, vain's all trust
  The fayrest proues vntrew, the best vniust.

2

Frosts how yow print the earth wth witherd face!
Storms, how wth lightning yow heauēs mantle lyne!
Fluds, how all to deuowr, yow hast yowr pace!
Fyre, how in beames of ruin yow doe shyne!
Plague, how wth killing arms, yow all embrace!
Dearth, how what death hath spared, in yow doth pine
  Frosts, storms, fluds, fyre, plague, dearth, answer wth mee
  Owr goods are ghests, owr losses homemates bee.

3

Thus whyle, the worlds fayre frame, such chang approues
Shee will as fals as it bee, as as fayre.
Thus from one mischeef, whyle another moues,
I feel the ils, wch worst cannot impayre.
whyle shee her fayth a prize sets to new loues,
in mee faith raines on wrongs, loue on despayre.
  Day, ayre, sea, brooke, trees, feelds, her falshood knowe
  Frosts, storms, fluds fyre, plague, dearth my merites showe.

Hencefourth

Pastoral 9

1

Day which so bright didst shine, how dark art thou?
Air even now sweet, how do mists in thee grow?
Sea late so calm, how high wrought are you now?
Brook once so clear, how doth sand in thee flow?
Trees so full blown, how bare now is each bough?
Fields, how do weeds your rich corn overgrow?
  Day, air, sea, brook, trees, fields, say 'Vain's all trust,
  The fairest proves untrue, the best unjust.'

2

Frosts, how you print the earth with withered face!
Storms, how with lightning you heaven's mantle line!
Floods, how all to devour you haste your pace!
Fire, how in beams of ruin you do shine!
Plague, how with killing arms you all embrace!
Dearth, how what death hath spared in you doth pine!
  Frosts, storms, floods, fire, plague, dearth, answer with me
  'Our goods are guests, our losses homemates be.'

3

Thus while the world's fair frame such change approves,
She will as false as it be, as as fair:
Thus from one mischief while another moves,
I feel the ills which worst cannot impair:
While she her faith a prize sets to new loves,
In me faith reigns on wrongs, love on despair.
  Day, air, sea, brook, trees, fields, her falsehood know;
  Frosts, storms, floods, fire, plague, dearth, my merits show.

4

Hencefourth then may, Fyre giue light to the Day:
and cleerest Ayre, a nurse to Plagues bee fownd.
Hencefourth may Frosts shutt vp the Seas large way
all vsefull
and Storms [the strongests] Trees teare frō the grownd.
Hencefourth no frute[s] of Feelds Dearth banish may,
all may
and smalest Brookes, in Fluds [the hils] surrownd
Since beauty growes the bed, where treason lyes
and faith is made the stayre to miseryes.

5

now wth
This sayd, the Shepheard, as [wth now] new eyes
wch had not
lookd vp and saw his flock [not from him] strayde
own vnknown
his [flock] wch hee for [others] did despise
whyle it stil kept his steps, his voice obeyde.
Then in his sowl the images did ryse
greeuing
of due and vniust loues: and [sighing] sayde
Ah Flock so louing, so regarded not:
are
how my faults [shew] yowr praise yor wrongs my blott

6

cure
So hee whose senses foild, no [help] could breed
in her faults, safety to his ruins fownd.
Those the good Dolfin were, the sauing threed,
wch stayde the seas deep iawes, the maze vnwound
fancies
He sees, how sweet, did [vices] poisons feed
how strongly follyes easy fetters bownd.
sais
Now loues his wrongs: [sais], vnder shame and sinn
I had bin lost, if lost I had not bin.

4

Henceforth then may fire give light to the day
And clearest air a nurse to plagues be found;
Henceforth may frosts shut up the sea's large way
And storms all useful trees tear from the ground;
Henceforth no fruit of fields dearth banish may
And smallest brooks, in floods, all may surround;
  Since beauty grows the bed where treason lies,
  And faith is made the stair to miseries.

5

This said, the shepherd—as now with new eyes—
Looked up and saw his flock which had not strayed,
His own, which he for unknown did despise,
While it still kept his steps, his voice obeyed.
Then in his soul the images did rise
Of due and unjust loves, and grieving said
  'Ah flock so loving, so regarded not,
  How my faults are your praise, your wrongs my blot.'

6

So he whose senses foiled no cure could breed,
In her faults safety to his ruins found;
Those the good dolphin were, the saving thread,
Which stayed the sea's deep jaws, the maze unwound.
He sees how sweet did fancy's poisons feed,
How strongly folly's easy fetters bound:
  Now loves his wrongs, says 'Under shame and sin
  I had been lost, if lost I had not been.'

Song. 10.

Yow whoe fauor doe enioy
and spend and keep loues treasure,
know
yow whoe [see] no end of ioy
nor limmits finde nor measure.
yow whose cares triumphing on anoy
giue yow a crown of pleasure

2

Beare ful sayles whyle fayre winds blowe
time what now is astranges.
Flowers chose this day wth best showe
tomorrow in dust ranges.
Beauty Queenlike not alone doth goe
but wayted on by changes.

3

Somewhat that yow are was I,
I throwgh a vayle saw glory
Ioies seemd wth my wings to fly
I was parte of loues story.
But if euer I did gladnes try
I time enowgh was sory.

4

When those beauties I did see
a hid worth I conceaued.
liking then grew rage to bee
I sowght, and was receaued
I did vowe, and had vowes made to mee
I trusted, was deceaued.

Happy

Song 10

You who favour do enjoy
And spend and keep love's treasure,
You who know no end of joy
Nor limits find nor measure,
You whose cares, triumphing on annoy,
Give you a crown of pleasure,

2

Bear full sails while fair winds blow,
Time what now is astranges,
Flowers chose this day with best show
Tomorrow in dust ranges,
Beauty, queen-like, not alone doth go
But waited on by changes.

3

Somewhat that you are was I,
I through a veil saw glory,
Joys seemed with my wings to fly,
I was part of love's story:
But if ever I did gladness try
I time enough was sorry.

4

When those beauties I did see
A hid worth I conceivèd,
Liking then grew rage to be,
I sought, and was receivèd,
I did vow, and had vows made to me,
I trusted, was deceivèd.

5

Happy they whoe did not loue,
or sitt down by theyr losses.
Nor left heer doe elswhere proue
new hopes are but new crosses.
Change of ship doth sicknes not remoue
one like the other tosses.

6

When from them no food doth growe
the hungry sowl liues dijng.
Soon as they some grace doe showe
they kill, to others flijng.
Equal weights, they on the louer throwe
or graunting or denijng.

7

yet fayre blessings women were
if they could one perseuer.
But the wheeles of time they beare
A whyle to them is euer.
Shee that sayd, my chang Frend, neuer feare
bownd
to one hower [tyde] her Neuer.

5

Happy they who did not love,
Or sit down by their losses,
Nor, left here, do elsewhere prove
New hopes are but new crosses:
Change of ship doth sickness not remove,
One like the other tosses.

6

When from them no food doth grow
The hungry soul lives dying,
Soon as they some grace do show
They kill, to others flying:
Equal weights they on the lover throw,
Or granting or denying.

7

Yet fair blessings women were
If they could one persever,
But the wheels of time they bear,
A while to them is ever;
She that said 'My change, friend, never fear'
To one hour bound her 'never'.

Sonet. 27.

Falshood: how long did I yowr stings endure
and lazerlike no sence had of yowr blowes
whyle yow not feard wrowght my close ouerthrows
and I deaf to all dowbts, did sleep secure.

Thorow the shadows of my loue, a sure
Standing yow tooke, to guyde yowr poisned blowes
My loue, wch made his ends, one wth his showes
and sure in his own cours like did assure.

Tel how yow could draw beauties pure and trew
to shrowd yow wth theyr wings? or so fayre minde
itself in league wth yowr fowl wayes to binde?

Relligious vowes are broken, labours new
reape of long faith the hyre: and all to late,
I learn, when help is past, my sicknes state.

Sonnet 27

Falsehood: how long did I your stings endure
And lazar-like, no sense had of your blows,
While you not feared wrought my close overthrows
And I deaf to all doubts, did sleep secure.

Thorough the shadows of my love, a sure
Standing you took to guide your poisoned blows—
My love, which made his ends one with his shows
And sure in his own course, like did assure.

Tell how you could draw beauties pure and true
To shroud you with their wings, or so fair mind
Itself in league with your foul ways to bind.

Religious vows are broken, labours new
Reap of long faith the hire: and all too late
I learn, when help is past, my sickness state.

Son: 28.

Ayre w[ch] about these wanton leaues dost play
comfort
and [sweetnes] draw from euery flower and tree
still storms and
so may thow [euer] from [fowl] mists bee free
might thow still inioy a Rosy
so [vnto thee bee still a flowry] May

hence goe and goe
As thow from [mee] wilt [fly], [but fly] that way
plenty garden treasures
where in most [store roses and vylets] bee
that in theyr bosomes sweet, they sweeten thee
Charys
and last on [Lysas] ruby lips thow stay.

There rest thy self, and those fayre cherries kiss
sucking fairness
and [kissing] them part of theyr [sweetnes] gett
Mirrh Amber
to w[ch] no [rose], no [vylett] equall is.

thirsting deer
Then to my [longing] sense [sweet] breath make hast
ritchess
that to my hart I may thy [sweetnes] lett
and of her lips the Nectar someway tast.

Sonnet 28

Air which about these wanton leaves dost play
And comfort draw from every flower and tree,
So may thou still from storms and mists be free,
So might thou still enjoy a rosy May,

As thou from hence wilt go, and go that way
Where in most plenty garden treasures be,
That in their bosoms sweet, they sweeten thee,
And last on Charys' ruby lips thou stay:

There rest thyself, and those fair cherries kiss,
And sucking them, part of their fairness get
To which no myrrh, no amber, equal is.

Then to my thirsting sense, dear breath, make haste,
That to my heart I may thy richesse let
And of her lips the nectar someway taste.

Son. 29.

Yowr hate to mee, must needs bee violent,
since to hurt mee, yowr self yow doe not spare.
Indeed the harms bee theyrs, wch wrongued are
but theyrs the sinn, whoe harm the innocent.

byde
yowr wrongs made mee, wth losses [ly] content
and now a safe thogh homely rest prepare
and as hopes had left mee, I leauing care
worck on the breaches, of time fondly spent.

when yow confessing faults, remission sowght
and for amends, large promises did make
But soon as I to my old bonds was browght
trusting on so fayre words, yowr word yow brake

See then yowr purchas, yowr ritch conquest see
yow poison yowr own faith, to infect mee.

Sonnet 29

Your hate to me must needs be violent
Since to hurt me, yourself you do not spare:
Indeed the harms be theirs which wrongèd are,
But theirs the sin, who harm the innocent.

Your wrongs made me with losses bide content
And now a safe though homely rest prepare,
And as hopes had left me, I leaving care
Work on the breaches of time fondly spent.

When you confessing faults, remission sought,
And for amends, large promises did make,
But soon as I to my old bonds was brought,
Trusting on so fair words, your word you brake.

See then your purchase, your rich conquest see:
You poison your own faith, to infect me.

Song. 11.

Thowghts vnto mee so deer
as vnto yow I liue.
Thowghts vnto whome I giue
a mind from all els [free] cleer
vniustly yow requyte mee
whoe will [not no] no more content mee
but wth what is torment mee
wth what will bee affright mee

2

Say if that euer I
sowght not yowr choicest food
what
and browght [was] ere was good
safe kept by memory.
But yow turn all betraijng
to poison in yow dwelling
and like an ill spleen swelling
yowr strength worcks my decaijng.

3

when in some blessed hower
I see those beauties shyne
and streight praye so deuine
bid yow thowghts to deuowr.
yow my well meaning wronging
reiect what I doe offer
and answer I things proffer
vnto some els belonging

Make

Song 11

Thoughts unto me so dear
As unto you I live,
Thoughts unto whom I give
A mind from all else clear,
Unjustly you requite me,
Who will no more content me,
But with what is torment me
With what will be affright me.

2

Say if that ever I
Sought not your choicest food,
And brought whate'er was good
Safe kept by memory:
But you turn all betraying
To poison in you dwelling,
And like an ill spleen swelling
Your strength works my decaying.

3

When in some blessèd hour
I see those beauties shine,
And straight prey so divine
Bid you thoughts to devour—
You, my well-meaning wronging,
Reject what I do offer
And answer, I things proffer
Unto some else belonging.

4

Make I not when hopes ryse
from worde or looke to yow
of them on comfort true
a smoking sacryfyze.
when yow say smokes are pleasing
the fainting sprytes perfuming
to bodyes but consuming
[They *smudged out*] Smokes yeald a soon past easing

5

Thus hope, sens memory
corrupted all are browght
to sooth vp Tirant thowght
and euen themselus deny
whyle lethargick I cherish
death in beguyling sleeping
and snakelike thowghts still keeping
preserue what makes me perish.

6.

Nor can I leaue to thinck
thogh thincking still I finde
More sight makes mee more blinde
My thirst more, more I drinck
like him whoe in fowl weather
will not cast out his Treasure
held
till for so deer [bowght] pleasure
The sea eates both together

7.

And so her Idol strang
wth my thowghts is made one
as yow may breake the stone
but can the forme not change

whoe

4

Make I not, when hopes rise
From word or look, to you
Of them on comfort true
A smoking sacrifice?
When you say, smokes are pleasing
The fainting sprites perfuming,
To bodies but consuming
Smokes yield a soon-past easing.

5

Thus hope, sense, memory,
Corrupted all, are brought
To sooth up tyrant thought
And even themselves deny,
While lethargic I cherish
Death in beguiling sleeping,
And snakelike thoughts still keeping
Preserve what makes me perish.

6

Nor can I leave to think,
Though thinking still I find
More sight makes me more blind,
My thirst more, more I drink:
Like him who in foul weather
Will not cast out his treasure
Till for so dear-held pleasure
The sea eats both together.

7

And so her idol strange
With my thoughts is made one,
As you may break the stone
But can the form not change:

whoe puld his eyes out euer
becaus they saw no better
or to cast of a fetter
his lims from him did seuer

8

Nor know I how to teare
the dross out of my hart
that wthall
but [at once] must part
the golde wch it doth beare
For whyle thowghts show full measure
in her of hate and scorning
they shew bliss fayrest morning
and high noonday of pleasure.

9

Thowghts therfore leaue not mee
for yow I will not leaue
what fortune [I *cancelled by*] yow receaue
the same my state shall bee
This one my loue requyreth
her hatred yow will couer
Alas a needy louer
soon thincks what hee desyreth.

10

Yow haue it often doon
when I best trusted you
and now I finde to true
Truth sowght out greef hath woon
In yowr fals arms then lay mee
as wth sleep drincks possessed
My paines will seem redressed
whyle yowr rest doth betray mee.

Who pulled his eyes out ever
Because they saw no better,
Or to cast off a fetter
His limbs from him did sever?

8

Nor know I how to tear
The dross out of my heart
But that withal must part
The gold which it doth bear:
For while thoughts show full measure
In her of hate and scorning,
They show bliss' fairest morning
And high noonday of pleasure.

9

Thoughts therefore leave not me
For you I will not leave,
What fortune you receive
The same my state shall be:
This one my love requireth—
Her hatred you will cover;
Alas, a needy lover
Soon thinks what he desireth.

10

You have it often done
When I best trusted you,
And now I find too true
Truth sought out grief hath won:
In your false arms then lay me
As with sleep drinks possessèd,
My pains will seem redressèd
While your rest doth betray me.

Song 12

To a french Tune
Ou estes vous allez mes belles amourettes

Since now those fayre eyes doe shyne in theyr cleer former light
why showld I refuse such guydes, to bring mee owt of paine
Ah whether will yow leade mee flattering delight
will yow then betray mee, once againe?

Since now from those sweetest lips flow words of Nectar right
why showld I my thirsting thowghts, from so deer cupp restraine
Ah whether will yow leade
will yow then etc

Meethincks I see in Glory, after a long cold night
ouer
the sun in beames of comfort, [after] sad darckness raine
Ah whether
will yow

Meethincks I see a haruest, wch of all dearths in spyte
a minde long hungerstarued, in plenty can mantaine
Ah whether
will yow

Triumph then late wrongued loue, hopes do put cares to flight
mischeefs now do turn theyr back, desert the feeld doth gaine
Ah whether
will yow

But stay memory wch did, my wrongs in marble wryte
wth the wounds wch falshood giues, my ioies doth entertaine
Ah whether
will yow

Song 12

To a French tune: Où êtes vous allées mes belles amourettes

Since now those fair eyes do shine in their clear former light
Why should I refuse such guides to bring me out of pain?
Ah whither will you lead me, flattering delight,
Will you then betray me once again?

Since now from those sweetest lips flow words of nectar right
Why should I my thirsting thoughts from so dear cup restrain?
Ah whither will you lead me, flattering delight,
Will you then betray me once again?

Methinks I see in glory after a long cold night
The sun in beams of comfort over sad darkness reign:
Ah whither will you lead me, flattering delight,
Will you then betray me once again?

Methinks I see a harvest, which of all dearths in spite,
A mind long hunger-starvèd in plenty can maintain:
Ah whither will you lead me, flattering delight,
Will you then betray me once again?

Triumph then late wrongèd love, hopes do put cares to flight,
Mischiefs now do turn their back, desert the field doth gain:
Ah whither will you lead me, flattering delight,
Will you then betray me once again?

But stay—memory which did my wrongs in marble write,
With the wounds which falsehood gives my joys doth entertain:
Ah whither will you lead me, flattering delight,
Will you then betray me once again?

True it is those Diamonds once so deer, still so bright
did proue fals when they were tryed, and all theyr luster vaine
  Ah whether
  will yow

True it is that bancket ritch so sweet sett owt to sight
sundry poisons of all sorts, did in each dish containe
  Ah whether
  will yow

worthy hee of wounds is, whoe twise tries the lions might
Hee deserus no pitty that, twise doth of falshood plaine
  Ah whether
  will yow.

whose
Farewell then eyes errors stars, [yowr] light doth mee benight
Farewell [then] venomstilling lips, whose words stings wth them
yow neuer more shall leade mee flattering delight [traine
yow shall not betray mee once againe.

True it is those diamonds once so dear, still so bright,
Did prove false when they were tried, and all their lustre vain:
Ah whither will you lead me, flattering delight,
Will you then betray me once again?

True it is that banquet rich so sweet set out to sight,
Sundry poisons of all sorts did in each dish contain:
Ah whither will you lead me, flattering delight,
Will you then betray me once again?

Worthy he of wounds is who twice tries the lion's might,
He deserves no pity that twice doth of falsehood plain:
Ah whither will you lead me, flattering delight,
Will you then betray me once again?

Farewell then eyes, error's stars, whose light doth me benight,
Farewell venom-stilling lips, whose words stings with them train:
You never more shall lead me, flattering delight,
You shall not betray me once again.

Son: 30.

Absence I cannot say thow hyd'st my light
darckned for ay sett
not [now Eclipst], but [quenched] is my Sun
No day sees mee, not when nights glass is rū
I present, absent ame; vnseen in sight.

Nothing but I doe paralele the night
act
in whome all [sense] of light and heate is doō
Shee that did all in mee, all hath vndoon
I was loues cradle once, now loues graue right

my mone to
Absence I vsde [of] to make [my plaints of] thee
when thy clowdes stayde my ioies they did not shyne
but now I may say ioies: cannot say mine

all I
Absent I want ^ what ^ care [most] to see
auaile mee not
present I see my cares [reiected grown]
[Absent I ame forgot: present not knoẇ]
present not harckned to, absent forgot.

Sonnet 30

Absence, I cannot say thou hid'st my light,
Not darkened, but for ay set is my sun;
No day sees me, not when night's glass is run;
I present, absent am; unseen in sight.

Nothing but I do parallel the night,
In whom all act of light and heat is done:
She that did all in me, all hath undone;
I was love's cradle once, now love's grave right.

Absence, I used to make my moan to thee,
When thy clouds stayed, my joys they did not shine;
But now I may say 'joys', cannot say 'mine'.

Absent, I want all what I care to see,
Present, I see my cares avail me not:
Present not hearkened to, absent forgot.

Son: 31.

Forsaken woods, trees wth sharpe storms opprest
whose leaues once hidd, the sun, now strew the grownd
once bred delight, now scorn, late vsde to sownd
of sweetest birds, now of hoars crowes the nest

Gardens w[ch] once in thowsand coulers drest
shewed natures pryde: now in dead sticks abownd
in whome prowd sum̃ers treasure late was fow̃d
now but the rags, of winters torn coate rest

Medows whose sydes, late fayre brookes kist now slyme
embraced holds: feelds whose youth greẽ and brave
promist long lyfe, now frosts lay in the graue

Say all and I wth them: what doth not tyme!
But they whoe knew tyme, tyme will finde again
I that fayre tymes lost, on tyme call in vaine

Sonnet 31

Forsaken woods, trees with sharp storms oppressed,
Whose leaves once hid the sun, now strew the ground,
Once bred delight, now scorn, late used to sound
Of sweetest birds, now of hoarse crows the nest;

Gardens, which once in thousand colours dressed
Showed nature's pride, now in dead sticks abound,
In whom proud summer's treasure late was found
Now but the rags of winter's torn coat rest;

Meadows whose sides late fair brooks kissed, now slime
Embracèd holds; fields whose youth green and brave
Promised long life, now frosts lay in the grave:

Say all, and I with them, 'What doth not Time!'
But they, who knew Time, Time will find again:
I that fair times lost, on Time call in vain.

Son: 32.

All yow fayre minds whome chois or destiny
wth humble hart deuoted haue to loue
and wth vnfained vowes, yowr faith will proue
and wth vnforced teares for pity cry.

Fly all blinde temples, all darck altares fly
from wch yowr lorde, yowr zeale doth not approve
and ioyfull hether yowr oblations moue
where hee stil raines, where his fyres neuer dy

See heer the eyes, by wch his power doth liue
Treasure
See heer the brest the [storehows] of his worth
See heer the lips his Oracles wch giue

Heer and but heer loue is beheld aright
Hid els to all: loucrs then bring henceforth
hether yowr rytes by day, yowr praiers at night

Sonnet 32

All you fair minds whom choice or destiny
With humble heart devoted have to love,
And with unfeignèd vows your faith will prove
And with unforcèd tears for pity cry—

Fly all blind temples, all dark altars fly,
From which your lord your zeal doth not approve,
And joyful hither your oblations move
Where he still reigns, where his fires never die.

See here the eyes, by which his power doth live,
See here the breast, the treasure of his worth,
See here the lips, his oracles which give.

Here, and but here, love is beheld aright,
Hid else to all: lovers then, bring henceforth
Hither your rites by day, your prayers at night.

Son: 32.

Fayrest of fayre, on whome the heauēs bestow
ritchly those gifts wch from all els they spare
whoe placing yow heer on earth did prepare
in sweetest body, sweeter minde to showe

In whose face beauties Oceans euer flow
whose eyes the Magazins of loues arms are
whose loueliness is garded wth such care
as bold desyres doe theyr own ruin know

whose chastest thowghts frō waywardnes are free
whose state affrighteth not the humble ey.
whose smalest motion lightneth Maiestee

Blame not in words nor fayre nor good if I
speake of yowr praise, wch euen conceit doth pass
Since Gods are pleased to see themselus in brass.

Sonnet 33

Fairest of fair, on whom the heavens bestow
Richly those gifts which from all else they spare,
Who placing you here on earth did prepare
In sweetest body, sweeter mind to show,

In whose face beauty's oceans ever flow,
Whose eyes the magazines of love's arms are,
Whose loveliness is guarded with such care
As bold desires do their own ruin know,

Whose chastest thoughts from waywardness are free,
Whose state affrighteth not the humble eye,
Whose smallest motion lightneth majesty,

Blame not, in words nor fair nor good if I
Speak of your praise, which even conceit doth pass,
Since gods are pleased to see themselves in brass.

Son: 33.

W^th how wyde iawes would I my poison drinck
and swallowing her hate, my last scores pay
if once for all the venumd cup would slay
and not that floting keep, that striues to sinck

For of my graue thogh I ly at the brinck
lead by the burial lights her eyes desplay
when heate of hate my spirits dries away
and cheynes of anger, sore to sore doe linck

yet what in beauty liues hate cannot kill
whose baulms, delaijng death make paines to liue
that euen my wounds my vaines wth new blood fill
whyle beawties brests milck to infections giue

Fast thus her sight, then light more lou'd, I fly
where hate torments, and beawty lets not dy.

Sonnet 34

With how wide jaws would I my poison drink
And swallowing her hate, my last scores pay,
If once for all the venomed cup would slay
And not that floating keep, that strives to sink.

For of my grave though I lie at the brink
Led by the burial lights her eyes display,
When heat of hate my spirits dries away
And chains of anger sore to sore do link,

Yet what in beauty lives hate cannot kill,
Whose balms, delaying death, make pains to live,
That even my wounds my veins with new blood fill
While beauty's breasts milk to infections give:

Fast thus her sight, than light more loved, I fly,
Where hate torments, and beauty lets not die.

Song. 13.

Vpon a wretch, that wastes away
consum'd wth wants: whose last decay
threatens each night to see no day
some speedy help bestow
whoe prostrat heer before yow lyes
and casting vp his begging eyes
sighs out to yow his hollow cryes
in whome his health must grow.
A poor wretch
but yowr wretch
whome misery so driueth
as onely that hee liueth
his sens of paine doth show.

Alas in yow loue chose to raine
becaus yowr treasures can sustaine
the charge to recompence theyr paine
whoe for him suffred haue
All other beauties but suffyse
of profferd loue to bee the prize
To yowrs no faith so high can ryse
as may requital craue
O do then
vndo then
the cheyne that grace foresloweth
no hand such beautie showeth
as that wch lyfe doth saue.

Song 13

Upon a wretch that wastes away
Consumed with wants, whose last decay
Threatens each night to see no day,
Some speedy help bestow:
Who prostrate here before you lies
And casting up his begging eyes
Sighs out to you his hollow cries
In whom his health must grow.
A poor wretch
But your wretch,
Whom misery so driveth
As only that he liveth
His sense of pain doth show.

Alas, in you Love chose to reign
Because your treasures can sustain
The charge to recompence their pain
Who for him suffered have.
All other beauties but suffice
Of proffered love to be the prize,
To yours no faith so high can rise
As may requital crave.
O do then
Undo then
The chain that grace forsloweth,
No hand such beauty showeth
As that which life doth save.

O yow fayre heauē wch blessings powers
on witherd mee, raine down yowr showrs
yow that my tyme are, graunt some howres
From loue deuowring death.
Or if yowr will my lyfe deny
and my will from yowrs cannot fly
so that truth wch knowes how I dy
my hearse wth mirtle wreath.
Receaue heer
Perceaue heer
a man that in paines ioijng
and but his faith enioijng
wth yowr praise shuts his breath.

O you fair heaven which blessings pours
On withered me, rain down your showers:
You that my time are, grant some hours
From love-devouring death:
Or if your will my life deny
(And my will from yours cannot fly)
So that truth, which knows how I die,
My hearse with myrtle wreathe—
Receive here,
Perceive here,
A man that in pains joying
And but his faith enjoying
With your praise shuts his breath.

Son: 34

Time cruel time how fast pass yow away
and in my case from yowr own custome fly
blackest
whyle I vnknown in [darkest] shadowes ly
and dum̄ wth feare, not that I loue dare say

Alas yowr wings doe to the light desplay
what choisest care in darkest bands doth ty
But thus forsaking mee yow make mee try
that whoe to tyme trusts doth himself betray

Speake time, and times child truth since first I saw
That bodied Angel: did my faith ere quaile
or was not spurd loue, held wth raines of awe?
But yow heare, not: pack on then yowr best saile

Leave mee behinde! Time yow shall nowhere moue
where whyle yow are yow shall not see my loue

Sonnet 35

Time, cruel Time, how fast pass you away
And in my case from your own custom fly,
While I unknown in blackest shadows lie
And dumb with fear, not that I love dare say:

Alas, your wings do to the light display
What choicest care in darkest bands doth tie;
But thus forsaking me, you make me try
That who to Time trusts doth himself betray.

Speak Time, and Time's child Truth: since first I saw
That bodied angel, did my faith e'er quail,
Or was not spurred love held with reins of awe?
But you hear, not:—pack on then you best sail,

Leave me behind! Time, you shall nowhere move
Where, while you are, you shall not see my love.

Vpon a Snufkin.

Goe happy furres the hands preserue
where beauty raines, and loue doth serue
Keep what the world like doth not showe
of stirring marble, fixed snowe.
when in blest yow, those liue pearles stay
to them from him that sends yow say
As is theyr christall wth out spott
his faith is pure, and faint will not.
and for each heare that in yow is
a thowsand times those ioies doth kiss.

Translated out of Spanish

Shee whome I loued, and loue shall still
sitting on this then blessed sand
wrate wth to mee heauē opning hand
first will I dy ere chang I will.
Oh vniust force of loue vniust
that thus a mans beleef showld rest
on words conceaued in womans brest
and vowes inroled in the dust.

Upon a Snuffkin

Go happy furs, the hands preserve
Where beauty reigns, and love doth serve;
Keep what the world like doth not show
Of stirring marble, fixèd snow.
When in blest you those live pearls stay
To them from him that sends you say,
As is their crystal without spot
His faith is pure, and faint will not;
And for each hair that in you is
A thousand times those joys doth kiss.

Translated out of Spanish

She whom I loved, and love shall still,
Sitting on this then blessèd sand
Wrate with to me heaven-opening hand
'First will I die ere change I will.'
O unjust force of love unjust!
That thus a man's belief should rest
On words conceived in woman's breast
And vows enrollèd in the dust.

Translated out of Seneca.

Yow vnto whome hee that rules sea and land
of lyfe and death grants the lawgiuing hand
puft vp and sullein hawty lookes forbeare
That wch from yow the meaner man doth feare
the same to yow, a greater lorde doth threate
All power is vnder heauyer power sett:
He whoe of coming day was lofty fownd
him the departing day saw on the grownd
let no man trust to much to seasons fayre
let none cast down of better tymes despayre.

In another place

So when wth out all noyse of mee
the dayes shall ouerpassed bee
a homely olde man I shall dy
On him a heauy death doth ly
whoe vnto all men to much known
vnto himself doth dy vnknown.

Translated out of Seneca

You unto whom he that rules sea and land
Of life and death grants the law-giving hand,
Puffed-up and sullen haughty looks forbear;
That which from you the meaner man doth fear
The same to you, a greater lord doth threat.
All power is under heavier power set.
He who of coming day was lofty found,
Him the departing day saw on the ground.
Let no man trust too much to seasons fair:
Let none cast down, of better times despair.

In another place

So when, without all noise, of me
The days shall overpassèd be,
A homely old man I shall die:
On him a heavy death doth lie
Who, unto all men too much known,
Unto himself doth die unknown.

Pastoral. 14.

Lycippe—Coridon.

Ly: What a change is this I see
altered so thow art as thee
I do not know?
Co: Such change haue yow often seen
in woods wch were fayre and green
and now cut low
show not to grow.

L. was thy loue so lightly sett
as some wrongs w[ch] thow hast mett
could make it dy?
C. No: but turn the springs away
how can ryuers but decay
and bare and dry
as vnknown ly

L. Tush when men themselus will change
they begin to lay the change
on them they lou'd!
C. So whome storms force to retourn
men will say theyr cours they [re]tourn
when I least mou'd
I was remou'd.

But perhaps

Pastoral 14

Lycippe. Corydon.

Lycippe What a change is this I see?
Altered so thou art as thee
I do not know.
Corydon Such change have you often seen
In woods which were fair and green
And now cut low
Show not to grow.

Lycippe Was thy love so lightly set
As some wrongs which thou hast met
Could make it die?
Corydon No: but turn the springs away
How can rivers but decay
And bare and dry
As unknown lie.

Lycippe Tush, when men themselves will change
They begin to lay the change
On them they loved!
Corydon So whom storms force to return
Men will say their course they turn:
When I least moved
I was removed.

L. But perhaps expect thow doost
greater matters then shee must
let from her pass?
C. Husbandmen no great thing moue
when they pray but that this proue
as frutfull as [the last]
the last yeare was.

L. Yet sometimes shynes in her face
that w[ch] of returning grace
a
might make the bost [? *altered to*] !
C. As a flattring winters day
[fals *altered to*] fayre and fals flowers doth desplay
w[ch] soon are lost
in next nights frost.

well
L. [when] bee constant still tyme may
what thow now thinckst gon away
againe restore!
C. waters to new currants lead
hardly come to theyr first [bead *altered to*] bedd
I yealde therfore
nor stryue will more.

Lycippe But perhaps expect thou dost
Greater matters than she must
Let from her pass?
Corydon Husbandmen no great thing move
When they pray but that this prove
As fruitful as
The last year was.

Lycippe Yet sometimes shines in her face
That which of returning grace
Might make the boast!
Corydon As a flatt'ring winter's day
Fair and false flowers doth display
Which soon are lost
In next night's frost.

Lycippe Well be constant still, time may
What thou now think'st gone away
Again restore!
Corydon Waters to new currents led
Hardly come to their first bed:
I yield therefore
Nor strive will more.

Songe. 15.

Heauen if any heauen there is
where loue[s] moues in spheares of bliss
is in yowr face.
In it loues light are beheld
from it whoe obscure is held
wth them vnder grownd hath place.

Heauen if any heauen bee fownd
where loues Angels ioies hims sownd
is in yowr voice
wth it loue sowles to him calls
from it whoe vngracious falls
[wth them vnder grownd hath place].
neuer truly can reioice.

Heauen if any heauen bee had
where loue like the Gods goes clad
is in yowr brest.
wth such whyte the Gods robes shyne
in that whyte, loues powers deuine
purely conuers wth his blest.

I alas whoe ame as farr
from them as from highest starr
the worms that creep
by theyr influence whoe liue
whoe ame by the lawes they giue
creaturlike theyr will whoe keep.

Vnto yow

Song 15

Heaven, if any heaven there is
Where love moves in spheres of bliss,
Is in your face;
In it love's lights are beheld,
From it who obscure is held
With them under ground hath place.

Heaven, if any heaven be found
Where love's angels joy's hymns sound,
Is in your voice;
With it love souls to him calls,
From it who ungracious falls
Never truly can rejoice.

Heaven, if any heaven be had
Where love like the gods goes clad,
Is in your breast;
With such white the gods' robes shine,
In that white love's powers divine
Purely converse with his blest.

I alas, who am as far
From them as from highest star
The worms that creep,
By their influence who live,
Who am by the laws they give,
Creature-like their will who keep,

Vnto yow lift vp mine eyes
on w[ch] my hart to yow flies
hart full of fyre
Fyre of Zeale, fyre of respect
w[ch] hath onely one aspect
to yowr presence to aspyre.

And thus say, the tyme may bee
when desyre shall shyne in mee
in loues lights true
when yowr iustice satisfied
wth my faith as golde pure tryed
yow will take mee vnto yow.

Unto you lift up mine eyes
On which my heart to you flies,
Heart full of fire,
Fire of zeal, fire of respect,
Which hath only one aspect—
To your presence to aspire,

And thus say: 'The time may be
When desire shall shine in me
In love's lights true;
When, your justice satisfied
With my faith as gold pure tried,
You will take me unto you.'

Elegy. 16.

Fayrest of Venus greate posteritee
what is, or what hath been, or what will bee
Charys cares of the heauens, heer speakes to you
the most vnhappy loue and the most true
as much the humblest will, and frutelest care
as yow all beawty and all chastnes are.
As many pleasures may yowr eyes attend
as showers of pearcing dartes, they frō them send
flow
and streames of blood in teares frō myne do [rū]
As many ioyfull thowghts yowr hart may know
as it doth cast on mee floods of desdaine
and my hart layde is vnder rocks of paine
As many comforts in yowr face shyne may
as thowand little loues about it play
and thowsand sorrowes trauail in my face
Neuer in yow what least is change embrace
still may yow bee yowr self, that is stil best
still in yowr own (what's fayre yowr own is) blest.
Till fownd bee of Venus posteritee
what is, or what hath been, or what will bee
A man as I so hapless and so true
or woman so fayre and so chast as yow.

Elegy 16

Fairest of Venus' great posterity,
What is, or what hath been, or what will be,
Charys, cares of the heavens: here speaks to you
The most unhappy love and the most true,
As much the humblest will, and fruitless't care,
As you all beauty and all chasteness are.
As many pleasures may your eyes attend
As showers of piercing darts they from them send
And streams of blood in tears from mine do flow:
As many joyful thoughts your heart may know
As it doth cast on me floods of disdain
And my heart laid is under rocks of pain:
As many comforts in your face shine may
As thousand little loves about it play
And thousand sorrows travail in my face:
Never in you what least is change embrace,
Still may you be yourself, that is still best,
Still in your own (what's fair your own is) blest:
Till found be of Venus' posterity,
What is, or what hath been, or what will be,
A man as I so hapless and so true
Or woman so fair and so chaste as you.

From fayrest brest, a shepheard tooke a knott
and on his head, this taking prize did sett
Thincking that of her thowghts, where faith cānot
obtaine beleef, hee had some strong band mett
But ah of loue how hidden is the lott
indeed what her brest lost, his hed did gett
  For her thowghts as vntyde, now show more free
  whyle in him captivd, sense and reason bee

~

Once to my lips my boyling hart did ryse
at heauen dew of her lips refresht to bee
when wth short sighs, swollen brest, and dazled eyes
I praied on Kiss, might press ioies wyne to mee
wth those lips where the sowle of kissing lyes
a parting kiss sayde shee, I will giue thee!
  Shee kist, I parted, parting in that kiss
  wth tast of loues ritch feast, first cup of bliss.

~

From fairest breast a shepherd took a knot
And on his head this taking prize did set,
Thinking that of her thoughts, where faith cannot
Obtain belief, he had some strong band met.
But ah, of love how hidden is the lot:
Indeed what her breast lost, his head did get,
For her thoughts as untied, now show more free,
While in him captived, sense and reason be.

Once to my lips my boiling heart did rise
At heaven-dew of her lips refreshed to be,
When with short sighs, swollen breast, and dazzled eyes,
I prayed one kiss, might press joy's wine to me.
With those lips where the soul of kissing lies
'A parting kiss,' said she, 'I will give thee!'
She kissed, I parted, parting in that kiss
With taste of love's rich feast, first cup of bliss.

I would bee blinde, when I might parfet see
and darckness finde, when I might light enioy
I would bee vexed when I might goe free
and to bee needy, would my goods destroy
I would bee sick, when I in health might bee
and would haue sorrows when I might feel ioy
  I would bee nothing that from her would bee
  who'is sight, light, rest, wealth, health, ioies, all to mee

Songe 17

The Suñ is set, and masked night
vailes heauens fayer eyes.
Ah what trust is there to a light
that so swift flyes.

A new world doth his flames enioy
New hartes reioice.
In other eyes is now his ioye
in other choice.

I would be blind, when I might perfect see,
And darkness find, when I might light enjoy,
I would be vexèd when I might go free,
And to be needy, would my goods destroy,
I would be sick, when I in health might be,
And would have sorrows when I might feel joy:
  I would be nothing that from her would be
   Who'is sight, light, rest, wealth, health, joys, all to me.

Song 17

The sun is set, and maskèd night
Veils heaven's fair eyes:
Ah what trust is there to a light
That so swift flies.

A new world doth his flames enjoy,
New hearts rejoice:
In other eyes is now his joy,
In other choice.

Song. 18

How oft sayd I, delaies are death
in wch still dijng, men do liue
for what ods is't to stop the breath
and to wth holde what doth lyfe giue

paines
Thus sense of present [ill], made not
the feare appeer of greater ill.
But importunity hath gott
denials, wch outright do kill.

Nor thowght I in denyalls lay
such vnentreatable a spell
as were not pleasd the lyfe to slay
vnless it sent the ghost to hell.

For thogh delaies did spare no smart
yet were they like, the purging fyre
throgh wch in time the faithfull hart
doth win the crown of true desyre.

But euen to hell denials cast
for what is it in hell to bee
but to see ioies for euer past
and of afflictions no end see.

Ah loue these are the glorious gaines
Faith doth ioine to thy deity
that thyne must bee not dijng paines
and no time may thy bands vnty

Song 18

How oft said I, delays are death
In which, still dying, men do live,
For what odds is't to stop the breath
And to withhold what doth life give?

Thus sense of present pains made not
The fear appear of greater ill:
But importunity hath got
Denials, which outright do kill.

Nor thought I in denials lay
Such unentreatable a spell
As were not pleased the life to slay
Unless it sent the ghost to hell.

For though delays did spare no smart,
Yet were they like the purging fire
Through which in time the faithful heart
Doth win the crown of true desire.

But even to hell denials cast,
For what is it in hell to be
But to see joys forever past
And of afflictions no end see?

Ah Love, these are the glorious gains
Faith doth join to thy deity—
That thine must be not-dying pains
And no time may thy bands untie.

Song. 19

Sun bee hencefourth from shyning parted
a greater wonder comes in sight.
loue is in mee from lyfe departed
whose time seemd surer, thē yowr light

The heauenly sweetnes wch loue formed
inspyring an eternal breath.
to hate and cruelty transformed
her own worck hath made praye to death

But what say I? loue no death trieth
it doth but pass from, hopes to paines
what's mortal in loue onely dyeth
th'immortal free from change remains.

Mortal in loue are ioye and pleasure
the fading frame, wherin loue moues
But greef and anguish are the measure
that do immortalyze owr loues.

Song 19

Sun, be henceforth from shining parted,
A greater wonder comes in sight—
Love is in me from life departed,
Whose time seemed surer than your light.

The heavenly sweetness which love formèd,
Inspiring an eternal breath,
To hate and cruelty transformèd
Her own work hath made prey to death.

But what say I? Love no death trieth,
It doth but pass from hopes to pains:
What's mortal in love only dieth,
Th'immortal free from change remains.

Mortal in love are joy and pleasure,
The fading frame wherein love moves,
But grief and anguish are the measure
That do immortalise our loves.

Song. 20

Senses by vniust force banisht
from the obiects of yowr pleasure
now of yow all end is vanisht:
yow whoe late possest more treasure
when eyes fed, on what did shyne
eares
and [eyes] dranck what was deuine
then the earths broad arms do measure

2

How haue I heauens for eyes praised
when her glories Charys showed?
what thancks for eares haue I raysed
words
heauenly flowers when her [voice] strowed
To ioy, to loue, to [admyre], desyre
wonders in hcr to admyre
nature, on mee, yow bestowed.

3

Now what are yow but confusions,
glasses to showe imperfections,
ministers to strang illusions,
organs of greefs deep infections.
whyle all I do heare and see
prisner from her brings to mee
stories full of lost perfections.

4

where then yow haue best deserued
try if owght will bee repaied.
To yowr selvs yow nowght reserued
when those deyties yow layed

Song 20

Senses by unjust force banished
From the objects of your pleasure,
Now of you all end is vanished:
You who late possessed more treasure,
When eyes fed on what did shine
And ears drank what was divine,
Than the earth's broad arms do measure.

2

How have I heavens for eyes praisèd
When her glories Charys showèd?
What thanks for ears have I raisèd
Heavenly flowers when her words strowèd?
To joy, to love, to desire,
Wonders in her to admire,
Nature on me you bestowèd.

3

Now what are you but confusions,
Glasses to show imperfections,
Ministers to strange illusions,
Organs of grief's deep infections:
While all I do hear and see
Prisoner from her, brings to me
Stories full of lost perfections.

4

Where then you have best deservèd
Try if aught will be repayèd,
To yourselves you naught reservèd
When those deities you layèd

in my reason and my harte
where since of them hath each part
as in theyr own temples staied.

5

For so in my brest I haue her
so haue yow her image traced
as like it no hands can graue her.
So throwgh yow, my thowght embraced
haue her worth, as knowledg right
of it in my reasons sight,
her fore what's calld best hath placed.

6

But how can wants bee releeued
where the help that is required
leaues the patient more agreeued.
Reason in mee neuer tyred
to consider her, doth say
that of sens not ledd astray
onely shee showld bee desyred.

7

Senses then yealde to yowr crosses.
yeald so as yow bee oppressed.
loose yowrselus in yowr greate losses
of all vse bee dispossessed.
Onely power of lyfe retaine
that yow may serue her againe
her
when [yo] presence makes yow blessed.

In my reason and my heart,
Where since of them hath each part
As in their own temples stayèd.

5

For so in my breast I have her,
So have you her image tracèd,
As like it no hands can grave her:
So through you my thought embracèd
Have her worth, as knowledge right
Of it in my reason's sight,
Her 'fore what's called best hath placèd.

6

But how can wants be relievèd
Where the help that is requirèd
Leaves the patient more aggrievèd?
Reason in me never tirèd
To consider her, doth say
That of sense not led astray
Only she should be desirèd.

7

Senses then yield to your crosses,
Yield so as you be oppressèd;
Lose yourselves in your great losses,
Of all use be dispossessèd:
Only power of life retain
That you may serve her again
When her presence makes you blessèd.

Song. 21

So did the morning crymson ryse
when Charys rosy cheekes it tooke.
So did the heauenly Charys looke
as when redd morning paints the skyes

So did the Moon the starres pryde marr
when shee had borrowed Charys light
So fayrest showed in Charys sight
as to the full moon smallest starr

Grace onely is what's Charys grace
No whyte but what her brest whyte tryes
The Sun shynes when hee is like her eyes
and fayre is that, that's like her face.

[O *overwritten*] Fayr heauens how are yow thus fayre still
and let her from yow somuch take
No yow of her a body make
when as among men walck yow will.

O that I onely eyes might bee
or that I onely hart might proue
that all I ame might Charys loue
and all I ame might Charys see

Song 21

So did the morning crimson rise
When Charys' rosy cheeks it took:
So did the heavenly Charys look
As when red morning paints the skies.

So did the moon the stars' pride mar
When she had borrowed Charys' light:
So fairest showed in Charys' sight
As to the full moon smallest star.

Grace only is what's Charys' grace,
No white but what her breast white tries,
The sun shines when he'is like her eyes,
And fair is that, that's like her face.

Fair heavens, how are you thus fair still
And let her from you so much take?
No, you of her a body make
When as among men walk you will.

O that I only eyes might be,
Or that I only heart might prove,
That all I am might Charys love
And all I am might Charys see.

Song. 22

But alas why do yow nowrish
poisnous weeds of colde despayre
in loues garden where would flourish
by hopes ritch soile, ioies sweet ayre
plants of hott zeale, trees of true faith
fast in there rootes, prowd in theyr haigth

2

Fertil is my sowle of louing
yeelding thowsand folde for one
But (as yow will) seasons prouing
yow heauens equal, whoe alone
loues summer are, heate, spring and showers
powers of first blowing, ripening powers.

3

Do yow hold it then a pleasure
to see yowrs to desert grown?
Meane yow to encreas yowr treasure
by wast leauing what's yowr own
Thinck yow, yow yowrs do not enioy
Vnless yow do it quite destroy.

4

Ah but that so nigh it lyeth
to my hart, scarse showld I know
mine own [loue] loue, so in it dyeth
what sweet was, and sower doth grow
Nettles of greef, bryars of care
where flowers of hope late were, now are.

The long

Song 22

But alas why do you nourish
Poisonous weeds of cold despair
In love's garden, where would flourish
By hope's rich soil, joy's sweet air,
Plants of hot zeal, trees of true faith,
Fast in their roots, proud in their heighth.

2

Fertile is my soul of loving
Yielding thousandfold for one,
But (as you will) seasons proving,
You heaven's equal, who alone
Love's summer are, heat, spring and showers,
Powers of first blowing, ripening powers.

3

Do you hold it then a pleasure
To see yours to desert grown?
Mean you to increase your treasure
By waste leaving what's your own?
Think you, you yours do not enjoy
Unless you do it quite destroy?

4

Ah but that so nigh it lieth
To my heart, scarce should I know
Mine own love, so in it dieth
What sweet was, and sour doth grow:
Nettles of grief, briars of care,
Where flowers of hope late were, now are.

5

The long fluds of yowr denijng
bring fourth store of what anoies
The heate of yowr hate still frijng
burns vp euen the root of ioies.
I choackt or staru'd, one choice haue stil
of blasted good, or growing ill.

6

But as when lands are forsaken
best they do theyr nature showe.
From my loue can not bee taken
what not in good place doth growe
The weeds w[ch] on my loue are fownd
are but in best conditiond grownd.

7

True deuotion far neglected
faith long tryed, yet not beleeued
smokes of burning hart reiected
praiers despised from a sowl greeued
The weeds are whence despayre doth grow
w[ch] in my loue yowr scorns do sowe

8

Fayrest eyes vnmatched glories
in whome worlds of ioies do moue
reade heer the still present stories
of yowr beawty, and my loue.
Beawty and loue, w[ch] onely true
wretch are in mee, and in blest yow.

5

The long floods of your denying
Bring forth store of what annoys,
The heat of your hate still frying
Burns up even the root of joys:
I choked or starved, one choice have still,
Of blasted good, or growing ill.

6

But as when lands are forsaken
Best they do their nature show,
From my love cannot be taken
What not in good place doth grow:
The weeds which on my love are found
Are but in best conditioned ground.

7

True devotion far neglected,
Faith long tried, yet not believed,
Smokes of burning heart rejected,
Prayers despised from a soul grieved,
The weeds are, whence despair doth grow,
Which in my love your scorns do sow.

8

Fairest eyes, unmatchèd glories,
In whom worlds of joys do move,
Read here the still present stories
Of your beauty, and my love:
Beauty and love, which only true
Wretch are in me, and in blest you.

Song. 23

Greefs sent from her whome in my sowle I bless
careful performers of her fierce desdaine
welcome to mee: receaue all, all possess.
there is no paine
wherwth I ame
not pleasd that comes, wth warrant of her name

Take on the face and force of all the ill
that euer louer felt, yow shall not finde
any resistance, since it is her will
in a sad minde
whose glory is
in greatest greefs that it no greef doth miss.

No meritt lookt vpon, no praier obtaind
no vowe accepted of, no loss restored
no hope auowed, no care nor feare restraind
wth yow thus stored
from paines I raise
not suffrance onely of her lawes, but prayse

yet this one ioy, will euer wth mee rest
do sorrows what yow can, that I do vaunt
I suffer for the fayrest and the best
that shee must graunt
and truth infers
yow could not gouern mee were I not hers.

For w^{ch}

Song 23

Griefs sent from her whom in my soul I bless,
Careful performers of her fierce disdain,
Welcome to me: receive all, all possess.
There is no pain
Wherewith I am
Not pleased, that comes with warrant of her name.

Take on the face and force of all the ill
That ever lover felt, you shall not find
Any resistance, since it is her will,
In a sad mind
Whose glory is
In greatest griefs that it no grief doth miss.

No merit looked upon, no prayer obtained,
No vow accepted of, no loss restored,
No hope avowed, no care nor fear restrained,
With you thus stored
From pains I raise
Not sufferance only of her laws, but praise.

Yet this one joy will ever with me rest
Do sorrows what you can, that I do vaunt
I suffer for the fairest and the best:
That she must grant,
And truth infers
You could not govern me were I not hers.

For wch another greef I will afforde
greef for her not for mee, that shee doth make
kindnes her scourg, obedience her sworde
wherwth to take
his lyfe that loues
whoe pitty not wth teares, but wth ioy moues

~

For which another grief I will afford,
Grief for her not for me, that she doth make
Kindness her scourge, obedience her sword,
Wherewith to take
His life that loves,
Who pity not with tears, but with joy moves.

Absence I fled to thee
as to a quiet shore
where I my barck from tempests free might thinck
But thow dost not helpe mee
already brused sore
and whoe leakes wth mee bring, wch make me sinck

Absence I fled to thee
as to a healthful shade
sun
from those [sun] beames, in wch my lyfe did fry
But thow dost not helpe mee
already in whome made
the feauer is, in wch consumd I ly

Then showld I thee haue known
when fond vnfortunat
my force against the conqueror I tryde
Now wounded ouerthrown
thy armour comes to late
to warde the arrowes wch haue pearst my syde

I will then back againe
where that high beawty liues
wch him, whoe in it ioies, wth sorrow Kils
And this ods is in paine
presence the green wounds giues:
Absence vncured sores, wth vlcers fils.

There shall

Song 24

Absence, I fled to thee
As to a quiet shore
Where I my bark from tempests free might think:
But thou dost not help me
Already bruisèd sore
And who leaks with me bring which make me sink.

Absence, I fled to thee
As to a healthful shade
From those sunbeams in which my life did fry:
But thou dost not help me
Already in whom made
The fever is in which consumed I lie.

Then should I thee have known
When (fond unfortunate)
My force against the conqueror I tried:
Now wounded, overthrown,
Thy armour comes too late
To ward the arrows which have pierced my side.

I will then back again
Where that high beauty lives
Which him, who in it joys, with sorrow kills:
And this odds is in pain—
Presence the green wounds gives,
Absence uncurèd sores with ulcers fills.

There shall I feel the heate
of pryde, and scorn and hate
as heer the coles of greef, and foild desyres
But where the sun rayes beate
the fyres strength doth abate
and greefs less burn, in sight of beawties fyres

And if that dy I must
fayrer on sworde to fall
of Tyrant eyes, then pined in fetters sterue
and when the time vniust
my lyfes light put owt shall
hate of
Shee of [fait] faith I, shall name deserue

There shall I feel the heat
Of pride and scorn and hate
As here the coals of grief, and foiled desires:
But where the sun rays beat
The fire's strength doth abate
And griefs less burn, in sight of beauty's fires.

And if that die I must
Fairer on sword to fall
Of tyrant eyes, than pined in fetters starve:
And when the time unjust
My life's light put out shall
She of hate, of faith I, shall name deserve.

COMMENTARY

Poems by Philip are identified by the abbreviations used in *The Poems of Sir Philip Sidney*, ed. William A. Ringler, Jr. (Oxford, 1962), as follows:

AS *Astrophil and Stella* (Sonnets 1–108 and Songs i–xi)
CS *Certain Sonnets* (1–32)
OA *Old Arcadia* poems (1–77)
OP Other Poems (1–7)
PP Poems Possibly by Philip (1–5)
PS Psalms (1–43)

In citing prose from the *Arcadia*, page references are given to *The Countess of Pembroke's Arcadia* (*The Old Arcadia*), ed. Jean Robertson (Oxford, 1973).

Quotations from Ficino's Latin Commentary on the *Symposium* are identified in each case by *Oratio* and *Caput*.

SONNET 1

Greville's *Caelica* iv starts from the same comparison and develops it in a way which suggests that Greville's first stanza may echo this sonnet. See Appendix B.

2 cf. Sonnet 13: 12–13.

8, 11 For the bringing together in the same sonnet of monosyllabic *heaven* and disyllabic *heaven's*, cf. Spenser's *Amoretti* lxxii (6, 8, 11, 14) and Shakespeare's Sonnet 21 (3, 8, 12). See also p. 23.

SONG 1

For the personal background to this poem, see pp. 79–80.

9 Robert himself spells the possessive singular either *liues* or *lifes* indifferently: cf. Song 6: 52 (*my lifes treasure*), 110 (*his liues delights*), Sonnet 22: 6 (*my lifes delight*).

21 cf. *Arcadia*, Book V (Robertson, p. 416) 'Gynecia (who, poor lady, thought she was leading forth to her living burial)'.

See p. 80 for the affinity of Song 1's imagery with that of Song 6.

25–6 Rowland Whyte addressed Robert in very similar terms (10 Mar. 1597/8): '. . . for from you and by you I breath and liue. . . . You haue bred me, and inabled me to serue you.' The comparison nicely illustrates how the courtly lover's service was closely modelled on the service which a feudal vassal owed his lord (cf. C. S. Lewis, *The Allegory of Love*, p. 2).

32 cf. AS ix: 50 'Her poor slave's unjust decaying'.

SONNET 2

9–12 cf. Spenser, *Amoretti* lxi: 13–14

> Such heavenly forms ought rather worshipt be,
> Than dare be loved by men of mean degree.

SONNET 3

6 *divinesse* divinity, divineness (see OED). Cf. Sonnet 16: 3.

10, 12 *devotions/perfections* See p. 21 for the pronunciation required by metre and rhyme here.

14 See p. 39 for the line by Ralegh which probably suggested this.

Robert addressed the Earl of Essex in very similar terms (12 Sept. 1596): 'I loue your Lordship for yowrself and for yowr vertues and whatsoeuer good fortunes may kome vnto me by yt shall bee but as accidents vnto yt.' See note on Song 1: 25–6.

SONNET 4

The idea behind this sonnet may be discerned in a sentence of the *Arcadia*, Book III (Robertson, p. 177): 'This is my hymn to you. . . . The temple wherein it is daily sung is my soul, and the sacrifice I offer to you withal is all whatsoever I am.' Cf. also Michael Drayton's sonnet *To the Vestals* (first published in 1599).

2 *assured by destiny* The first reference to the idea that the poet's love is predestined, an idea which provides the theme of Sonnets 12–14 (= Sonnets 2–4 of the unfinished Crown).

4 *which are what I am* a favourite Sidneian expression: cf., for example, CS 25: 34 'All what I am, it is you'.

Robert addressed the Earl of Essex more than once in very similar terms: e.g. (31 May 1597) 'For what I ame, is wholy yowrs'. See notes to Song 1: 25–6 and Sonnet 3: 14.

PASTORAL 2

For the structure of this dialogue poem see p. 29. This is the only poem of Robert's sequence where the lover addresses his beloved as *thou* (cf. head-note to Pastoral 8).

15–20 This imagery recalls OA 17 'My sheep are thoughts . . . What wool my sheep shall bear, while thus they live, In you it is, you must the judgement give'.

17 *thy care* i.e. my concern for thee (with play on Latin *carus* = dear). Cf. Shakespeare's Sonnet 48: 7 'Thou best of dearest, and mine only care'.

41 *What's past* = *all the time I loved not thee* (37).

42 *what will be* = *what remains* (39).

SONG 3

This poem introduces into the sequence the theme of the beloved's desertion, and the Winter imagery which becomes the dominant symbol of the lover's deserted condition.

That this poem directly parodies the *Pervigilium Veneris* is made clear to the informed reader at the start in the two unrhymed lines which subsequently recur as a refrain: these lines are not only an inverted verbal echo of the *Pervigilium Veneris*, they also echo its 'trochaic catalectic' metre. See p. 32.

9 *Divorced . . . marry* This imagery, unparalleled in Robert's sequence, is an inverted echo of that which runs through the *Pervigilium Veneris*: cf. 'vere nubunt alites, Et nemus comam resolvit de maritis imbribus . . . Cras erit cum primus aether copulavit nuptias', etc.

24–6 cf. Song 10: 41–2 and see p. 119.

45 cf. OP 5: 108 'To hit, but kissing hit'.

63 The comma shows that *once* is here to be taken with what follows and has the force *once for all*: cf. Robert to the Earl of Essex (22 Oct. 1596) 'I would once that the Queen for matters of warr would repose all care vpon your Lordship'.

There is probably calculated effect in the way *once* occurs in lines 58, 63, and 65, the sense being varied each time.

SONNET 6

Although the theme is touched on at Sonnet 3: 3–4, this is the first 'night' poem in the sequence. The poet's 'inward night' is the essential subject, and the theme reappears in Sonnets 20 and 22. Cf. AS 96–99.

12–14 cf. Samuel Daniel's *Delia* (1592), Sonnet xvi: 9–10

> But still the Hydra of my cares renewing
> Revives new sorrows of her fresh disdaining.

SONNET 7

Sonnets 6 and 7 face each other in the notebook, and are the only two sonnets whose sestets are undivided in layout (see p. 18). The conjunction of *scorn* and *repulse* in both (Sonnet 6: 12–13, Sonnet 7: 5 and 12) constitutes a verbal link.

SONNET 8

6 cf. Pastoral 14: 41–2 and Greville's *Caelica* lxxv: 201–2 'Feeling he had of his woe, Yet did love his overthrow'.

7 *idol* image or likeness: cf. Spenser, *Amoretti* xxvii

> Fair proud now tell me why should fair be proud . . .
> That goodly Idol now so gay beseen,
> Shall doff her flesh's borrowed fair attire

—but where Spenser's theme is the transience of mortal beauty, Robert perceives in his beloved's beauty the Platonic *truth* (essence, reality) of the beauty which is beyond change.

SONNET 9

The imagery of returning *home* into oneself as a refuge or *rest* from the pains of love is echoed in Sonnet 29.

9 *my proud will* immediately abandoned its pride and knelt in prayer to the beloved. Cf. *Hamlet* III. iii. 70 'Bow, stubborn knees'.

12 *than erst* than in my former loves.

12-14 Behind these lines is the notion of fire as a purifying element which consumes the baser elements of physical desire.

SONG 4

For the metre of this poem see pp. 32-4.

4-6 cf. Greville's *Caelica* iv: 15-16 'For I have vowed in strangest fashion, To love, and never seek compassion'.

16-18 cf. Ficino II. ii 'unus quidam continuus astractus est a deo incipiens, transiens in mundum, in deum denique desinens, qui quasi circulo quodam in idem unde manavit iterum remeat'.

52-4 cf. CS 24: 26-7

> For if those flames burn my desire,
> Yet shall I die in Phoenix fire.

SONNET 10

4 The qualities here enumerated are reflected back in the succeeding lines: *joy and love* in line 6, *grace* is echoed in the *blessèd words* of line 7, *beauty* in line 8, *sweetness* is evoked by lines 9-10.

9-10 cf. Song 12: 5.

A CROWN OF SONNETS, BUT UNFINISHED

For the symbolic significance of this abortive Crown, see pp. 26-7 and 112.

SONNET 12

1–4 These lines echo two poems by Philip, OA 47: 13–14

> My heart my word, my word hath given my heart.
> The giver given from gift shall never part

and PP 3: 1

> Who gives himself may well his picture give.

2 cf. Sonnet 29: 12 for the *words/word* verbal play.

Robert addressed the Earl of Essex in very similar terms (6 Nov. 1595): 'But such as I ame, I haue of long giuen myself vnto yow.' See note on Sonnet 3: 14.

5–8 i.e. Predestination and Free Will are reconciled in the poet's love. Cf. CS 17: 9 'I, whom free choice slave doth make'. Cf. also the phrase *choice or destiny* in Sonnet 32: 1.

10–11 *upon the day Sacred to you* because on that day was born your predestined lover. See pp. 91–2.

12 *since* balances *ere* in line 9.

13 *fatal* decreed by fate, predestined.

13–14 i.e. until I can fulfil my destiny by sealing with my death a life wholly devoted to your service.

SONNET 13

7 i.e. it is only reasonable to forgive faults which are predestined (hence inescapable).

12–14 cf. Sonnet 1: 1–2 and Spenser's *Hymne in Honour of Beautie*: 197–8.

> For Love is a celestial harmony
> Of likely hearts composed of stars' consent.

SONNET 14

1–3 i.e. your matchless worth may assure your judgement that you are the proper object of so great a love.

9–11 cf. Ficino II. ii 'Ibi amantium ardor quiescit, nec extinguitur sed impletur.'

SONG 5

It will assist the modern reader to understand this poem if he remembers that religious persecution was a familiar reality in the sixteenth century. (See p. 68.)

3–4 The switch within these lines from the present to the past tense is significant: *eyes* must always *admire* ('Lucem illam corporis . . . oculus percipit' Ficino II. ix) but the outward devotion of *hands, lips*, and *knees* has been suppressed.

14 *truth of beauty* cf. Sonnet 8: 9 and note to line 7 of that sonnet.

SONG 6

In its form and phrasing this Song evokes the popular ballad of 'Walsingham', the original words of which are mostly lost (see pp. 35-7). The tune, however, survives in various early settings and Robert's words can be effectively sung to it:

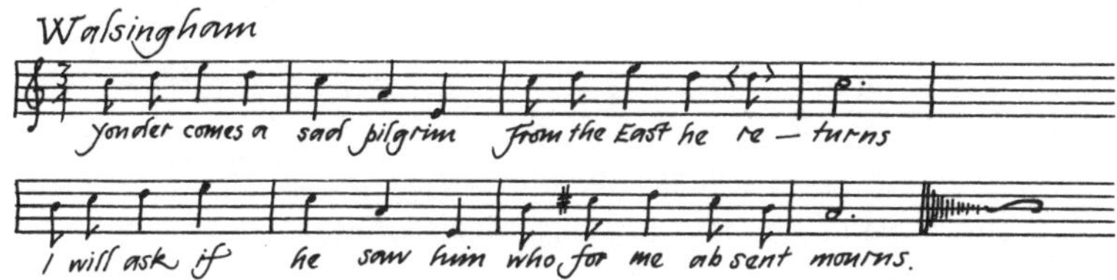

For the personal background to Robert's poem, its unique role within the sequence, and for the comparison it implicitly invites with AS viii—a comparison which brings out both important resemblances and important differences—see Introduction, *passim.*

2 *from the East* when taken in conjunction with the clues contained in lines 17, 65, 69, and 73-4, this intimates that Penshurst is the scene of the imagined meeting between Lady and Pilgrim, and Flushing the scene of the Knight's imagined death whence the Pilgrim is returning.

9-12 cf. lines 5-8 of the 'Ralegh' version of the popular ballad:

> How should I know your true love
> That have met many one
> As I came from that holy land
> That have come, that have gone.

16 cf. AS 70: 7 'Grief but Love's winter livery is'.

21 cf. line 13 of the 'Ralegh' version

> Such an one did I meet good Sir

and note *good Sir* in place of the *lady* who appears both in Robert's version and in the version recalled by Ophelia (see p. 36).

33-4 cf. Ficino II. viii 'Quotiens duo aliqui mutua se benivolentia complectuntur, iste in illo, ille in isto vivit'. Also OP 3: 1-2

> His being was in her alone,
> And he not being, she was none.

69 *On a sand hill* evokes the sand dunes of the coast near Flushing.

74 *Near Medway's sandy bed* the only non-fictitious proper name

anywhere in Robert's verse and, in the context, an unmistakable allusion to Penshurst: the *lady* is thus identified as Barbar. See p. 79.

76 The Knight always speaks of himself as already dead—cf. lines 92, 95, 97–100. See pp. 47 and 80.

79–80 See p. 12 for the *feign/true* antithesis (found in a complementary sense at Song 1: 35–6, i.e. applied not to the lady's worth but to the poet's love).

95 *what I am* cf. Sonnet 4: 4 and note.

99–100 cf. Spenser, *Amoretti* viii: 13 'Dark is the world, where your light shinèd never'.

109 *They* i.e. those things which she enumerates in the succeeding stanzas, her *arms* (113–16), her *hair* (117–20), her *eyes* (121–4), her *lips* (125–8).

129–32 cf. Henry Constable, *Diana* (1594), The fourth Decad, Sonnet v: 11–12

> Would God that I might hear my last bell toll,
> So in your bosom I might dig my grave.

133 This distilled expression of mutual love may echo Catullus xlv: 20 'mutuis animis amant amantur'.

136 This line implicitly evokes and finally answers line 97.

SONNET 15

5 *No weak or foe or force* i.e. the united force of *virtue, fortune, skill* described as *foe* to the victorious beloved because of their vain attempt to defend him from submitting to the fate of loving her.

PASTORAL 7

See pp. 90–1 for the significance of *Lysa* and *Rosis*, and for the connection between this poem and Sonnet 28. It is probably no accident that this, the only poem where Robert himself figures under a transparent pastoral persona, should be the central poem of the diversified series in the sequence as originally conceived (i.e. the sequence which concluded with Sonnet 35, wherein the diversified series concluded with Song 13). A wryly humorous tone, especially to be recognized in the third stanza, distinguishes the poem (other touches of humour or irony within the sequence may be discerned in Pastorals 2 and 8 and in Sonnet 25).

7 This poem contains the only occurrence of *lad* in Robert's verse and was evidently prompted by OP 5: 1 'The lad Philisides'.

10–11 cf. OP 4: 453 'Proudly bedecked in April's livery'.

18 The shepherd lad takes advantage of the embrace primarily to gratify his sense of sight (see p. 58).

25–30 cf. Spenser, *Amoretti* xxx: 1–6

My love is like to ice, and I to fire;
How comes it then that this her cold so great
Is not dissolved through my so hot desire,
But harder grows the more I her intreat?
Or how comes it that my exceeding heat
Is not delayed by her heart frozen cold. . . .

SONNET 16

This is the first of a widely spaced series of three reproachful sonnets, culminating in Sonnet 29 with direct reproach of the beloved (see p. 96).

2 cf. Ficino V. v 'cum in illo perspicue divini decoris scintilla refulget'.

3 *divinesse* cf. Sonnet 3: 6 and note.

4 *vows and prayers* a favourite expression with Robert in his correspondence though usually with the nouns reversed, e.g. Robert to Essex (6 June 1597) 'I wil follow yow with my best praiers and vowes, the onely arms which hetherunto I haue bin able to serue you withall.'

8 *love and rage* cf. Ficino I. iv 'appetitio vero, quae reliquos sequitur sensus, non amor sed libido rabiesque vocatur'.

SONNET 17

1 *endless* almost certainly echoes AS 97: 6 'endlessly despairing of his grace'.

7–11 This sailing imagery is closely related to a passage in a letter to the Earl of Essex (9 Jan. 1596/7) wherein Robert describes the political frustrations of his position as Governor of Flushing: see p. 98.

Cf. also Spenser, *Amoretti* lxiii

After long storms and tempest's sad assay,
Which hardly I endurèd heretofore,
In dread of death and dangerous dismay
With which my silly bark was tossèd sore,
I do at length descry the happy shore
In which I hope ere long for to arrive . . .

—but while Spenser confidently expects to arrive, Robert knows that in his case any such hope must be a delusion.

13 cf. CS 19: 17 'I yield and strive, I kiss and curse the pain'.

14 *nor end with joys nor end from cares* echoes the opening *endless* and thus gives the whole sonnet an appropriately circular movement (see p. 26).

PASTORAL 8

For the internal structure of this poem see p. 30, and for its relationship with Pastoral 9 see p. 109. The Nymph here always addresses the Shepherd as *thou* while he always addresses her as *you* (compare and contrast Pastoral 2).

3 *with comfort greet* in this phrase *greet* is the Kentish form of *great*: for the use of a single dialect form to add a touch of bucolic colour cf. the refrain 'hey ho chill [= I'll] love no more' of the poem 'Though Amaryllis dance in green' from William Byrd's *Psalmes, Sonets and Songs* (1588).

21–4 In these lines the masculine *Sun* represents the Nymph and the feminine *earth* represents the Shepherd: see pp. 44–5 for the characteristic Neoplatonic indifference to the anomaly involved.

27–8 The same image recurs several times (see Pastoral 9: 30, Sonnet 31: 9–10, Song 22: 25–6) and probably contains a memory of the water meadows at Penshurst which the 'high swoln Medway' floods each year.

36 cf. AS 46: 7–8. See pp. 55–6 for the Neoplatonic source and the different responses of the two brothers thereto.

41 *that by which I am* cf. Sonnet 4: 4 and note.

45–6 Note how easily the *Moon*—in her capacity as 'governess of floods'—is for the moment equated with the beloved, though the *Sun* is the dominant symbol for her in this poem as throughout the sequence: in lines 9–12 the inferior power of *Moon* and *stars* is implicitly contrasted with the sun-beloved who alone is able to renew the year and to give day.

48 *I cold and dark* echoes line 12 and again implies that the Shepherd is deprived of his sun.

SONNET 18

This sonnet, where the poet-lover takes pleasure in his helpless enslavement, is directly followed by a sonnet where he is bitter about that same enslavement ('Unstaid and skittish in all motions else Save in the constant image of the creature That is beloved': see pp. 106–8).

4 The poet wears the emblem of victory in celebration of his defeat by the beloved.

SONNET 19

9 *Chained to those beauties* as the galley-slave is chained to his oar. For the significance of the plural *beauties* see note to Sonnet 27: 9.

SONNET 20

This 'full Allegorie' (see p. 44) is an expansion of a theme suggested by AS 88: 6 'When Sun is hid, can stars such beams display?'

1 *these eyes* which (as the next line makes clear) have never been blessed with the sight of the poet's beloved.

4 cf. Henry Constable, *Diana* (1592), Last sonnet: 7

Which praise to you, and joy should be to me.

5-8 cf. AS 97: 5-8

But ah, poor Night, in love with Phoebus' light,
And endlessly despairing of his grace,
Herself (to show no other joy hath place)
Silent and sad in mourning weeds doth dight.

10 *store* plenty, abundance: cf. Robert to the Earl of Essex (6 June 1597) 'I wil eate with them which haue store'.

11 *ere long* the beloved is either asleep and he expects her awakening, or she is temporarily absent and he expects her return.

13-14 cf. OA 51: 14

Till her eyes shine, I live in darkest night.

SONNET 21

This is the only sonnet of Robert's sequence to use the stock situation of the lover addressing an unsympathizing friend: cf. AS 14: 1 'Alas have I not pain enough, my friend'. Compare and contrast Sonnet 24.

For the political background to this sonnet see pp. 98-9.

6 Matthew 23: 27 'For ye are like unto whited sepulchres . . . within full of dead men's bones and of all uncleanness.'

SONNET 22

The first of three consecutive sonnets whose opening quatrains all evoke a shore and a storm-beaten mariner: see pp. 100-1.

This is Robert's only poem on the stock theme of the 'missed meeting': see pp. 80-1 for the possible association of Barbara with the situation here portrayed.

5-8 He is shortly to depart from the beloved and, having been blessed hitherto only with the sight of her, he now hopes that his hearing also is about to be blessed with the sound of her voice. See p. 58.

9 *condition* metre and rhyme show that the *ion* termination has here its full disyllabic value (see p. 21).

12-14 For this fusion of outer and inner darkness cf. AS 96-9, especially AS 98: 9-10

While the black horrors of the silent night
Paint woe's black face so lively to my sight.

SONNET 23

The first in a series of three widely spaced poems addressed to Absence: see p. 110. For the reflections of all three in Greville's *Caelica* xlv, see Appendix B.

3–4 This imagery of shore and tempest-tossed bark is echoed at Song 24: 1–6.

5 *fettered* cf. Robert to Essex from Flushing (6 June 1597) 'For neuer yet since I was a Captein vnder yow . . . haue I bin so happy to see yow in the feeld, which I onely attribute to the fetters which this place doth ty me in.' The same association of *fetters* with Absence occurs at Song 24: 33.

7–8 evokes the proverb 'The remedy is worse than the disease'.

8 *grief* is likewise associated with Absence at Song 24: 27.

14 *pain* is likewise associated with Presence at Song 24: 22.

SONNET 24

The person addressed here is manifestly not the unsympathizing friend addressed in Sonnet 21, but a man whose experience is paralleled with the poet-lover's own experience: for the identification of this man as Sir Walter Ralegh, see pp. 99–100.

1, 3 *thou* as distinct from *you* in Sonnet 21.

2 *bitter storms* cf. Ralegh's narrative of his Guiana voyage 'when we were arrived at the sea side then grew our greatest doubt, and the bitterest of all our iourney forepassed . . . for the same night . . . there arose a mighty storme'.

5–8 See p. 101 for the passage from Robert's letter to Essex of 28 Mar. 1597 disclosing the reality behind these lines.

SONNET 25

For the meaning of this sonnet, which depends for its proper understanding on a knowledge of the Neoplatonism expounded by Ficino, see pp. 58–60.

Note the changes of pace, reflected in the punctuation or lack thereof, from the first quatrain to the rapid second quatrain to the measured articulation of the third quatrain.

2, 6, 7 See p. 21 for these trisyllabic rhymes.

SONNET 26

This sonnet probably reflects both a passage in Philip Sidney's *Arcadia* and the physical reality of his last illness: see pp. 45–6.

6 Robert's deletions here suggest that this line stood in the draft *whose loss of part ransom of rest must bee.*

10 cf. Ficino II. viii 'tibi propinquior quam mihi sum'.

PASTORAL 9

For the correlative structure of this poem, cf. CS 18 and OP 5.

The poem as originally entered in Robert's notebook was complete in four stanzas: the fifth stanza introduces into the sequence the theme of the lover's rejection of his bondage. See pp. 15-16.

The first two stanzas contain what seem clear verbal echoes of Samuel Daniel, *Delia* (1592), Sonnet xxxiiii: 1-4

> When winter snows upon thy golden hairs
> And frost of age hath nipped thy flowers near:
> When dark shall seem thy day that never clears,
> And all lies withered that was held so dear

—but where Daniel's theme is the transience of the beloved's beauty, Robert's Shepherd applies the same imagery to the transience of the beloved's affections and equates her beauty with the permanent *frame* of the world which contains vicissitude within itself.

25-30 Robert did not use initial capitals for any of the nouns in these lines at the first writing, but later changed *fyre* to *Fyre*, etc.

30 See note on Pastoral 8: 27-8.

33 The absolute construction here recalls Philip, e.g. OP 5: 114-15 'This said, at length he ended His oft sigh-broken ditty'.

42, 47 The mention of *faults* and *sin* in these two lines links this poem with Sonnet 29 (lines 4, 9), the most intense expression of personal bitterness in the Sonnet series.

43-4 The *good dolphin* who *stayed the sea's deep jaws, the saving thread* which *the maze unwound*, come respectively from the story of Arion and the story of Theseus and Ariadne.

48 In its form this final line closely echoes AS 87: 14

> I had been vexed, if vexed I had not been

but in its essence Robert's line is more akin to the classical 'periissem nisi periissem'. (Cf. Richard Simpson, *Moral Considerations touching the Duty of Contentedness* (1686), p. 77 'Thus once a noble Heathen, after he had experienced the great Advantage his Banishment gave him, as to his Temporal Preferment, cryed out *Periissem, ni periissem*'—a reference I owe to the kindness of Professor Nancy Brown.) In a Christian society, the saying naturally acquired a spiritual meaning (it was, for example, adopted as a motto by the Anstruther family).

SONG 10

See p. 31 for the metre of this poem.

The theme of the lover's rejection of his bondage was introduced in the last two stanzas of the previous poem and is continued here, but Song 10's buoyant cynicism—after the ideal vision of its opening stanza—is in marked contrast to the tone of the previous poem.

1–6 cf. Ficino II. ii 'Amor igitur in voluptatem a pulchritudine desinit. Id sibi voluit Hierothei et Dionysii Aeropagitae hymnus ille praeclarus, ubi sic hi theologi cecinerunt: *Amor circulus est bonus a bono in bonum perpetuo revolutus*.'

7 recalls the proverb 'Hoist your sail when the wind is fair'.

11–12 see p. 65 and cf. Greville, *Caelica* vii: 3 'Nature, the queen of change, to change is loving'.

14 cf. Samuel Daniel, *Delia* (1592), Sonnet xxxvii: 9–11

> Why then though Delia fade let that not move her
> Though time do spoil her of the fairest veil
> That ever yet mortality did cover

but Robert's evocation of these lines brings out an important difference, for where Daniel perceives the mortal body under the outward beauty Robert perceives the immortal spirit.

21 *rage* cf. Sonnet 16: 8 and note.

25–8 i.e. happy are they who (1) have not loved, or (2) have not remained near their lost loves, or (3) have not become amorously entangled elsewhere since their departure hence.

39 This evokes the emblem of Fortune as a woman balancing a wheel on her hand and standing on a globe. (The sixteenth-century Antwerp printer Jean Richard used this traditional representation as his device with the motto *Fortuna rotat omne fatum*.)

41–2 See p. 119 and cf. Song 3: 24–6.

SONNET 27

This is the second in the series of three 'reproachful' sonnets beginning with self-reproach (Sonnet 16) and ending in direct reproach of the beloved (Sonnet 29). This middle sonnet reproaches neither himself nor her but Falsehood (see p. 96). For the link between this sonnet and the disappointments Robert experienced in his public career, see p. 97.

9 *beauties* the beloved's beauties (enumerated at Sonnet 6: 2 as her *face*, her *eyes*, her *voice*, her *hands*, her *breast*). The singular *mind* (line 10) shows that all the *beauties* belong to one woman.

12–13 recalls Luke 10: 7 'for the labourer is worthy of his hire'.

14 *my sickness state* referring back to *lazar-like* (line 2).

SONNET 28

This evocation of springtime fragrance is inserted between two 'poisonous' sonnets on the beloved's treachery. This sonnet has a special role as the only poem in the sequence which concentrates its appeal on the lower triad of senses and is thus the exception which confirms the rule that beauty is revealed only to sight and hearing (see p. 111). For an assessment of the unusually extensive revisions, see pp. 14–15.

8 *Lysa's* revised to *Charys'*—see pp. 90–1 for the significance of this and for the link with Pastoral 7 (the only other poem in the sequence effectively to acknowledge the lower senses).

10 *fairness* replaces *sweetnes* in the notebook and is itself written directly on top of an earlier replacement, or attempted replacement, which I have failed to decipher. In this tangle of revision the deleted original reading is all that remains clearly legible, but *fairness* seems to represent Robert's final intention and deliberately to echo *fair* in the previous line. For the association with *cherries* cf. the street cry which begins Herrick's lyric 'Cherry-ripe, ripe, ripe, I cry, Full and fair ones; come and buy'.

14 *nectar* cf. Sonnet 10: 9.

SONNET 29

The culmination of the series of three 'reproachful' sonnets (see headnote to Sonnet 27).

3–4 cf. Samuel Daniel, *Delia* (1592), Sonnet xv: 14 'The fault is hers, though mine the hurt must be'.

5–8 See pp. 97–8 for the real-life background and for Robert's letter to his wife (20 Mar. 1597) containing essentially the same self-counsel. The same advice can be recognized again in one of Robert's annotations in his copy of Tacitus: 'Many men who haue come into disgrace and danger also haue escaped with shewing themselus quiet in theyr misfortune: wheras if they had giuen any token of discontentment would doutlesly haue browght themselus to an extremity.' (*Cornelii Taciti Opera quae exstant*, Antwerp, 1585, p. 64, annotating the passage in the text about Pomponius who 'dum adversam fortunam aequus tolerat, Tiberio superstes fuit'. The copy in question contains Robert's autograph motto *Fata viam inuenient*, signature and date 20 *Jan*: 1585: it is now British Library, C 142. e. 13).

7 evokes the proverb 'Past cure, past care'.

12 cf. Sonnet 12: 2 for the verbal play.

SONG 11

6 The correction suggests that this line stood in the draft *who will not now content me.*

23–4 The implication that the beloved is legally another's has already appeared at Pastoral 8: 8 and 32.

31–2 his thoughts tell him that the smokes of sacrifice bring no more than a brief respite to bodies which can only consume in the fire.

33 *hope, sense, memory* referring back respectively to stanzas 4, 3, and 2: stanza 3 shows that the *sense* in question is the sense of sight.

39–40 recalls the proverb 'To nourish a snake in one's bosom'.

43 cf. CS 1: 4 'Since force doth faint, and sight doth make me blind'.

45–8 cf. Henry Constable, *Diana* (1592), sonnet 19: 11–14

> But like a ship that's overcharged with gold
> Must either sink, or hurl the gold away.
>   But hurl out love thou canst not, feeble heart:
>   In thine own blood thou therefore drownèd art.

49–50 i.e. and so her extraneous image is incorporated into my thoughts. (For *idol* see Sonnet 8: 7 and note; *strange* here retains its root sense from Latin *extraneus*.)

51–2 recalls the proverb 'It will sooner break than bow'.

69–70 i.e. his love requires from his thoughts this one condition, namely that they will conceal from him his beloved's hatred.

75–6 cf. AS 67: 13–14

> I am resolved thy error to maintain
> Rather than by more truth to get more pain.

77–80 The most sexual image in this Neoplatonic sequence: it may recall Shakespeare's Sonnet 138 about his deceiving mistress

> Therefore I lie with her, and she with me,
> And in our faults by lies we flattered be

—but the *arms* where poet-lover Robert asks to be laid are the purely metaphorical arms of his own deceiving thoughts.

SONG 12

Robert had to turn the notebook sideways when entering this poem in order to fit its long lines on the page.

The tune of *Où êtes vous allées* is discussed on pp. 52–3. It survives in MS Egerton 815 (fo. 350) in a version to which Robert's words can be effectively sung:

Song 12 reintroduces the theme of the lover's rejection of his bondage, a theme which has already appeared in Pastoral 9 (stanzas 5 and 6) and in Song 10. Song 11 has continued the theme of woman's falsehood but the false hope which the poet-lover there clings to is here decisively rejected: the transition from the embittered cynicism of Song 11 to the buoyant cynicism of Song 12 echoes the similar transition in moving from Pastoral 9 to Song 10.

The use of *betray* in the refrain echoes the last line of Song 11 in a way which highlights the contrast between the two poems (see p. 108).

5 cf. the Countess of Pembroke's metrical version of Psalm 45: 8 'Thy lips, as springs, do flow with speaking grace'.

21 cf. the reference to *memory* in Song 11, stanzas 2 and 5.

SONNET 30

See head-note to Sonnet 23. This middle poem of the widely spaced three addressed to Absence and all revolving round the Presence versus Absence theme asserts that presence and absence are equally painful.

1–8 cf. the first quatrain of the sonnet by Daniel first published in *Syr P. S. His Astrophel and Stella* (1591) and in a revised version in the second of the two editions of *Delia* published in 1592:

> My cares draw on my everlasting night,
> In horror's sable clouds sets my life's sun,
> My life's sweet sun, my dearest comfort's light,
> Shall rise no more to me, whose day is done

4 cf. AS 60: 13 'Whose presence, absence, absence presence is'.

SONNET 31

This 'full Allegorie' (see p. 44) reflects the frustrations which Robert experienced at Flushing both in his personal life and in his political career.

1 *Forsaken woods* cf. Robert to the Earl of Essex from Flushing (10

Jan. 1597/8) '. . . this place heer, which as yet seemes to bee neglected or forsaken, and in few words to participat with the fortune of the Gouernor of yt'.

9–10 see note on Pastoral 8: 27–8.

11 *now frosts lay in the grave* cf. Robert to Essex (24 May 1597) 'since I see Flushing must bee the graue of my yowth and I feare of my fortune' and see p. 101.

12 *Say all and I with them* this expression occurs identically at OP 5: 93.

SONNET 32

1 *choice or destiny* alluding to the idea of predestined love, an idea which runs through Sonnets 12–14 (= Sonnets 2–4 of the unfinished Crown).

SONNET 33

Another pure celebration of the beloved's beauty, like the previous poem: the fact that Robert has numbered both these sonnets '32' can be seen therefore as significant (cf. head-note to Song 21).

4 *sweetest body* the theme of lines 5–8.

4 *sweeter mind* the theme of lines 9–11.

5 cf. AS 69: 4 'What oceans of delight in me do flow'.

11 cf. AS 20: 12 'But straight I saw motions of lightning grace'.

13 *which even conceit doth pass* i.e. which surpasses even what the mind can conceive.

SONNET 34

The same notion underlies the sonnet by Michael Drayton, first published in the 1605 edition of *Idea*, which begins 'As in some countries far remote from hence' and concludes

> Even so my mistress works upon my ill,
> By curing me and killing me each hour,
> Only to show her beauty's sovereign power.

5–6 cf. Song 6: 121–4. There is irony in the way a sonnet on the beloved's hatred echoes Robert's only poem portraying a wholly mutual love.

8 this recalls the imagery of the galley-slave chained to his oar in Sonnet 19.

SONG 13

This, the final poem of the diversified series in the sequence as originally conceived, itself consists of thirteen-line stanzas. We discern here the same 'conceit' involving the number 13 as can be recognized in the unfinished Crown and in the design of the alternative sequence (see pp. 27 and 112, and head-note to Pastoral 7 in this Commentary).

This Song was evidently suggested by the hymn which survives in several early manuscript and printed versions, was included in *The Paradise of Dainty Devices* (1576 and later editions) and was popularly supposed to have been sung by Walter Devereux, Earl of Essex, on his deathbed in 1576:

O heavenly God, O father dear,
  Cast down thy tender eye
Upon a wretch that prostrate here
  Before thy throne doth lie,
O pour thy precious oil of grace
  Into my wounded heart,
O let the drops of mercy 'suage
  The rigour of my smart.

20–4 We cannot in ourselves *crave* (justly claim) *requital* or reward and therefore we must depend on *grace*.

20 *yours* i.e. your beauties.

24 *foresloweth* hinders, holds back.

29 cf. Pastoral 8: 17 'The time that me restores moves in your eyes'.

31–4 cf. the Ode which concludes Samuel Daniel's *Delia* (1592)

But her will must be obeyed,
  And well he ends for love who dies.

33 *So that* provided that.

34 *myrtle* is sacred to Venus, goddess of love.

SONNET 35

This finale of the sequence as originally conceived is founded on the idea variously expressed in contemporary proverbs: 'Time brings the truth to light', 'Time is the father of truth', 'Truth is time's daughter'.

See pp. 66–7 for the relationship between this sonnet and sonnets to Time by Drayton and Daniel.

2 *your own custom* namely, of bringing truth to light.

8 evokes the proverb 'In trust is treason'.

11 cf. AS 98: 7–8 'Spurred with love's spur, though galled and shortly reined With care's hard hand'.

13–14 cf. Sir John Davies, *Nosce Teipsum* (1599) line 1595 'And Time itself, in Time shall cease to move'.

This final couplet intimates that the object of the poet's unattainable love is an ideal and not ultimately to be identified with any particular embodiment.

UPON A SNUFFKIN

The first of the unnumbered poems, i.e. the first of the poems falling outside the sequence. The sequence itself—while it includes poems to the stars (Sonnets 1 and 20), to the Air (Sonnet 28), and others addressed to such abstractions as Absence—contains no poem addressed to a specific object such as the snuffkin (= muff) made of fur which the poet addresses in this poem as he sends it to his beloved. The poet finally imagines himself repeatedly *kissing* the hands which the muff is to cover: in the sequence itself the only *kisses* mentioned are those metaphorically bestowed by the air and the brooks (see pp. 57–8).

TRANSLATED OUT OF SPANISH

A translation of the last stanza of the first song in Montemayor's *Diana* (1559). This is the only poem where Robert invites direct comparison with his elder brother, since Philip had translated the whole of Montemayor's five-stanza song (CS 28). The final stanza reads in the original Spanish

> Sobre el arena sentada
> de aquel rió la vi yo
> do, con el dedo escrivió:
> antes muerta que mudada,
> Mira el amor lo que ordena
> que os viene a hazer creer
> cosas dichas por mujer
> y escritas en el arena.

and in Philip's version

> On sandy bank of late
> I saw this woman sit
> Where 'sooner die than change my state'
> She with her finger writ:
> Thus my belief was stayed
> (Behold Love's mighty hand)
> On things were by a woman said
> And written in the sand.

Robert is more faithful than Philip to the formal aspects of the Spanish original in that he retains its octosyllabic structure and its chiasmal rhyme-scheme.

Robert has turned the single stanza of his original into a self-contained poem by expanding Montemayor's *la* (Philip's *this woman*) into *She whom I loved, and love shall still*. In Robert's version the *sand* which when the beloved sits on it is *then blessèd* becomes *dust* at the end when it is seen as the emblem of her falsehood. These touches are Robert's own, as is the epithet *heaven-opening* (line 3) which continues the idea inherent in *blessèd*.

That in entering this translation Robert was again resuming the note-book after a break is indicated by the fact that it is written across the terminal flourish made below *Upon a snuffkin*.

TRANSLATED OUT OF SENECA

A line-for-line translation of Seneca, *Thyestes*, lines 607–16:

Vos quibus rector maris atque terrae
ius dedit magnum necis atque vitae
ponite inflatos tumidosque vultus;
quidquid a vobis minor expavescit
maior hoc vobis dominus minatur;
omne sub regno graviore regnum est.
quem dies vidit veniens superbum,
hunc dies vidit fugiens iacentem.
nemo confidat nimium secundis,
nemo desperet meliora lapsis.

6 for the two pronunciations of *power* required by the metre here, see pp. 22–3.

IN ANOTHER PLACE

A line-for-line translation of Seneca, *Thyestes*, lines 398–403:

sic cum transierint mei
nullo cum strepitu dies,
plebeius moriar senex.
illi mors gravis incubat
qui notus nimis omnibus,
ignotus moritur sibi.

Sir Thomas Wyatt had translated the same passage as part of a longer extract (lines 391–403) from the same Chorus, and a complete version of *Thyestes* 'faithfully Englished' by Jasper Heywood had been published in 1560 and republished in *Seneca his Tenne Tragedies, translated into English* (1581). Both Wyatt's and Heywood's versions of the present passage are in decasyllabics, and both contain some phrases which have no equivalent in Seneca to meet the requirements of their metre. What distinguishes Robert's translations is his evident care to reproduce as closely as possible not only the sense but also the syllabic structure of his original in each case. Notable among later poets who have translated the same passage is Andrew Marvell, who translated lines 391–403 into seven-syllable (i.e. catalectic) trochaics.

Robert's two translations from Seneca are the only two poems in his notebook which are not concerned with love.

PASTORAL 14

With this poem the numbered sequence is resumed. The *change* in the lover which surprises his friend Lycippe at the outset is revealed as the poem proceeds to arise from his simple acceptance that the beloved has deserted him—and he firmly rejects all Lycippe's attempts to revive his hopes. This particular mood has not been encountered before and will not appear again in the sequence.

Lycippe represents a variation on the conventional 'unsympathising friend' addressed in Sonnet 21.

11-14 cf. OP 5: 37-9 'Tell me, if your diverted springs become Absented quite from you, Are you not dried? Can you yourself renew?'

41-2 evoke Sonnet 8: 6 'love foiled yields to his overthrow'—but in Sonnet 8 the poet-lover finally returns to his bondage and ends grieving: in the present poem the lover ends as he began in a mood of quiet resignation, all passion spent.

SONG 15

4 *love's lights* echoed at line 33: the beloved's eyes are also referred to as *lights* at Song 1: 1 and 7, Song 4: 22 and 49, Song 6: 100, and at Sonnet 34: 6 they become *burial lights*. In Robert's MS the phrase appears in line 4 as *loues light* but this must be a slip (the only *uncorrected* scribal slip in the notebook) for the notion of 'light loves' would be quite at variance with the context.

7-12 cf. AS vii: 18 'The very essence of their tunes, when Angels do rejoice'.

20 *them* = her *face* (stanza 1), her *voice* (stanza 2), and her *breast* (stanza 3).

21 cf. Psalm 22: 6 'But I am a worm, and no man'.

24 *creaturelike* cf. the subscription of Robert's letter to Penelope Rich (October 1596) 'your most humble creature and seruant'.

36 cf. Psalm 27: 10 'then the Lord will take me up'. For the surface similarity of Robert's line to, and its real difference from, the lover's repeated entreaty in AS iv, see pp. 67-8.

ELEGY 16

For the formal design of this celebratory poem, and for the appropriateness of its circular movement to conclude the sequence, see pp. 24-5. For the significance of Charys, see p. 91.

2, 20 echoes both Catullus xlix: 2-3 'quot sunt quotque fuere, Marce

Tulli, quotque post aliis erunt in annis' and the *Corde natus* of Prudentius —'Omnium quae sunt, fuerunt, quaeque post futura sunt'.

13–14 cf. Spenser, *Amoretti* xvi: 5–6

I mote perceive how in her glancing sight
Legions of loves with little wings did fly.

'FROM FAIREST BREAST'

This introduces the second of the two groups of unnumbered poems which interrupt the numbered sequence. This second group consists of three poems, each of which is untitled and each of which consists of a single eight-line stanza.

'ONCE TO MY LIPS'

This description of an actual kiss would have broken the decorum of the numbered sequence had it been included therein: cf. *Upon a snuffkin* and head-note.

1 cf. AS x: 25–7

Think of that most grateful time
When my leaping heart will climb
In my lips to have his biding

2 *heaven-dew of her lips* cf. OA 62: 44 'Her heavenly-dewèd tongue'.

8 *taste of love's rich feast* Compare and contrast Sonnet 28: 12–14 asking the air to visit the poet after visiting the distant beloved so that he may 'of her lips the nectar someway taste'.

I WOULD BE BLIND

An exercise in a popular genre, the 'paradox-poem'. The reiterated *would be* round which the poem revolves means *wish to be*: cf. Thomas Lodge, *Phillis* (1593), Sonnet 25: 10 'I would be thralled, and yet I freedom love'.

SONG 17

With this poem the numbered sequence is resumed for the second time. The shortest poem in the numbered sequence, it is a 'full Allegorie' which can be recognized as an expansion of a theme supplied by AS 91: 3–4 (see pp. 44–5).

That Robert was again resuming the notebook after a break is confirmed by the fact that this Song crosses the terminal flourish he had made below the previous poem.

5–6 The same idea is more 'wittily' expressed by Greville, *Caelica* lxix: 15 'With them that walk against me is my sun'.

SONG 18

3 *what odds is't* what difference is it.

3–4 cf. *The Merchant of Venice*, IV. i. 375–6 'you take my life When you do take the means whereby I live'.

13–16 cf. Spenser, *Hymne in honour of love* (1596): 278–9

> So thou thy folk, through pains of purgatory,
> Dost bear unto thy bliss, and heaven's glory.

SONG 19

The third and fourth stanzas continue the idea introduced in the last stanza of the previous poem, that love's immortality consists in the lover's suffering.

1–4 let the sun cease to shine for a greater wonder than that has occurred, namely, I have ceased to love.

5–8 the *heavenly sweetness* which created love and gave it an immortal soul is now transformed to *hate and cruelty* and has destroyed her own creation.

SONG 20

This imaginatively realizes the advice given in the Fourth Book of Castiglione's *Courtier* about how the lover is to endure absence from the beloved (see pp. 60–1).

Stanzas 1–3 make clear that the senses being addressed are the *eyes* and *ears*: stanzas 4–5 concern the *outward fair* and the *inward worth* (cf. Shakespeare, Sonnet 16: 11), which are the twin aspects of the beloved's beauty respectively perceived by *eyes* and *ears* and respectively treasured as *deities* in the twin *temples* of the poet's *heart* (or *breast*) and *reason* (or *thought*).

11 cf. George Chapman, *Ovid's Banquet of Sense*: 'All rhetoric's flowers in less than in a word.'

20 *Prisoner from her* cf. Sonnet 23: 6.

29–31 cf. Ficino II. viii 'Accedit quod amans amati figuram suo sculpit in animo'.

34 cf. AS xi: 29–30 'Never doth thy beauty flourish More than in my reason's sight'.

36–8 cf. AS 35: 5–6 'What Nestor's counsel can my flames allay Since reason's self doth blow the coal in me?'

37 *the help that is requirèd* i.e. reason, proverbially known as the physician to love (cf. Shakespeare, Sonnet 147: 5).

SONG 21

The sense pattern is matched to the chiasmal rhyme-scheme in the first, second, and fifth stanzas (see p. 27). For the notion of the beloved as the criterion of all beauty in the created universe, cf. Amour 48 in Drayton's *Ideas Mirrour* (1594) which begins 'Who list to praise the day's delicious light, Let him compare it to her heavenly eye'.

This pure celebration of the beloved's beauty recalls the two companion sonnets both of which Robert numbered 32: those two sonnets viewed as a unit constitute the fourth item from the end of the sequence as originally conceived, just as Song 21 constitutes the fourth item from the end of the expanded sequence.

9 for the verbal play in this line, see p. 91.

17–20 cf. AS 88: 12 'That where before heart loved and eyes did see'.

SONG 22

For the metre of this poem, see p. 31.

2, 5 *cold despair, hot zeal* In Renaissance botany plants had 'temperatures', *cold* being applied to the earlier blooming plants which 'have a quicker perception of the heat' (Bacon, *Sylva Sylvarum*): *hot* seems also to have been the designation for the more strongly scented plants, cf. Perdita's 'Hot lavender, mints, savory, marjoram' (*The Winter's Tale*, IV. iv. 104).

9–12 cf. Song 13: 29 and note, and Amour 47 in Drayton's *Ideas Mirrour* (1594)

> But my fair planet, who directs me still,
> Unkindly such distemperature doth bring,
> Makes summer winter, autumn in the spring,
> Crossing sweet nature by unruly will.

14 *yours* your garden (= me your lover).

25–6 cf. Pastoral 8: 27–8 and note.

31–2 cf. Erasmus, *De parabolis sive similibus* 'Ut terra quo melior est natura, hoc magis corrumpitur, si negligatur', and Shakespeare, *2 Henry IV*, IV. iv. 54 'Most subject is the fattest soil to weeds'.

35–6 i.e. the weeds found on my love are the kind found only in the most fertile soil. The *weeds* in question are itemized in lines 37–40.

45–6 cf. Sonnet 22: 4, Song 10: 16, and AS 45: 12–13

> Then think, my dear, that you in me do read
> Of lover's ruin some sad tragedy.

47–8 see p. 28 for the design of this final couplet.

SONG 23

30 recalls the conclusion—*in pains joying*—of Song 13, the penultimate poem in the sequence as originally conceived.

SONG 24

The last poem in the notebook, and the last in the widely spaced series of three addressed to Absence (see head-note to Sonnet 23). The present poem, which finally decides in favour of presence, contains deliberate echoes of the first poem in the series which concluded in favour of absence as less painful than presence: see notes to Sonnet 23.

22 i.e. there is this advantage in pain; cf. AS 96: 12 ‘night’s side the odds hath fur’.

APPENDIX A

TWO SONNETS RELATED TO ROBERT'S SONNET 35

(see Introduction, pp. 66–7)

Stay, stay, sweet Time: behold, or ere thou pass
From world to world, thou long hast sought to see,
That wonder now wherein all wonders be,
Where heaven beholds her in a mortal glass.
Nay, look thee, Time, in this celestial glass,
And thy youth past in this fair mirror see:
Behold world's beauty in her infancy,
What she was then, and thou, or ere she was.
Now pass on, Time: to after-worlds tell this,
Tell truly, Time, what in thy time hath been,
That they may tell more worlds what Time hath seen,
And heaven may joy to think on past world's bliss.
  Here make a period, Time, and say for me,
  She was the like that never was, nor never more shall be.

(Michael Drayton, Amour 7 in *Ideas Mirrour*, 1594)

Time, cruel Time, come and subdue that brow
Which conquers all but thee; and thee too stays,
As if she were exempt from scythe or bow,
From love or years, unsubject to decays.
Or art thou grown in league with those fair eyes,
That they may help thee to consume our days?
Or dost thou spare her for her cruelties,
Being merciless like thee, that no man weighs?
And yet thou see'st thy power she disobeys,
Cares not for thee, but lets thee waste in vain;
And prodigal of hours and years betrays
Beauty and youth t'opinion and disdain.
  Yet spare her, Time, let her exempted be,
  She may become more kind to thee or me.

(Samuel Daniel, Delia xxiii in *The Works*, 1601)

APPENDIX B

ROBERT, FULKE GREVILLE, AND SHAKESPEARE

(See pp. 339–41 for texts of the poems by Greville and Shakespeare discussed here.)

While Robert was not known as a poet to the contemporary reading public (see p. 2), there are indications that a few at least of the poems which he collected in his notebook had previously circulated among a select readership. These indications are contained in what appear on comparison to be conscious echoes of particular poems by Robert in (1) Fulke Greville's *Caelica*, and (2) Shakespeare's *Love's Labour's Lost*. If Robert did indeed allow any of his poems to be read by a select few outside his own family, then his known connections readily explain why both Greville and Shakespeare should have been included in the privileged circle.

What we know of the social background of Elizabethan courtly verse suggests that the 'private friends' who—as we learn from Francis Meres, *Palladis Tamia* (1598)—were allowed to read Shakespeare's 'sugred Sonnets' in manuscript during the 1590s may well have been reciprocating with sonnets of their own. Characteristic of these poets is the way they respond to each other's work, so that where a relationship between two poems has been detected it may still be impossible to say which is echoing which. The nature of the relationships between the particular poems here examined, however, suggests that in these cases Greville and Shakespeare are both (independently) responding to Robert rather than he to them.

Fulke Greville's renowned friendship with Robert's elder brother began when the pair were schoolboys together at Shrewsbury, was fostered by their joint concern for the future of English poetry, and was commemorated by Philip upon his deathbed when he bequeathed all his books 'to my dear friends Mr Edward Dyer and Mr Fulke Greville'. Many years later, when Greville composed the epitaph for his own tomb in St Mary's church, Warwick, he ensured that posterity remembered him as 'Servant to Queen Elizabeth, Counsellor to King James, Friend to Sir Philip Sidney'. Greville remains in himself something of an enigma, manifestly gifted but preserving a cynical detachment which Philip's younger brother may have found somewhat less than endearing. Of the various references to Greville among the Sidney papers, the passage which evokes him most vividly occurs in one of Rowland Whyte's letters dating from what can be seen as the 'dark period' of Robert's career (see pp. 81–3). Writing from Court on 19 May 1597, Whyte reports to Robert a conversation which had taken place the previous night:

Mr. foulke Grivell yesternight told me, that you had forgotten your frends in court and that he had not hard from you a great while. Sir, sayd I, if he doe soe I cannot much blame hym, because yt is a very hard matter to know who are frends now a dayes. but for you, I am sure he esteemes you as his frend, and wold be glad to heare from you that liue in place to know all, how things doe pass here. You cold not shew your loue in any thing more pleasing vnto hym, then by doing this. And with a great protestacion of his loue, the ordinary infection of this place, he assured me that no man knew better the tyme then your self, nor their humors better, that had most power here, and that you were wise enough to gouern your self accordingly.

It is characteristic of Greville that the relationships which have been detected between certain poems in *Astrophil and Stella* on the one hand, and certain poems in *Caelica* on the other, reveal Greville giving an ironical twist to ideas contained in Philip's work.[1] The same sort of relationship can be detected between Robert's Sonnet 1 and *Caelica* iv. The opening quatrain of Sonnet 1 and the first stanza of *Caelica* iv develop in the same way—(1) the stars of heaven are addressed, (2) they are told they rule the world, (3) they are likened to the beloved's eyes. But a sophisticated turn is imparted by Greville to ideas which are given simple expression in Sonnet 1. Where Robert addresses the stars of heaven with due reverence, Greville addresses them patronizingly as 'You little stars that live in skies' and boldly tells them to rejoice at being compared to his lady's eyes. In the second line of Sonnet 1 Robert simply tells the stars of heaven that they *rule the world below*: the same idea is more esoterically expressed in lines 3–4 of Greville's poem, where he tells those same stars that in their *aspects conjoinèd lies / The Heaven's will, and Nature's story*. Robert's simple statement (line 12) that in his beloved's eyes *all eyes on earth are blessed* is mirrored with an added wit in line 6 of Greville's poem, which states that his beloved's eyes *make all eyes glad, or sorry.*

Caelica xlv reads very much as though it had been composed as a counter-exercise in response to Robert's three interlinked poems on the theme of presence versus absence (Sonnet 23, Sonnet 30, Song 24: see p. 110). Both poets compare absence to clouds before the sun (Sonnet 30: 10, *Caelica* xlv: 21–4) and refer to the wounds inflicted by presence which are not healed by absence (Song 24: 23–4, *Caelica* xlv: 11–14). The final stanza of Greville's poem (*But thoughts be not so brave / With absent joy . . . Absence is pain*) seems deliberately to recall the conclusion of Sonnet 23 (*As present pain than absent joy is worse*). The gist of Greville's poem is that absence from the beloved is painful because it encourages erotic fantasies but prevents their realization. His conclusion

For thought is not the weapon
Wherewith thought's ease men cheapen,
Absence is pain

[1] See John Buxton, *Sir Philip Sidney and the English Renaissance* (1954), pp. 105–9.

implicitly points to the 'weapon' wherewith men actually *can* 'cheapen' (i.e. procure) ease for their lovesick thoughts, and this allusion is balanced by the allusion to 'Cupid's shadowed centre'—signifying the female counterpart of the male 'weapon'—in the corresponding lines of the previous stanza. Under the veil of its figurative language *Caelica* xlv is one of the most insistently sexual of Greville's poems, and the clue to this may be that it represents Greville's ironic response to Robert's physically pure Neoplatonism.

Although the Sidney papers contain no mention of Shakespeare by name, they afford clear glimpses of a familiar friendship between Robert and the Earl of Southampton—the only man whom Shakespeare ever acknowledged as his patron. It was to Southampton that Shakespeare dedicated the only two volumes for whose publication he was personally responsible, *Venus and Adonis* (1593) and *The Rape of Lucrece* (1594): the warmth and assured tone of the dedicatory epistle to the latter transcend the conventions of its genre.

An already quoted letter to Robert from Thomas Edmondes is particularly interesting for its disclosure of Southampton, during a diplomatic mission to Paris in 1598, procuring songs for Robert from the Parisian music-seller Léon Cavellat (p. 52). The intimacy implicit in Edmondes's postscript is illustrated again in an undated letter from Sir Charles Danvers written to Robert when he was expected at court. Although Lady Hoby 'in whose Chamber this letter is written' had just commanded Danvers to write no more, 'I cannot forgett to lett you know that my Lord of Southampton is at his howse and wilbe very glad to see yow there as yow come vp, and if yow come on munday or tusday I may chance meete yow there.' Southampton was evidently hoping that Robert would break his journey up to court in order to pay him a social visit. Thomas Edmondes's wry remark to Robert about Southampton's slothfulness in the matter of letter-writing helps explain the absence of letters from the Earl himself among the Sidney papers.

In February 1600/1 Southampton, for his part in Essex's rebellion, was stripped of his honours and sent to the Tower, where he was lucky to keep his head on his shoulders. He remained a prisoner until the accession of James I in March 1603, when he was pardoned without delay. The new king began to shower favours on Southampton almost at once: in 1603 he was restored to his former honours and was also appointed Master of Game to the new queen, and a member of her Council. When, during the Christmas season of 1604–5, Southampton wished to entertain the queen at his house in London, the play chosen for the occasion was *Love's Labour's Lost.*[1] The reason which (so Walter Cope told Cecil)

[1] The performance in question can be identified as that recorded in the Revels Account for 1604–5 'Betwin Newers Day and Twelfe Day a play of Loues Labours Lost'. That this performance was at Southampton's house, and in the queen's presence, can be deduced from two letters taken in conjunction: (1) Sir Walter

Burbage gave for the choice was 'ther ys no new playe that the quene hath not seene' but we may none the less ponder on the choice for such an occasion of a play which (as commentators agree) abounds in highly topical satire yet which by 1604–5 was far from new: the implication is that *Love's Labour's Lost* had a special appeal for Southampton and his circle. Robert Sidney belonged to that circle, and had recently been appointed Chamberlain to the new queen: we can reasonably assume, on both counts, that he would have attended this performance. (It was during this same festive season that Robert's daughter Mary Wroth danced at court in Ben Jonson's *Masque of Blackness*, the queen's Twelfth Night entertainment.)

Although the top-dressing of local allusions in *Love's Labour's Lost* may never now be completely understood, the play's central target can still be recognized as the Neoplatonist philosophy which by the end of the sixteenth century had become a fashionable cult in courtly circles throughout Europe. In the opening dialogue of Shakespeare's play the idealistic young King of Navarre outlines his programme in discussion with his three 'fellow-scholars', revealing his eagerness to transcend the body, to exclude sex, and to turn his court into 'a little academe' for contemplation and study. Discernible behind all this are the main features of the philosophy expounded by Marsilio Ficino, whose Commentary on the *Symposium* is set in 'a little academe' (its occasion being the annual banquet held by the Platonic Academy of Florence to celebrate Plato's birthday). The play's opening dialogue wittily touches on the esoteric aspect of the philosophy (see I. i. 56–69 about the end of study being to know 'things hid and barred from common sense') and introduces the recurrent theme of 'eyes' and 'light' (a theme which reflects the Neoplatonic preoccupation with the *ray* or *beam* whose ultimate source is the divine radiance).

Intimately linked with Neoplatonism was the sonnet vogue which reached its height in England in the 1590s and gave to the fashionable philosophy its most popular expression. *Love's Labour's Lost* portrays this aspect in the poetical tributes addressed by the King and his three companions to the four ladies with whom they have respectively fallen in love (IV. ii and IV. iii). Here, if anywhere, we might look for echoes of Robert's verse, and the first intimation that these may exist occurs in line 10 of the King's sonnet

So ridest thou triumphing in my woe.

The image of the Roman triumph was no doubt available to any Elizabethan poet, but it would be difficult to find another sonnet which uses that image in such a similar way as does Robert's address to his cruel

Cope to Robert Cecil, Lord Cranborne, and (2) Dudley Carleton to John Chamberlain, 15 Jan. 1604/5. All three documents are printed in E. K. Chambers, *William Shakespeare* (1930), ii, pp. 331–2.

beloved in Sonnet 25: in the version of Sonnet 25 originally entered in the notebook, line 4 reads

And triumphs lead in my captivity.

If this were an isolated link it might be rash to build anything on it: its evidential value, however, is greatly strengthened when it is taken in conjunction with the curious entreaty to the beloved in lines 13–14 of the King's sonnet

But do not love thyself—then thou wilt keep
My tears for glasses, and still make me weep.

The abrupt *But do not love thyself* seems to require some further justification than can be found within the sonnet itself, where it merely serves to give a ludicrous turn to the conceit about the lady's reflection in her lover's tears. The wit is enhanced if we see in these lines a direct parody of Robert's entreaty to his beloved in Sonnet 25

O love yourself: be you yourself your care

—an entreaty whose esoteric significance would be understood by those versed in Neoplatonism but would be 'hid and barred' from the uninitiated (see pp. 58–9).

It is possible also to detect a relationship between Robert's Sonnet 28 and Dumain's 'Ode' in the same scene. Both start from the same image—of the spring wind playing among leaves—and the verbal correspondences between two short poems include *air* and *breath* (as synonyms for the wind), *wanton, play(ing), leaves*, and *May*. These surface resemblances suggest that Sonnet 28 may have supplied the initial impulse for Dumain's lyric, but it is important to observe that the resemblances serve ultimately to bring out the real difference between the two poems. Dumain's lyric quickly develops into an erotic fantasy, as the lover identifies in imagination with the *wanton air* while the *blossom passing fair* merges into the image of his beloved. No such erotic development occurs in Sonnet 28, where the lover is left at the end aspiring only to receive the chaste kiss of the air which had previously rested on the distant lips of his beloved —a type of kiss which would scarcely have satisfied Dumain's lover. In the play Dumain's lyric is the last of the poetical tributes by the four lovers, and it contrasts vividly with the other three. Dumain's eroticism implicitly reflects on the orthodox Neoplatonic decorum observed in their poems by Berowne, the King, and Longaville. With Sonnet 28 in mind, we may also recognize in Dumain's lyric an oblique reflection on the sexual purity of Robert's verse—a reflection akin to the ironic response which can be discerned behind Greville's insistently sexual *Caelica* xlv when that poem is seen in relation to Robert's three interrelated poems on the theme of presence versus absence.

APPENDIX B

You little stars that live in skies
And glory in Apollo's glory,
In whose aspects conjoinèd lies
The Heaven's will, and Nature's story,
Joy to be likened to those eyes
Which eyes make all eyes glad, or sorry,
  For when you force thoughts from above
  These overrule your force by love.

(Fulke Greville, *Caelica* iv,
first stanza)

Absence, the noble truce
Of Cupid's war,
Where, though desires want use,
They honoured are.
Thou art the just protection
Of prodigal affection,
Have thou the praise;
When bankrupt Cupid braveth
Thy mines his credit saveth
With sweet delays.

Of wounds which presence makes
With beauty's shot
Absence the anguish slakes,
But healeth not.
Absence records the stories
Wherein desire glories,
Although she burn;
She cherisheth the spirits
Where constancy inherits
And passions mourn.

Absence, like dainty clouds
On glorious bright,
Nature's weak senses shrouds
From harming light.
Absence maintains the treasure
Of pleasure unto pleasure,
Sparing with praise;
Absence doth nurse the fire
Which starves and feeds desire
With sweet delays.

Presence to every part
Of beauty ties,
Where wonder rules the heart
There pleasure dies.
Presence plagues mind and senses
With modesty's defences,
Absence is free;
Thoughts do in absence venture
On Cupid's shadowed centre,
They wink and see.

But thoughts, be not so brave
With absent joy,
For you with that you have
Yourself destroy.
The absence which you glory
Is that which makes you sorry
And burn in vain;
For thought is not the weapon
Wherewith thought's ease men cheapen,
Absence is pain.

(Fulke Greville, *Caelica* xlv)

So sweet a kiss the golden sun gives not
To those fresh morning drops upon the rose,
As thine eye-beams when their fresh rays have smote
The night of dew that on my cheeks down flows:
Nor shines the silver moon one half so bright
Through the transparent bosom of the deep,
As doth thy face through tears of mine give light;
Thou shin'st in every tear that I do weep.
No drop but as a coach doth carry thee,
So ridest thou triumphing in my woe;
Do but behold the tears that swell in me
And they thy glory through my grief will show.
But do not love thyself—then thou wilt keep
My tears for glasses, and still make me weep.
O queen of queens, how far dost thou excel
No thought can think, nor tongue of mortal tell.

(William Shakespeare, *Love's Labour's Lost*, IV. iii)

APPENDIX B

On a day, alack the day!
Love, whose month is ever May,
Spied a blossom passing fair
Playing in the wanton air:
Through the velvet leaves the wind
All unseen can passage find,
That the lover, sick to death,
Wished himself the heaven's breath.
Air, quoth he, thy cheeks may blow—
Air, would I might triumph so.
But, alack, my hand is sworn
Ne'er to pluck thee from thy thorn:
Vow, alack, for youth unmeet,
Youth so apt to pluck a sweet.
Do not call it sin in me,
That I am forsworn for thee:
Thou for whom Jove would swear
Juno but an Ethiop were,
And deny himself for Jove,
Turning mortal for thy love.

(William Shakespeare, *Love's Labour's Lost*, IV. iii)

APPENDIX C

ECHOES OF ROBERT'S SEQUENCE IN HIS DAUGHTER MARY WROTH'S VERSE

The Countesse of Mountgomeries Urania. Written by the right honorable the Lady Mary Wroath was published in folio at London in 1621. The *Urania* is a prose romance interspersed with poems and is directly followed by a separately paginated (1–48) sonnet-and-song sequence entitled *Pamphilia to Amphilanthus* which concludes a volume whose overall indebtedness to the authoress's uncle, Philip Sidney, is manifest. With the publication of her father's verse a previously concealed debt to him is also disclosed.

1. Unheard, unseen, will pray and love (Song 5: 24)

   Unseen, unknown, I here alone complain (*Urania*, p. 2)

2. You who favour do enjoy
   And spend and keep love's treasure,
   You who see no end of joy
   Nor limits find nor measure,
   You whose cares, triumphing on annoy,
   Give you a crown of pleasure (Song 10: 1–6)

   You, who ending never saw
   Of pleasures best delighting (*Urania*, p. 355)

3. For as the condemned man from dungeon led
   Who with first light he sees, ends his last breath
   (Sonnet 23: 9–10)

   Like one long kept in prison, brought to light;
   But for his end, condemnèd ne'er to be,
   Freed from his dungeon, till that wretched he
   Conclude his living with his latest sight. (*Urania*, p. 514)

4. Shepherd, why dost thou so look still on me (Pastoral 8: 1)

   Fond agèd man, why do you on me gaze (*Urania*, p. 515)

5. I cannot part from that by which I am (Pastoral 8: 41)

   For love is blind, and though I agèd be,
   I can nor part from it, nor it from me (*Urania*, p. 515)

6. You that take pleasure in your cruelty (Sonnet 25: 1)

Nor pleasure take, your cruelty to show
(*Pamphilia to Amphilanthus*, p. 3)

7. Winter is come at last,
Cold winter, dark and sad (Song 3: 3–4)

The spring now come at last . . .
Cold winter yet remains (*Pamphilia to Amphilanthus*, p. 3)

8. Thus said a shepherd, once
With weights of change oppressed (Song 3: 63–4)

A shepherdess thus said,
Who was with grief oppressed
(*Pamphilia to Amphilanthus*, p. 4)

9. Most fair, the field is yours—now stay your hands;
No power is left to strive, less to rebel.
I pleasure take, that at your blows I fell,
And laurel wear, in triumph of my bands . . .
O save: do not destroy what is your own
(Sonnet 18: 1–4, 13)

Love leave to urge, thou knowst thou hast the hand;
'Tis cowardice to strive where none resist:
Pray thee leave off, I yield unto thy band,
Do not thus still in thine own power persist.
(*Pamphilia to Amphilanthus*, p. 4)

10. Delights departed are,
Labours do only tarry:
Divorced from pleasures, marry
Henceforth we do with care (Song 3: 7–10)

Joys are bereaved me, harms do only tarry,
Despair takes place, disdain hath got the hand:
Yet firm love holds my senses in such band
As (since despisèd) I with sorrow marry.
(*Pamphilia to Amphilanthus*, p. 5)

11. The endless alchemist, with blinded will,
That feeds his thoughts with hopes, his hopes on shows,
And more his work proves vain more eager grows
While dreams of gold his head with shadows fill,

Feels not more sure the scourge of flatt'ring skill,
When in false trust of wealth true need he knows,
Than I, on whom a storm of losses blows (Sonnet 17: 1–7)

The weary traveller, who tirèd sought
In places distant far, yet found no end
Of pain or labour, nor his state to mend:
At last with joy is to his home back brought,

Finds not more ease though he with joy be fraught,
When past his fear content like souls ascend,
Than I, on whom new pleasures do descend
(*Pamphilia to Amphilanthus*, p. 6)

12. My wants, another's store, grudge not to see
(Sonnet 20: 10)

Making your loss a gain to other's store
(*Pamphilia to Amphilanthus*, p. 13)

13. Time, cruel Time, how fast pass you away
And in my case from your own custom fly
(Sonnet 35: 1–2)

How fast thou fliest, O Time, on love's swift wings
(*Pamphilia to Amphilanthus*, p. 17)

14. O eyes, O lights divine,
Which in unmatchèd face
Like two fair suns in clearest heaven do shine,
And from so glorious place
Vouchsafe your beams to move
On humble me to raise my thoughts to love (Song 1: 1–6)

You happy blessèd eyes,
Which in that ruling place
Have force both to delight, and to disgrace;
Whose light allures and ties
All hearts to your command,
O look on me who do at mercy stand.
(*Pamphilia to Amphilanthus*, p. 21)

15. O heavenly eyes then say
'Ah smokes of feignèd fires,
He is not here, that burns in true desires'. (Song 1: 34–6)

But (Dear) on me cast down
Sweet looks, for true desire,
That banish do all thoughts of feignèd fire.
(*Pamphilia to Amphilanthus*, p. 22)

16. You purest stars, whose never-dying fires
Deck heavenly spheres, and rule the world below,
Grudge not if I in your clear beauties know
The fair maid's eyes, the stars of my desires (Sonnet 1: 1–4)

You blessèd stars, which do heaven's glory show
And at your brightness make our eyes admire,
Yet envy not though I on earth below
Enjoy a sight which moves in me more fire.

I do confess such beauty breeds desire,
You shine, and clearest light on us bestow
(*Pamphilia to Amphilanthus*, p. 24)

17. The pains which I uncessantly sustain,
Burning in hottest flames of love most pure,
Are joys, not griefs (Sonnet 2: 1–3)

Blest in my bands (Sonnet 2: 7)

Love is true Virtue, and his ends delight,
His flames are joys, his bands true Lovers' might
(*Pamphilia to Amphilanthus*, p. 36)

18. Strengthened by love, assured by destiny (Sonnet 4: 2)

Strengthened by worth, renewed by carefulness
(*Pamphilia to Amphilanthus*, p. 39)

APPENDIX D

PHYSICAL DESCRIPTION OF ROBERT'S NOTEBOOK

Dr Nicholas Pickwoad has made a careful physical examination of the notebook (now British Library, Add. MS 58435) and I am indebted to him for the accompanying diagram of its make-up and for the description which now follows.

The diagram is based on the physical evidence available from the manuscript in its present green morocco binding, which was made for Viscount Kingsborough between 1834 and 1837 (see p. 7). The physical evidence I believe to be firmly established. While the conclusions based on that evidence cannot all be completely demonstrated from the manuscript in its present condition they represent, so far as I can see, the only probable explanation of the facts. The leaves of the manuscript measure approximately 198 × 149 mm.

Watermarks

The watermarks (see p. xiv, footnote) are all bisected by the spine folds, which indicates that each leaf represents one quarter of the full sheet. To arrive at this quarto format each full sheet must have been folded twice, and sheets thus folded could be made up into gatherings of four or multiples of four as desired. The watermarks are represented on the diagram, which shows that—allowing for the leaf apparently excised between fos. 26 and 27 (see below)—the leaves in the body of the volume can be divided into five eight-leaf gatherings: in addition, there are three leaves at the beginning (probably the remains of a four-leaf gathering, i.e. one folded sheet) and four leaves plus a stub at the end, probably the remains of another eight-leaf gathering.

On this arrangement, the halves of the watermarks match up in the complete gatherings in a manner which is entirely consistent with two sheets of paper, one on top of the other, folded together twice to make each gathering. Where parts of the watermark are visible in the leaves, it is quite possible to see which side of the sheet lay against the paper-maker's mould in the course of manufacture, and this mould-side of the paper conforms without exception to the make-up shown in the diagram. Without resorting to betaradiographs of each leaf containing a part-watermark, or without dismembering the manuscript, it is not possible to give any more evidence in support of this make-up: I would suggest, however, that the evidence presented is fairly conclusive.

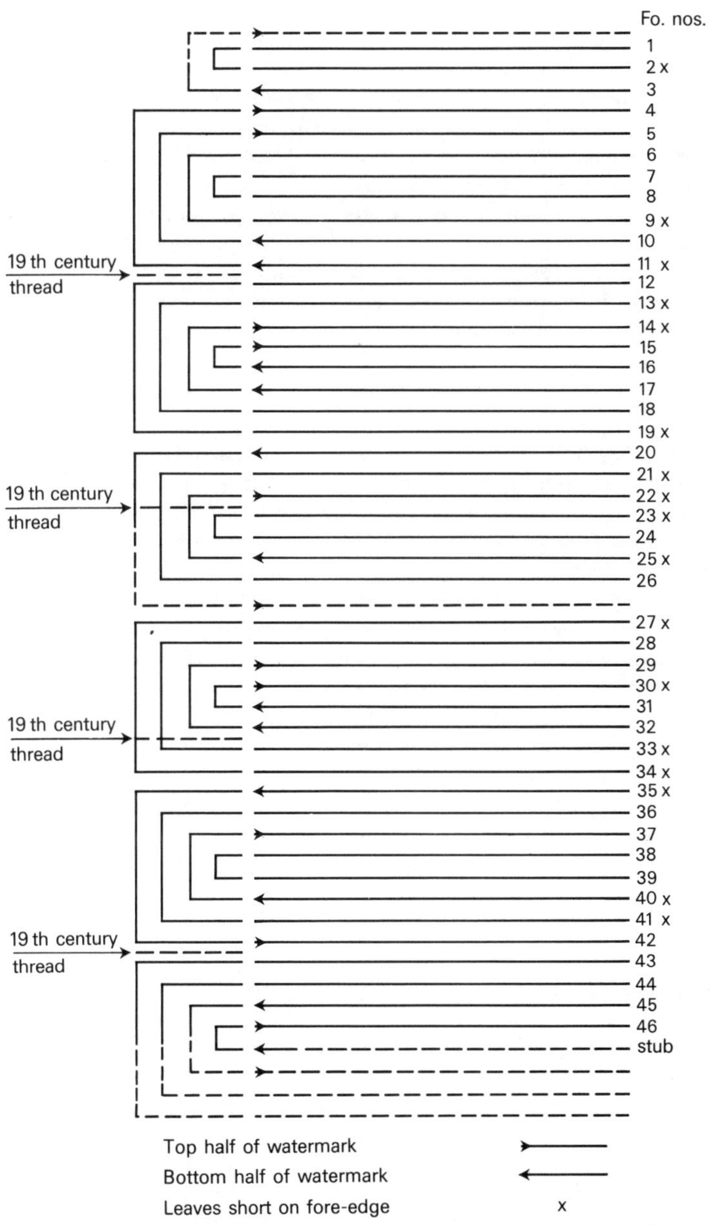
Fo. nos.
1
2 x
3
4
5
6
7
8
9 x
10
11 x
19 th century thread
12
13 x
14 x
15
16
17
18
19 x
20
21 x
19 th century thread
22 x
23 x
24
25 x
26
27 x
28
29
30 x
31
19 th century thread
32
33 x
34 x
35 x
36
37
38
39
40 x
41 x
19 th century thread
42
43
44
45
46
stub
Top half of watermark
Bottom half of watermark
Leaves short on fore-edge
x

APPENDIX D

Chronology

Robert wrote on trimmed leaves with a border ruled in red ink to each page. The red ruling must have been done after the leaves had been folded to their final size, and knife cuts visible on head-, tail-, and fore-edges show that in fact the sheets were first folded and then marked up for ruling. That Robert wrote on trimmed leaves is proved by the fact that on four of the seventeen leaves which are short on the fore-edge the ink goes over the cut edge (on fos. 9, 21, 22, and 33). Robert's ink on many leaves can be seen to go over the red lines. One can therefore state that Robert wrote after the sheets had been folded, cut, and ruled: there is no positive indication, however, as to whether the leaves were sewn or unsewn when he wrote on them.

Excisions

The diagram shows six leaves as having been excised. It is not possible to say when the (presumably blank) leaves at the beginning and end were excised. For the excision between fos. 26 and 27 there is physical evidence in the form of a crease on fo. 27 recto running parallel to the spine close into the gutter towards the tail-edge of the leaf: the most probable explanation is that the crease was made by the knife which excised the missing leaf. The resulting stub was presumably lost either while the manuscript was in a damaged state (see below) or when it was re-bound between 1834 and 1837: since the stub was on the outside of a gathering it would have been particularly vulnerable. The excision between fos. 26 and 27 has left no hiatus in the text and was therefore probably made during the period of writing.

The stub at the end of the volume remains and the short knife cut at the tail of the preceding leaf (fo. 46) aligns exactly with the edge of the stub, showing that the missing leaf was cut out of the folded gathering.

Gilding

The fact that the top and bottom edges of the manuscript are uneven is conclusive proof that the gilding pre-dates the present binding. The colour and generally worn condition of the gilding suggest a date for it not long after the completion of writing.

The seventeen leaves which are short on the fore-edge have escaped gilding, which suggests that the leaves were gilded after they had been sewn. There is confirmation of this in the way several of the full-width leaves (e.g. fo. 15) lying next to short leaves were crushed into the spaces left at the fore-edge by the short leaves. This happened either when the edge was scraped smooth prior to gilding or when it was burnished after the gold leaf had been laid on: in either case, the volume must already have been sewn. At the top of fo. 44 recto the initial S of *Song* in the heading was shaved when preparing the leaf for gilding: there is no trace of ink on the gilt edge itself, as there must have been had the pen gone over the edge of the already gilt leaf. We know from the presence of ink on the edges of the short leaves that Robert wrote after the leaves had been trimmed: the evidence just given shows that he wrote before they had been gilded. The '12 quire of gilt paper' mentioned in Rowland Whyte's account book on 30 June 1596 as purchased for 'your Lordship's store' cannot have been used for the notebook, despite the suggestion which was tentatively put forward in the *British Library Journal*, i, 1975, p. 113. Equally untenable is the assumption made there that Kingsborough's binder was mainly responsible for the gilding.

Binding

There is no visible evidence of the previous binding: the remains of adhesive on fo. 1 recto seem to represent some later attempt at repair. Thomas Thorpe's catalogue entry of 1833 (item 944) records that the binding was then of vellum, which suggests a binding more or less contemporary with the manuscript itself.

The worm-holes at the foot of fos. 1–28 provide evidence that the original sewing had broken down some time before the volume was rebound for Viscount Kingsborough between his acquisition of the volume in 1834 and his death in 1837. If the worm-holes in adjacent leaves are lined up, it will be found that the edges of the leaves do not then line up with each other. This can only mean that the leaves were in that uneven state when the worm attacked them. Since the worm-holes do not line up in the present binding either, they must pre-date it, just as they must post-date the collapse of the original structure.

The structure of the present binding is not entirely clear, as the volume will not open far enough to allow thorough examination of the spine folds. Thread is visible in four openings through the volume (see diagram), but these positions have no logical relation to the positions of the watermarks and cannot represent centre-folds of original gatherings. There is evidence indicating that Kingsborough's binder overcast groups of leaves together and then sewed these artificial 'gatherings' in a conventional manner on five recessed cords. The fact that the previous structure had loosened if not disintegrated suggests that Kingsborough's binder used the method of overcasting in order to avoid the need to repair damaged spine folds. It would not be unknown for a binder of this period to cut a damaged manuscript into single leaves before overcasting. If this was done here, then the binder's choice of openings for his sewing thread would be entirely arbitrary. There is always a tendency for the artificial 'gatherings' produced by overcasting not to lie flush with each other at head and tail. In the present case, there are distinct 'steps' between fos. 16 and 17 and between fos. 37 and 38 respectively, both of which would correspond to ten-leaf 'gatherings' with the main sewing thread (which runs parallel to the spine and is the thread represented on the diagram) in the middle of each 'gathering'.

Any attempt to relate the present sewing to the volume's original make-up can only lead to confusion. Reliance on the sewing evidence may help to explain why the watermarks have been found to show 'a marked lack of matching halves' (*British Library Journal*, i, 1975, p. 112). This mistaken view entailed the unjustified assumption that in the course of compiling the notebook Robert must have excised many leaves.

TABLE OF ROBERT'S VERSE FORMS

In order to facilitate comparison between the technique of the two brothers, this table is modelled on the table of Philip's verse forms published by Ringler (*Poems of Sir Philip Sidney*, 1962, pp. 569–72). The diversified forms are arranged first according to their metre, and then according to number of lines per metrical unit, order of rhymes, and line length (subscript numbers indicate syllables per line): the sonnets are treated separately at the end of the table—a modification of Ringler's system. While, apart from sonnets, each poem in the numbered sequence extends that sequence's metrical diversity, each poem is itself divided into metrical units of uniform length and structure and all line numbers cited in the table refer to these metrical units. The total number of lines in each poem is given in brackets after the title, and this number divided by the number of lines per metrical unit (the number which begins each entry) gives the number of metrical units—though Song 3 contains seven ten-line stanzas and seventy-two lines because the two-line refrain is also used to begin the poem. All Robert's verse is composed in stress metres and the term accentual, employed by Ringler to distinguish Philip's native from his quantitative metres, has been discarded here as superfluous. Of Robert's twenty-six diversified verse forms (i.e. excluding sonnets) only six had been used by Philip: each of the six entries concerned is distinguished by an asterisk in the table and the poem or poems by Philip employing that form cited within square brackets at the end of the entry. Ringler's abbreviations for Philip's poems have been used.

IAMBIC (OTHER THAN SONNETS)

*2 aa_8. Upon a Snuffkin (10); In another place (6). [Cf. OA 6, 62; OP 3]

*2 aa_{10}. Translated out of Seneca (10); Elegy 16 (22). [Cf. OA 27]

4 $a_8b_4a_8b_4$. Song 17 (8).

4 $abab_8$. Song 18 (24).

4 $a_9b_8a_9b_8$. Song 19 (16).

4 $abba_8$. Translated out of Spanish (8); Song 21 (20).

*6 $aabccb_{10}$. Pastoral 8 (48). [Cf. PS 31]

6 $ab_6a_{10}bc_6c_{10}$. Song 1 (36).

*6 $ababcc_8$. Song 5 (24). [Cf. OA 5, 25]

6 $aba_{10}bc_4c_{10}$. Song 23 (30).

6 $ab_6b_{10}ac_6c_{10}$. Pastoral 7 (30).

6 $ab_6c_{10}ab_6c_{10}$. Song 24 (36).

8 $abababaa_{10}$. 'I would be blind' (8).

*8 $ababab cc_{10}$. Pastoral 9 (48); 'From fairest breast' (8); 'Once to my lips' (8). [Cf. OA 35, 54; OP 4]

8 $abba_6cddc_7$. Song 11 (80).

10 $a_8b_4a_8bcc_4d_8e_4d_8e_4$ (only four rhymes used in stanza 3 to give ababcccdcd) Pastoral 2 (70).

13 $aaa_8b_6ccc_8b_6dd_3ee_7b_6$. Song 13 (39).

TROCHAIC

7 $abab_8cc_7b_8$. Song 20 (49).

TABLE OF ROBERT'S VERSE FORMS

MIXED TROCHAIC AND IAMBIC

(Iambic lines specified: all other lines trochaic)

4 $ab_{13}A_{12}B_9$ on two rhymes throughout, lines 3-4 refrain, line 3 iambic. Song 12 (40). Discussed on pp. 52-3.

6 $aa_7b_4ccb_7$ line 3 iambic. Song 15 (36).

6 $abab_7a_9b_7$ lines 2, 4, 6 iambic. Song 10 (42).

6 $a_8b_7a_8b_7cc_8$ lines 5-6 iambic. Song 22 (48).

7 $aa_7b_4cc_7bb_4$ lines 3, 6-7 iambic. Pastoral 14 (42).

10 $ababc_6dd_7c_6E_6F_7$ lines 1-8 iambic, lines 9-10 unrhymed refrain also used to begin the poem. Song 3 (72).

UNCLASSIFIABLE

4 $a_7b_6a_7b_6$ stress patterns freely varied within fixed syllabic structure. Song 6 (136). Discussed on pp. 34-7.

*6 $a_6a_4bc_6c_4b_6$ variably mixed iambic and anapaestic within fixed syllabic structure. Song 4 (54). [Cf. PS 33: discussed on pp. 32-4]

POEMS CONTAINING FEMININE RHYMES

Song 3 (lines 6-7), Song 6 (non-typical: see p. 35), Song 10 (lines 2, 4, 6), Song 11 (lines 5-8), Song 13 (lines 9-12), Song 19 (lines 1, 3), Song 20 (lines 1-4, 7), Song 22 (lines 1, 3).

SONNETS

Each of Robert's sonnets consists of fourteen iambic pentameters, all eschew feminine rhyme, and all employ the same rhyme-scheme in the octave: *abba abba.* Each sestet employs three rhymes, and these are always different from the two rhymes in the octave. The sonnets can be formally distinguished (1) according to the four different rhyme-schemes in the sestets, and (2) according to whether the sestet is (a) undivided, or divided into (b) groups of three and three, or (c) groups of four and two lines. This classification by sestets yields the following:

ccd eed. Sonnets 5, 24.

cdcdee. Sonnets 6, 7.

cdc dee. Sonnets 15, 21, 33.

cdcd ee. Sonnets 2, 3, 10, 18, 19, 20, 23, 25, 29, 34, 35.

cdc ede. Sonnets 1, 4, 11, 12, 13, 14, 28, 32.

cdd cee. Sonnets 8, 9, 16, 17, 22, 26, 27, 30, 31.

INDEX OF FIRST LINES